Gender and Politics

Series Editors

Johanna Kantola
Helsinki University
Finland

Sarah Childs
School for Policy Studies
University of Bristol
United Kingdom

The Gender and Politics series celebrates its 5th anniversary at the 4th European Conference on Politics and Gender (ECPG) in June 2015 in Uppsala, Sweden. The original idea for the book series was envisioned by the series editors Johanna Kantola and Judith Squires at the first ECPG in Belfast in 2009, and the series was officially launched at the Conference in Budapest in 2011. In 2014, Sarah Childs became the co-editor of the series, together with Johanna Kantola. Gender and Politics showcases the very best international writing. It publishes world class monographs and edited collections from scholars - junior and well established - working in politics, international relations and public policy, with specific reference to questions of gender. The 15 titles that have come out over the past five years make key contributions to debates on intersectionality and diversity, gender equality, social movements, Europeanization and institutionalism, governance and norms, policies, and political institutions. Set in European, US and Latin American contexts, these books provide rich new empirical findings and push forward boundaries of feminist and politics conceptual and theoretical research. The editors welcome the highest quality international research on these topics and beyond, and look for proposals on feminist political theory; on recent political transformations such as the economic crisis or the rise of the populist right; as well as proposals on continuing feminist dilemmas around participation and representation, specific gendered policy fields, and policy making mechanisms. The series can also include books published as a Palgrave pivot.

More information about this series at
http://www.springer.com/series/14998

Koen Slootmaeckers • Heleen Touquet • Peter Vermeersch
Editors

The EU Enlargement and Gay Politics

The Impact of Eastern Enlargement on Rights, Activism and Prejudice

Editors
Koen Slootmaeckers
School of Politics and International
   Relations
Queen Mary University of
   London
United Kingdom

Leuven International and European
   Studies (LINES)
KU Leuven – University of Leuven
Belgium

Heleen Touquet
Leuven International and European
   Studies (LINES)
KU Leuven – University of Leuven
Belgium

Peter Vermeersch
Leuven International and European
   Studies (LINES)
KU Leuven – University of Leuven
Belgium

Gender and Politics series
ISBN 978-1-349-69407-5   ISBN 978-1-137-48093-4   (eBook)
DOI 10.1057/978-1-137-48093-4

Library of Congress Control Number: 2016945000

Cover illustration: © Grzegorz Gajewski/Alamy Stock Photo

Printed on acid-free paper

This Palgrave Macmillan imprint is published by Springer Nature
The registered company is Macmillan Publishers Ltd. London

PREFACE AND ACKNOWLEDGEMENTS

The idea for this book emerged from a conversation between its editors at the University of Leuven, Belgium, back in 2013. Heleen Touquet, who had been studying social movements and post-ethnic mobilizations in the Western Balkans, and Koen Slootmaeckers, who had begun to work on sexualities and LGBT issues, were joined in their discussions by Peter Vermeersch, a specialist in Eastern European affairs and Europeanization. We asked ourselves a series of questions we thought were becoming increasingly urgent but which could not fully explore on our own: Why and how have LGBT rights become such a controversial topic in international politics in Central and Eastern Europe and the Western Balkans? What is the role of the EU within this larger context? What can be expected from the external transformative power of the EU on an issue like that of LGBT rights, at a time when the EU itself is so evidently grappling with an internal crisis on so many other fields? What does this mean for LGBT rights in the Western Balkans? And what was the situation of LGBT rights in 2004 when the CEE countries acceded? What changed?

In this book, with the aid of our contributors, we seek to provide some answers. Rather than tackling these rather substantial questions head-on, the volume brings together case studies from several layers of politics around LGBT issues in and around the EU. It looks specifically at the role of the EU in the promotion of LGBT rights throughout the enlargement process, but also considers diverse responses (and non-responses) to it in selected member and candidate member states.

We brought together a group of authors who not only were doing excellent research on these and related questions, but were also keen to

vi PREFACE AND ACKNOWLEDGEMENTS

share their findings with fellow researchers in our group and to write about their work for the common enterprise that this book has become. The end result is a series of broad, nuanced and diverse explorations that are nevertheless tied together by a common conceptual thread, that of EU enlargement and Europeanization.

Of course, no book bringing different research streams together can cover everything, and this one is no exception. From the outset, we thought it important that our topic should be addressed from different perspectives and should cover a variety of dimensions. But we very soon came to realize that there are too many dimensions to this topic to cover it in its entirety in one volume. The book therefore should not be seen as a reflection of our aspiration to be exhaustive; rather, it shows our ambition to be diverse and to highlight particular studies that we found crucial in particular subareas of the larger question. We have put these together in the context of the introductory and opening chapters, which introduce the broader theme and address mostly the EU side of the matter.

In addition, to some extent, the book seeks to bridge academia and activism. We have included not only research of established academic authors in the field; we also offer here insight into some of the practical knowledge of both young and experienced researchers from international civil society. In particular, we have solicited the input of ILGA-Europe—the European section of the International Lesbian, Gay, Bisexual, Trans and Intersex Association (ILGA), an international non-governmental umbrella organization bringing together 422 organizations from 45 European countries.

We want to thank all the authors who have enthusiastically contributed to this volume. We have learned a great deal from their work, and we hope they have also benefited from the discussions and exchanges we have organized with them.

This book is also part of a conversation with people who were not contributors—with a wider group of academic researchers, activists and policymakers. In preparation for the ultimate selection of papers, we participated in several international meetings and initiated a number of meetings ourselves. In April 2014, we organized a panel on "EU enlargement and LGBT rights in Central Eastern Europe and the post-Yugoslav space" at the conference of the British Association for Slavonic and East European Studies (BASEES) in Cambridge, and in that same month we brought together a panel with the same title at the 19th Annual Association for the Study of Nationalities (ASN) World Convention, Columbia University, New York. In February 2015, we held a special two-day conference in

Brussels on "EU enlargement, democracy and the politics of sexual orientation and gender identity," which we were so lucky to be able to organize on the premises of the European Parliament (EP) and the Royal Flemish Academy of Belgium for Science and the Arts. We want to thank the co-organizers of this event: the European Parliament (the LGBTI Intergroup, Evert Jacobsen, Tanko Jure), ILGA-Europe and Queen Mary University of London. And we want to thank all the people who have generously participated in our panels and conferences with smaller or larger contributions—first, the authors whose work appears in this volume, but also the people who discussed and helped shape this work through their participation: in particular, Phillip Ayoub (Drexel University), Emina Bošnjak (Sarajevo Open Center), Tanya Domi (Columbia University), Adam Fagan (Queen Mary University of London), Vjosa Musliu (Ghent University), David Patternotte (Université libre de Bruxelles), Łukasz Szulc (University of Antwerp) and Lien Verpoest (University of Leuven). We also want to extend our thanks to the MEPs who have given their support to the initiative and also participated in the conference with their own contributions, in particular Tanya Fajon (head of the Slovenian delegation within the political group the Progressive Alliance of Socialists and Democrats, and a vice-president of the Social Democrats) and Ulrike Lunacek (head of delegation of the Austrian Greens, vice-president and foreign affairs spokesperson of the Greens/EFA group in the European Parliament, Kosovo-Rapporteur and co-president of the Intergroup on LGBT Rights).

Koen Slootmaeckers
London, UK

Heleen Touquet
Leuven, Belgium

Peter Vermeersch
Leuven, Belgium

CONTENTS

NOTES ON CONTRIBUTORS

Uladzislau Belavusau is assistant professor of EU Law at the Department of European Studies of the University of Amsterdam (the Netherlands). He has previously taught at the law faculty of the Vrije Universiteit Amsterdam (2011–2015). He holds a Ph.D. from the European University Institute (Florence, Italy) and an L.L.M. from the *Collège d'Europe* (Brussels, Belgium). In addition, he has been a visiting scholar at the University of California at Berkeley (USA), *Max-Planck-Institut für ausländisches öffentliches Recht und Völkerrecht* (Heidelberg, Germany), Tel Aviv University (Israel) and York University (Toronto, Canada). His research interests cover EU non-discrimination law, human rights, comparative constitutional law, law and society. He is an author of a monograph on freedom of speech (Routledge, 2013). Currently he is co-editing a book on memory laws and conducting research for the ACCESS-Europe project on EU sexual rights.

Bojan Bilić is Marie Curie Intra-European Fellow at the Amsterdam Institute for Social Science Research, University of Amsterdam, where he is working on a research project (*Post-*)*Yugoslav LGBT Activism: Between Nationalism and Europeanisation*, 2014–2016. He is the author of *We Were Gasping for Air:* (*Post-*) *Yugoslav Anti-War Activism and Its Legacy* (2012) and co-editor (with Vesna Janković) of *Resisting the Evil:* (*Post-*)*Yugoslav Anti-War Contention* (2012).

Metka Mencin Čeplak is Assistant Professor of Psychology at the University of Ljubljana (Faculty for Social Sciences, Department of Sociology) and researcher at the Institute of Social Sciences, Centre for Social Psychology. Her main theoretical and research interests are in the area of critical (social) psychology, social construction of otherness, (re)production of power relations and education. She is the co-author of *Social Vulnerability of young people* (2000) and *Time-out for the students' youth* (1996). Her recent articles include 'On critical psychology in Slovenia' (with

M.N. Ule, 2013), 'Heteronormativity: school, ideology, and politics' (2013) and 'The individualisation of responsibility and school achievement' (2013).

Erwan Fouéré born in 1946 of Irish nationality, joined the Centre for European Policy Studies as an Associate Senior Research Fellow in 2013. Prior to that, his most recent appointment was Special Representative for the Irish 2012 Chairmanship of the OSCE with special responsibility for the Transdniestrian settlement process, a post he assumed after pursuing a career spanning 38 years with the European Union institutions. He was the first to assume joint responsibilities of EU Special Representative and Head of Delegation in the EU External Service when he was appointed in this double capacity in Macedonia (2005), where he served for 5 years, up to his retirement from the EU institutions. Before that he was Head of Delegation in Slovenia leading to accession, the first Head of Delegation in South Africa (1994), and the first Head of Delegation in Mexico and Cuba (1989). He was awarded the Order of Good Hope, Grand Officer, by President Nelson Mandela (1998).

Dimitry Kochenov is Visiting Professor and Crane Fellow in Law and Public Affairs at Woodrow Wilson School of Public and International Affairs, Princeton University (2015–2016). He holds a Chair in EU Constitutional Law at the University of Groningen and is also Visiting Professor at the College of Europe, Natolin campus. His research deals with the role of the individual in shaping and reshaping legal orders, focusing on minority rights and citizenship in the European Union context. His latest edited volumes include *Europe's Justice Deficit?* (with Gráinne de Búrca and Andrew Williams, 2015, Hart Publishing, Oxford), *EU Citizenship and Federalism: The Role of Rights* (Cambridge University Press, 2016) and *The Enforcement of EU Law and Values: Methods against Defiance* (with András Jakab, Oxford University Press, 2016)). His monograph on EU citizenship law entitled *Ius Tractum of Many Faces* is under contract with Hart Publishing, Oxford.

Mattias Kristoffersson holds Bachelor's degrees in political science and human rights studies, and a Master's degree in political science from Lund University, Sweden. His area of study was EU Affairs, and his theses covered the subjects of LGBTI rights during and after the EU accession process. He has previously done an internship at ILGA-Europe. Mattias has a strong commitment to LGBTI rights. He is a member of the Board of Stockholm Pride and of the European Pride Organiser's Association (EPOA), where he serves as Human Rights Coordinator.

Roman Kuhar is Associate Professor of Sociology at the University of Ljubljana (Faculty of Arts, Department of Sociology) and researcher at the Peace Institute, Ljubljana. His research topics include GLBT/queer topics, intolerance and equality, media, citizenship and sexuality. He is the author of several books, including *Media Construction of Homosexuality* (2003), *At the Crossroads of Discrimination* (2009), co-author (with A. Švab) of *The Unbearable Comfort of Privacy* (2005) and co-editor (with J. Takács) of *Beyond The Pink Curtain: Everyday life of LGBT people in Eastern Europe* (2007) and *Doing Families: Gay and Lesbian Family Practices* (2011).

Richard C.M. Mole is Senior Lecturer in Political Sociology at the School of Slavonic and East European Studies, UCL. His research focus is the relationship between identity and power, with particular focus on nationalism, sexualities, migration and diaspora. He has a theoretical interest in discourse—particularly the post-structuralist discourse theories of Laclau and Mouffe—and a regional interest in Russia, Poland and the Baltic states. His research on the discursive constructions of identities has found expression in his monograph *The Baltic States from the Soviet Union to the European Union: Identity, Discourse and Power in the Post-Communist Transition of Estonia, Latvia and Lithuania*, his edited volume *Discursive Constructions of Identity in European Politics*, and in articles and reviews in *Nations and Nationalism, European Journal of Social Psychology, Ethnicity and Health, Slavonic and East European Review, Sexualities, Journal of Baltic Studies* and *Sexually Transmitted Infections*.

Conor O'Dwyer is Associate Professor of Political Science at the University of Florida. His book *Runaway State-Building: Patronage Politics and Democratic Development* (Johns Hopkins University Press, 2006) examines the relationship between party-building and state-building in new democracies, looking specifically at the relationship between party competition and patronage politics in post-communist Eastern Europe. His current research explores how the expansion of the European Union affects the terrain of domestic politics in post-communist Europe. This research is particularly focused on the development of gay rights movements in the region. He has been an Academy Scholar at the Weatherhead Center for International Affairs at Harvard University (2003–2004 and 2006–2007) and has published in *World Politics, Studies in Comparative International Development, East European Politics, Comparative European Politics* and the *Journal of European Integration*.

Lilit Poghosyan is a Senior Programmes and Policy officer at ILGA-Europe, where her work focuses on EU enlargement and foreign policy. She has led ILGA-Europe's advocacy work on EU enlargement since 2008 and has been working closely with LGBTI organizations in the Western Balkans and Turkey, building their capacity for strategic advocacy and maximizing the impact of joint advocacy actions. She had devised and implemented advocacy strategies, monitored developments at the EU and target country levels, written advocacy documents and maintained relationships with relevant stakeholders. She advises national organizations on strategic advocacy, and has organized study and advocacy visits to European institutions. She holds an M.Sc. in Human Rights from the London School of Economics and Political Science. Before joining ILGA-Europe, she worked at *Médecins Sans Frontières* (Doctors Without Borders), where she developed and oversaw HIV/AIDS and mental health projects in Africa and Asia.

Bjorn van Roozendaal is responsible for the overall management of ILGA-Europe's Programmes Service Area and its team. He directs the implementation of ILGA-Europe's strategy on building the capacity of the LGBTI movement throughout Europe. Before joining ILGA-Europe, Björn worked with COC Netherlands, first as a project consultant and later as International Advocacy Officer. His activist work started with the Dutch LGBT youth magazine *Expreszo*. He later became a board member of IGLYO, and advised the subsequent board. He is a currently a member of the board of trustees of the Planet Romeo Foundation and also serves on the LGBT rights working group of Liberal International. Björn holds a degree in communications from the Inholland University in Rotterdam, the Netherlands. His thesis covered the subject of philanthropy fundraising in the Netherlands. His work was recognized by his election as Dutch European young person of the year in 2007.

Koen Slootmaeckers is a Ph.D. candidate at the School of Politics and International Relations, Queen Mary University of London, and a research affiliate at Leuven International and European Studies (LINES) at KU Leuven, University of Leuven (Belgium). His doctoral research deals with the impact of the EU accession on LGBT rights and activism in Serbia, with special focus on the adoption and implementation of the anti-discrimination legislation as well as the politics surrounding Belgrade Pride. Koen's primary research interests lie within the field of gender and sexuality studies, (sexual) nationalism and European Union politics, with a specific interest in lesbian, gay, bisexual and transgender (LGBT) topics. His work has been published in, amongst others, *Politics* and the *Journal of Homosexuality*.

Safia Swimelar is Associate Professor of Political Science and Policy Studies at Elon University and the coordinator of the International Studies program. She attained her B.A. and M.A. in government from the University of Texas-Austin and her Ph.D. in political science at the University of Nebraska-Lincoln. She teaches courses in international relations, European politics, international human rights, international law, and peace and conflict studies. She was a Fulbright Scholar at the University of Sarajevo in Bosnia-Herzegovina, where she investigated post-war human rights and nationalism. She has also done research on the role of images in teaching and understanding human rights issues. Safia has published articles in the *International Journal of Human Rights*, *Human Rights Quarterly*, *Ethnopolitics* and *International Studies Quarterly*. Her current research investigates and compares LGBT rights, politics and activism in the Balkans.

Heleen Touquet is a post-doctoral researcher and part-time Professor of International Relations at the University of Leuven (KU Leuven). She has published works about post-ethnic mobilization and nationalism in Bosnia-

Herzegovina and reconciliation in the Western Balkans in *Nationalism and Ethnic Politics, Studies in Ethnicity and Nationalism, Europe-Asia Studies* and other journals. Her current work focuses on gender politics and sexual violence in conflict and post-traumatic mobilization.

Peter Vermeersch is a professor of social science and a writer of literary non-fiction. He has a background in Eastern European Studies and is affiliated with the University of Leuven (KU Leuven) in Belgium, where he is research coordinator of the LINES Institute (Leuven International and European Studies). His previous roles have included researcher-in-residence at the OSCE Secretariat in Prague and a visiting scholar at the Minda de Gunzburg Center for European Studies, Harvard University (2007–2008). Vermeersch's research and writing covers topics such as minority politics, the Roma movement, nationalism, everyday citizenship and the politics of reconciliation and democratization. His academic papers have appeared in a wide range of academic books and journals, including *The European Journal of Sociology, Europe-Asia Studies, Ethnic and Racial Studies, The Journal of Ethnic and Migration Studies* and *East European Politics and Societies.*

LIST OF ABBREVIATIONS

CEE	Central and Eastern Europe
CFF	Campaign for All Families
CIFRC	Civil Initiative for the Family and the Rights of Children
CoE	Council of Europe
COHOM	Council Working Group on Human Rights
DPA	Dayton Peace Agreement
DUI	Albanian Democratic Union for Integration
EC	European Community
ECHR	European Court of Human Rights
ECJ	European Court of Justice
EEC	European Economic Community
EP	European Parliament
EU	European Union
EUSR	EU Special Representative
FREMP	Council Working Group on Fundamental Rights and Freedom of Movement
ICTY	International Tribunal for the Former Yugoslavia
IGO	Inter-Governmental Organization
ILGA	International Lesbian, Gay, Bisexual, Trans and Intersex Association
IPA	Instruments for Pre-accession Assistance
KPH	*Kampania Przeciw Homofobii* (Campaign Against Homophobia)
LDS	Liberal Democracy of Slovenia
LGBT	Lesbian, Gay, Bisexual, Transgender
LGBTI	Lesbian, Gay, Bisexual, Transgender, Intersex
LPR	League of Polish Families

LSYS	The League of Socialist Youth of Slovenia
MEP	Member of European Parliament
MP	Member of Parliament
ODIHR	Office for Democratic Institutions and Human Rights
OHR	Office of the High Representative
OSCE	Organisation for Security and Cooperation in Europe
PiS	*Prawo i Sprawiedliwość* (Law and Justice)
PO	*Platforma Obywatelska* (Civic Platform)
RCC	Roman Catholic Church
RS	Republika Srpska
SAA	Stabilisation and Association Agreement
SDP	*Socijaldemokratska partija Hrvatske* (Social Democratic Party Croatia)
SDS	*Srpska Demokratska Stranka* (Serbian Democratic Party)
SDSM	*Socialdemokratski Sojuz na Makedonija* (Social Democratic Union of Macedonia)
SEE	Southeast Europe
SFRY	Socialist Federal Republic of Yugoslavia
SLD	*Sojusz Lewicy Demokratycznej* (Democratic Left Alliance)
SOC	Sarajevo Open Center
TEC	Treaty establishing the European Community
TEU	Treaty on the European Union
TFEU	Treaty on the Functioning of the European Union
TR	*Twój Ruch* (Your Movement)
VMRO-DPMNE	Internal Revolutionary Organisation –Democratic Party for Macedonian National Unity

CHAPTER 1

Introduction: EU Enlargement and LGBT Rights—Beyond Symbolism?

Koen Slootmaeckers, Heleen Touquet, and Peter Vermeersch

Over the last decade, the rights of lesbian, gay, bisexual, and transgender (LGBT)[1] people have become an ever more salient and controversial topic in international politics. LGBT rights are increasingly considered a litmus test for a country's broader human rights record. As Kenneth Roth, executive director of Human Rights Watch, so eloquently articulated:

> The status of the LGBT community is a good litmus test for the status of human rights in society more broadly, precisely because it is such a vulnerable minority—similar to the proverbial canary in the coal mine. Where the rights of LGBT people are undermined, you can be sure that the rights of other minorities and critical members of civil society will soon also be in jeopardy.[2]

K. Slootmaeckers (✉)
School of Politics and International Relations, Queen Mary University of London, Belgium
Leuven International and European Studies (LINES), KU Leuven – University of Leuven, Belgium

H. Touquet • P. Vermeersch
Leuven International and European Studies (LINES), KU Leuven – University of Leuven, Belgium

© The Editor(s) (if applicable) and The Author(s) 2016
K. Slootmaeckers et al. (eds.), *The EU Enlargement and Gay Politics*, DOI 10.1057/978-1-137-48093-4_1

1

The monitoring of these rights has become not only a powerful tool for leverage in the hands of international advocacy groups, but also a topic of direct political contestation, both within and among countries. In international relations, politicians have increasingly referred to the subject of LGBT rights in their criticism of other countries. One of the most visible examples was the speech by President Barack Obama on July 25, 2015, in Kenya (see Holmes and Scott 2015). Obama said:

> With respect the rights of gays and lesbians, I have been consistent all across Africa on this. I believe in the principle of treating people equally under the law [...] and that the state should not discriminate against people based on their sexual orientation. [...] When you start treating people differently not because of any harm they are doing to anybody, but because they are different, that's the path whereby freedoms begin to erode, and bad things happen.

While Obama's address was applauded by international LGBT nongovernmental organizations (NGOs), it was strongly condemned by Kenyan president Uhuru Kenyatta. He replied by relegating LGBT rights to the realm of culture:

> The fact of the matter is Kenya and the United States share so many values: common love for democracy, entrepreneurship, value for families—these are some things that we share. [...] But there are some things that we must admit we don't share—our culture, our societies don't accept. It is very difficult for us to be able to impose on people that which they themselves do not accept. This is why I repeatedly say for Kenyans today the issue of gay rights is really a non-issue.

Kenyatta's response to Obama is an interesting example of what some authors have called resistance to 'homonationalism'. Jasbir Puar (2007, 2013), who coined the term, defines homonationalism as 'a facet of modernity and a historical shift marked by the entrance of (some) homosexual bodies as worthy of protection by nation-states, a constitutive and fundamental reorientation of the relationship between the state, capitalism, and sexuality' (Puar 2013, p. 337). Homonationalism thus describes a historical moment in which states can advance their exceptionalism or modernization by demonstrating their tolerance of homosexuality, which is contrasted with 'homophobic others'. Furthermore, there is no way to opt out from homonationalism; like modernity, Puar (2013) argues, it can only be resisted or re-signified. In other words, homonationalism structures global politics, as gay-friendliness becomes a key factor in assessing a country's modernity which cannot be escaped—a country will be judged on its gay-friendliness regardless of whether it believes in LGBT rights. Opponents can resist this historical moment only by depicting LGBT rights as a Western, non-universal concept, or they can attempt to re-signify it by linking the meaning of modernity to so-called traditional values.

Similar instances of homonationalism and resistance to it can be found in geographical areas closer to the European Union (EU). Take, for example, the recent developments in Russia and Ukraine. Since 2012, Russia has engaged in 'a conscious and consolidated effort to build a "sexual sovereignty" of the nation' (Makarychev and Medvedev 2015, p. 51), which has had strong implications for the politics around LGBT issues not only in Russia, but also in countries in its sphere of influence. In 2013, President Vladimir Putin signed into law a bill prohibiting 'homosexual propaganda'. With this and other laws, Russia aims to reenter the world stage by providing an alternative political and cultural model against the Western EU- and US-led model (Ayoub and Paternotte 2014). In this alternative model, Russia promotes 'traditional values' and seeks to defend 'authentic' national cultures, whilst resisting democratic and 'modern' values imposed from abroad. LGBT rights in this model are a powerful symbol. The clash between the two opposing models was highly visible in Ukraine when the country was about to sign an association agreement with the EU in 2013. In the run-up to this event, posters were put up in the streets of Kiev with the slogan 'Association with the EU means same-sex marriage'. In his *Ukraine Diaries*, the Ukrainian writer Andrey Kurkov (2014, p. 17) noted, 'In Kiev, this propaganda campaign is considered laughable, but I am afraid that in the east and in the provinces, people will naively believe that universal conversion to homosexuality is the condition imposed by Europe on Ukraine for the signature of the treaty'. Alexey Pushkov, the chair of the Duma's foreign affairs committee, tweeted that signing the association agreement would mean that Pride parades would be held instead of parades for Victory Day (in Birnbaum 2015).

The events in Ukraine show that LGBT rights have become increasingly salient in the relations between the EU and the countries in its close proximity, and have provided a fulcrum for political contestation. Association with the EU is often equated with support of same-sex marriage by opponents, and the EU similarly gauges countries' modernization by examining their stance on LGBT rights. For example, (former) EU Commissioner Füle (2014) called the 2014 Pride in Belgrade a 'milestone in the modern history of democratic Serbia'. And Member of the European Parliament (MEP) Tanja Fajon said, 'After three last-minute bans over the last three years, this year, the Serbian government will have the opportunity to right these wrongs. The values of tolerance and diversity that will be highlighted this Sunday are European, and Serbia fully belongs in Europe'.[3]

These examples are striking, in that they clearly demonstrate that LGBT rights have acquired important symbolic value in EU politics and discourse—e.g. Pride parades, for example, can now serve to illustrate a candidate country's endorsement of European norms—yet such symbolic politics stands in stark contrast to the amount of actual EU power and EU legislation in this field. The EU's *acquis* on LGBT rights is rather limited.

The aim of this book, therefore, is to disentangle the symbolism from the actual advances on the ground and to more precisely determine the influence of the EU on LGBT rights in former or current 'enlargement countries'. Specifically, we ask the question: what is the impact of the EU enlargement on the political and legal contexts in which these LGBT people live and claim rights? Today, a little over a decade since the first Eastern EU enlargement, we believe it is high time to analyze the impact of this process in the newer member states in Central Europe, as well as to take stock of the lessons learned for the Western Balkans.

CONCEPTUAL BACKGROUND OF THE BOOK

In this book, we strive to offer a balanced, thorough, well-investigated, and accessible picture of the state of affairs in LGBT rights and activism in Central Europe and the Western Balkans by providing not only thoughtful reflections, but also a wealth of new empirical findings—arising from legal and policy analysis, large-scale sociological investigations, and country case studies. The authors use different theoretical concepts from institutional analysis, the study of social movements, law, and Europeanization literature. In their chapters, they analyze such issues as the tendency of nationalist movements to turn 'sexual others' into 'national others', the actions and rhetoric of church actors as powerful counter-mobilizers against LGBT rights, and the role of the domestic state on the receiving end of EU pressure in the field of fundamental rights. The chapters offer the reader insight into emerging Europe-wide activism (Have activists been able to utilize the new European opportunity structure arising from the EU enlargement process to buttress their activism?), into the politics of activism in domestic contexts, and into the complicated relationship between activism and the larger LGBT community (Do highly visible forms of activism such as pride parades manage to connect to and unite 'LGBT communities'?).

Although we did not ask the contributors to use a specific theoretical approach in their chapters, insights from the literature on 'Europeanization via Enlargement' are a central theme throughout the book.[4] Europeanization' is often conceptualized as

> processes of (a) construction, (b) diffusion, and (c) institutionalization of formal and informal rules, procedures, policy paradigms, styles, 'ways of doing', and shared beliefs and norms which are first defined and consolidated in the EU policy process and then incorporated in the logic of domestic (national and subnational) discourse, political structures, and public policies. (Radaelli 2003, p. 30)

More simply, it refers to the process of transferring the EU's policies, institutions, rules, beliefs, and values to other countries (Bulmer 2007). Rational choice institutionalism (RCI) and sociological institutionalism (SI) (Börzel and Risse 2003; Grabbe 2006; Schimmelfennig and Sedelmeier 2005) explain why third countries comply with EU rules and norms. Both perspectives start from the premise that the EU has existing standards that third countries must adhere to. The RCI perspective argues that third countries comply with EU rules when the benefits outweigh the costs of domestic change. This is also the reasoning behind the *conditionality* principle of the EU, in which the advancement towards EU integration is conditioned upon compliance with EU rules and norms. The SI perspective focuses on the soft transfer of EU policies and norms (Vermeersch 2005). Compliance is seen as an outcome of third countries' changing preferences, and EU rules are deemed appropriate. Here the notion of (international) socialization plays an important role, with the EU being the socializing agent, actively promoting its norms and values (Börzel and Risse 2012; see also Manners 2002). Both perspectives emphasize *vertical* processes of diffusion in which the EU is the initiator and third states the recipients of the EU's norms and rules.

Europeanization is treated more broadly here, to encompass *horizontal* processes of diffusion as well (see e.g. Ayoub 2013; Kuhar 2011, 2012; Kuhar and Mencin Čeplak 2016). These horizontal processes emphasize transnational (activist) cooperation and policy transfer (or cross-loading) via state-to-state learning and informal policy networks (Börzel and Risse 2007; Kollman 2009). This horizontal diffusion is particularly important when there is no hard *acquis*, or when considering 'soft law'. In terms of LGBT policies, Kollman (2009) and Paternotte and Kollman (2013) have studied the policy convergence of same-sex union legislation in the Western European countries, emphasizing the role of international norm diffusion and transnational networks (for an analysis of same-sex union policies in two Central European countries, see the chapter by Kuhar and Mencin Čeplak 2016; or that by O'Dwyer and Vermeersch 2016).

The book also contributes to the emerging research agenda on LGBT rights in the enlargement process (see e.g. Ayoub 2014, 2015; Kahlina 2015; O'Dwyer 2010, 2012; O'Dwyer and Schwartz 2010), by analyzing the impact of the EU enlargement on the new member states from the different iterations of the Eastern enlargement, as well as on those countries currently in the EU's 'waiting room'. These contributions provide an analysis of the importance of the transnational network of LGBT activists (see e.g. the chapter by Kristofferson, Roozendaal and Poghosyan 2016) and the role of changes in domestic political configurations (see, e.g., the chapters by Kuhar and Mencin Čeplak 2016; and O'Dwyer and Vermeersch 2016), reveal the hurdle of (nationalist) opposition to the imposition of decadent foreign values (see the chapters by Mole 2016 and Swimelar 2016), and draw attention to some unintended consequences of EU pressure on LGBT activism (see the chapter by Bilić 2016). In doing so, the book corroborates the recent 'domestic turn' in Europeanization via enlargement (see Elbasani 2013), which 'bring[s] in more prominently domestic factors as the key to explaining successful rule transfer' (Elbasani 2013, p. 8). It also highlights state identity as an important factor in understanding the limited impact of Europeanization (Freyburg and Richter 2010; Subotic, 2010, 2011).

Critical scholars have argued that, ironically, the EU's enlargement has contributed to the reification of an East–West divide (Kulpa and Mizielińska 2011), which has reinforced the notion of Western exceptionalism in LGBT rights. Ammaturo (2015) described this as the 'Pink Agenda', which creates and promotes a fault line between presumably LGBT-friendly and homophobic countries, and suggests that the EU is unique in its open-mindedness and tolerance of LGBT persons. According to critics, the EU enlargement has contributed to the advancement and popularization of this idea by subjecting candidate countries, through the use of conditionality, to what Kulpa (2014) has called a 'leveraged pedagogy' (Kulpa 2014; see also Kulpa and Mizielińska 2011). Through this leveraged pedagogy, Western Europe condemns candidate countries as not sufficiently European or modern to merit full acceptance into the European fold, but European enough to be offered redemption and help in their attempts to Europeanize. Within this framework, old (Western) EU member states are cast as the 'knowledgeable teachers of democracy, liberalism, and tolerance' (Kahlina 2015, p. 74), whilst Central and Eastern

European countries are rendered as permanently in transition (i.e. not yet sufficiently liberal), post-communist, and—especially important for our discussion—homophobic (see Kulpa 2014; Kahlina 2015). The earlier-mentioned statements by both (former) Commissioner for Enlargement Štefan Füle and MEP Tanja Fajon on the 2014 Belgrade Pride (see supra) illustrate this tendency.

The contributors to this book have steered clear from reintroducing an East–West divide that unnecessarily simplifies the complexity of the issue at hand (see also Kulpa and Mizielińska 2011; Kulpa 2014; Ammaturo 2015), even though it is clear that LGBT rights can be, and often are, politicized as inherently European (see e.g. the chapters that address domestic opposition to LGBT rights in the new EU member states in Central Europe. Several of these chapters (Mole 2016; Kuhar and Mencin Čeplak 2016; O'Dwyer and Vermeersch 2016) show how politicians employ homophobic political rhetoric to oppose EU integration.[5] In order to defend the 'traditional' culture of their country from Western (EU) influence, the political elite employ 'political homophobia' (Weiss and Bosia 2013, see also Currier 2010) as a 'purposive strategy' to depict LGBT people as the ultimate 'other'. In Central European EU member states, the LGBT issue has been positioned onto the schism between pro- and anti-EU politics (Mole 2011). In Latvia, for example, the pressure for equal rights for LGBT persons is seen as a direct attack on the nation's future by the so-called international gay lobby (Mole 2011). In Poland, the Kaczyński government declared that it needed to prevent the 'aggressive promotion of homosexuality' because it felt that 'although Poland may have joined the EU, they will have none of the "loose" attitudes toward sex' (Graff 2006, p. 436). In other words, LGBT rights may sit comfortably with the EU as part of its effort to abolish discrimination and promote human rights, and they may to a large extent have been accepted as such by a substantial segment of the population in many EU member states, but it may be precisely for this reason that opposition to such rights in the form of criticism of the EU resonates well with a number of politicians in the new EU member states, as well as with sizeable portions of their electorate.

To add further nuance to the topic of LGBT politics and EU enlargement, we need to acknowledge the ongoing debate on terminology. What we discuss in this book can be categorized under a variety of labels, a fact that is not without its consequences for the politics that relates to such categories. Whilst 'gay and lesbian', along with the acronym LGBT (and sometimes LGBTI to include 'intersex'), are now commonplace terms (Paternotte and Tremblay 2015), there are authors who prefer to place the topic under the rubric of 'sexual orientation and gender identity' (SOGI) (see e.g. Lennox and Waites 2013), or simply prefer to use the term 'gay'. In the title of this book we have used the word 'gay' because it is short and may speak to a wide audience. As such, the term serves as practical shorthand for the great variety of concepts that appear in this field, and may therefore be understood in a way that is similar to the early gay liberation movement's understanding of it—as an 'all-embracing collective term, uniting men and women, young and old, black and white, transvestites and transsexuals' (Weeks 2015, p. 47). Readers will notice that throughout the chapters of the book, the term 'LGBT' is rather prominent. The reason is straightforward: the acronym is dominant in EU policies and documents, as well as in the world of Central European and Balkan activism. Nevertheless, we should clarify that this acronym, like other terms, is not without its problems. 'LGBT' is described by Binnie and Klesse (2012, p. 445) as signifying a 'coalitional practice between different collectivities of actors [...]. [It] is controversial because it insinuates a quasi-natural confluence of interests around certain gender and/or sexual subjectivities'. Furthermore, in EU policies and documents, its meaning is often somewhat reductionist—it is used mostly to refer to same-sex sexual orientations—i.e. lesbian and gay—while trans* and bisexual issues remain invisible. The acronym has been further criticized as a hegemonic and homogenizing term, and one that does not always allow for local expressions of identity—indeed, it may even oppose such expressions (as Kulpa and Mizielińska 2011 have clearly argued in their edited volume). In light of these critiques, we have asked our contributors to remain sensitive to local expressions of identity. Hence, although LGBT appears in practically all chapters, it can have various connotations depending on the context in which it is used, and it can be used in slightly varying form. For example, in their chapter, Kristofferson, Roozendaal, and Poghosyan largely use the acronym 'LGBTI' (the 'I' stands for 'Intersex'), as this is ILGA-Europe's preferred terminology, yet at times they amend the acronym to accurately reflect the preferred terms among local Central European activists. Alternatively, Bilić uses the term 'LGBT' for practical reasons, but warns the reader that despite the prominence of the term in the Serbian context, bisexual and trans* issues usually remain under the radar.

STRUCTURE OF THE BOOK

We have opted to structure the book along the chronology of the iterations of the Eastern enlargement. The impact of EU enlargement on rights, activism, and prejudices are part of a bigger system, and trying to separate them would not do justice to its complexity. The first part of the book, *The Broader Picture: LGBT Issues in the EU*, focuses on the EU and sketches the wider backdrop against which previous and current enlargements have taken place. It examines institutional changes at the European level (particularly in terms of its foreign, and more specifically, its enlargement policies), the influence of the EU legal structure, and the role of the European LGBT movement in effecting change.

In the first, introductory chapter, Koen Slootmaeckers and Heleen Touquet trace the evolution of LGBT rights within the context of the enlargement process from the 1990s onwards, and take stock of the changes in procedures over time. They show how, with the first enlargement to Eastern Europe, the EU has contributed to an increased focus on fundamental rights, including LGBT rights, in its enlargement policy. The chapter continues with an analysis of the impact of the EU enlargement on LGBT rights in Central Europe and Croatia, and it concludes with insights into the future of LGBT rights among the current candidate countries in the Western Balkans.

Matthias Kristofferson, Björn Roozendaal, and Lilit Poghosyan complement Slootmaeckers and Touquet's account by writing from the perspective of ILGA-Europe, a pan-European umbrella organization for LGBT rights, about the EU's influence on LGBT rights. We see a detailed picture of how mobilization and advocacy by LGBT rights activists from across the continent have helped to position LGBT rights as one of the central issues of the EU's enlargement and foreign policy agenda. We can also see, from an activist's perspective, how the gradual inclusion of sexual orientation and gender identity in the EU agenda has created opportunities to push for advances for LGBT people in accession countries.

The third and final chapter of Part I, by Ulad Belavusau and Dimitry Kochenov, takes a legal perspective and illustrates how the how quasi-federal elements embedded in EU law (Beaud 2007; Schütze 2009), on the one hand, have created opportunities for mobilizing transnational LGBT litigation and, on the other hand, have steadily Europeanized the discourse on LGBT rights. Citizenship, anti-discrimination, and fundamental rights developments have all contributed to the minimum

'European' standards of LGBT rights protection. Additionally, the chapter explores avenues for future LGBT litigation, capitalizing on the current opportunities in EU law. Through their study of a European Court of Justice case (the Romanian *Asociaţia ACCEPT* against a Romanian football club), Belavusau and Kochenov are able to show that legal opportunities in the EU are providing an unprecedented impetus for Central European activists. Their example shows the 'value of pragmatic cause litigation [...] for the benefit of a disempowered minority and the rise of an active form of citizenship mobilizing EU sexual rights' (Belavusau and Kochenov 2016).

The second part of the book, *Zooming In: Central and Eastern Europe*, takes a closer look at the 2004 enlargement wave. It begins by examining the role of nationalism in LGBT politics. As such, the initial chapter of this section relies on a more sociological discussion of the EU's impact on LGBT rights. Richard Mole considers the implications of nationalism in Central and Eastern Europe and the Western Balkans. He argues that the adoption of EU norms in Eastern Europe has failed largely because they conflict with domestic national identity discourse. He examines the links between nationalism and political homophobia, demonstrating that EU support for LGBT equality can also have a negative impact on attitudes towards non-heteronormative individuals. He contends that nationalist politicians use the EU's more liberal position towards LGBT rights to draw a boundary between the 'decadent West' and the 'traditional East' for their own social and political purposes—an observation that will be corroborated in several of the remaining chapters of the book.

The last two chapters of Part II, Chaps. 6 and 7, look at the history of same-sex union proposals in Poland and Slovenia, respectively, examining the role of the EU in the political debate around the topic. The conversation between the two chapters cannot go unnoticed by the reader. Not only do both chapters focus on a similar topic, i.e. same-sex partnership regulations, but they also highlight the interaction between the LGBT movements and party politics in each country, and its consequences for the adoption of same-sex union legislation. Additionally, the vast time span of their research presents an important contribution to the Europeanization literature. Not only do both chapters show that the notion of same-sex partnership legislation had been debated in both countries even before they joined the EU, they also show the time-limited impact of EU enlargement and the significant role of domestic politics on this same-sex partnership debate.

Conor O'Dwyer and Peter Vermeersch examine the steady advances the gay rights movement has made in Poland over the last decade. Despite the distinct lack of a broader social acceptance of homosexuality in this post-communist country, registered partnerships became an issue of political debate. O'Dwyer and Vermeersch identify two key moments that significantly shaped new opportunities for Polish LGBT activists. First, the EU accession and its requirements regarding LGBT rights caused a period of heightened political homophobia. During this time, LGBT activists received unprecedented public visibility, which helped them forge new alliances. Secondly, the arrival of a new niche party, *Twój Ruch*, created a new opportunity structure for LGBT activists, who as a result managed to expand their political influence.

Roman Kuhar and Metka Mencin Čeplak offer the reader an analysis of the impact of EU and international norms on LGBT rights in Slovenia. They argue that domestic political dynamics have caused delays in and resistance to the adoption of marriage equality legislation. Their research reveals the ambivalence and discontent on both ends of the political spectrum. The liberal center-left declared their support for the idea of equal treatment, but continuously postponed acting on their commitment. In contrast, the conservatives used a discourse of tolerance and adopted a very limited law on registered partnerships, which put the issue on the back burner. The chapter also discusses the major role of the conservative movement, including the Roman Catholic Church.

In the last part of the book, *Close-ups of the Western Balkans*, three authors analyze a current candidate member state from the Western Balkans: Bosnia-Herzegovina, (the Former Yugoslav Republic of) Macedonia, and Serbia. Among the three, Serbia has evolved furthest in the process of accession. Macedonia seemed to be on a steady track to speedy accession in the early 2000s, but the country has recently been in the throes of a political crisis that has stalled its progress on the road to EU membership. Bosnia is another of the so-called laggards of EU accession, caught up in a seemingly perpetual crisis. The chapters by Erwan Fouéré and Safia Swimelar very clearly show the difficulties faced by LGBT activists in these two post-conflict areas. Bojan Bilić, on the other hand, raises important questions about the use of Pride in Serbia.

Safia Swimelar demonstrates how domestic norms influence the diffusion of EU norms. She argues that Bosnia's post-war identity—emphasizing ethno-nationality—prohibits the recognition and acceptance of other identities, especially those based on gender identity and sexual orientation.

These identities are seen by political elites as a threat to the dominant national identities, as they cross ethno-sexual boundaries. Swimelar describes in detail how religious and nationalist political homophobia affects the work of local NGOs that are supported by the EU. Following insights from norm diffusion theory, she finds that the existing, albeit limited, EU conditionality policy has contributed to a shift in Bosnian LGBT politics. She also highlights, however, the backlash that has come with the increased visibility of the LGBT community in this country.

In his chapter (Chap. 9), Bojan Bilić examines the symbolic politics of the Belgrade Pride parade, and asks whether it actually serves to advance the LGBT cause in Serbia. He discusses disparities in wealth, education, and professional status, but also in skills, connections, and geographical locations within the Serbian LGBT population, and argues that these differences seriously hamper the country's acceptance of grassroots LGBT activism. Bilić's chapter speaks to the more critical scholarship on EU enlargement and LGBT rights, and asks urgent questions for the EU. Its current reliance on symbolic politics, he points out, might negatively affect the goals of anti-discrimination it seeks to pursue. Bilić's questions invite us to think about the future of LGBT rights in the EU and introduce us to an important new research agenda—one that focuses on how to deal with the unintended consequences of EU pressure on the experiences of LGBT people in candidate countries.

The last chapter of the book, by Erwan Fouéré, offers a unique insider perspective on the place of LGBT rights in the enlargement process. As a former EU Special Representative and Head of EU Delegation to Macedonia, he explains how domestic politics in Macedonia have limited the possible EU impact on LGBT rights. After early pro-EU governments, in 2006 the political climate shifted towards heightened nationalism, thriving under the influence of political homophobia. Fouéré discusses the obstacles encountered by an EU official dealing with the enlargement process in a post-conflict state.

NOTES

1. We will discuss the decisions in relation to use of 'gay' and 'LGBT' in more detail later in the introduction.
2. Quoted from Roth (2014).
3. Quoted in a press release from the European Parliament Intergroup on LGBT Rights (Intergroup on LGBT Rights 2014).

4. The chapter by Swimelar utilizes the more general norm diffusion theory. However, Europeanization via enlargement is a closely linked process which can be seen as a specific case of the norm diffusion theory. For more on norm diffusion, see Swimelar's chapter.
5. The chapter by Kuhar and Mencin Čeplak does indeed refer to political homophobia; however, the authors have chosen not to use the term homophobia in their work, as they see the concept as not fit to describe the rationalized nature of sexual prejudices.

References

Ammaturo, F. R. (2015). The "Pink Agenda": Questioning and challenging European homonationalist sexual citizenship. *Sociology*, Online first, pp. 1–16.

Ayoub, P. M. (2013). Cooperative transnationalism in contemporary Europe: Europeanization and political opportunities for LGBT mobilization in the European Union. *European Political Science Review*, 5(2), 279–310.

Ayoub, P. M. (2014). With arms wide shut: Threat perception, norm reception, and mobilized resistance to LGBT rights. *Journal of Human Rights*, 13(3), 337–362.

Ayoub, P. M. (2015). Contested norms in new-adopter states: International determinants of LGBT rights legislation. *European Journal of International Relations*, 21(2), 293–322.

Ayoub, P. M., & Paternotte, D. (Eds.) (2014). *LGBT activism and the making of Europe: A rainbow Europe?* Basingstoke, England: Palgrave Macmillan.

Beaud, O. (2007). *Théorie de la federation*. Paris: Presses Universitaires de France.

Belavusau, U., & Kochenov, D. (2016). Federalizing legal opportunities for LGBT movements in the growing EU. In K. Slootmaeckers, H. Touquet, & P. Vermeersch (Eds.), *The EU enlargement and gay politics*. London: Palgrave Macmillan.

Bilić, B. (2016). Whose pride? LGBT 'Community' and the organisation of pride parades in Serbia. In K. Slootmaeckers, H. Touquet, & P. Vermeersch (Eds.), *The EU enlargement and gay politics*. London: Palgrave Macmillan.

Binnie, J., & Klesse, C. (2012). Solidarities and tensions: Feminism and transnational LGBTQ politics in Poland. *European Journal of Women's Studies*, 19(4), 444–459.

Birnbaum, M. (2015). Gay rights in Eastern Europe: A new battleground for Russia and the West. *The Washington Post* [Online], 25 July. Retrieved September 22, 2015, from http://www.washingtonpost.com/world/europe/gay-rights-in-eastern-europe-a-new-battleground-for-russia-and-the-west/2015/07/24/8ad04d4e-2ff2-11e5-a879-213078d03dd3_story.html.

Börzel, T. A., & Risse, T. (2003). Conceptualizing the domestic impact of Europe. In K. Featherstone & C. M. Radaelli (Eds.), *The politics of Europeanization* (pp. 57–80). Oxford: Oxford University Press.

Börzel, T., & Risse, T. (2007). Europeanization: The domestic impact of European Union politics. In K. Jorgensen, M. Pollack, & B. Rosamond (Eds.), *Sage handbook of European Union politics*. London: Sage.

Börzel, T. A., & Risse, T. (2012). From Europeanisation to diffusion: Introduction. *West European Politics, 35*(1), 1–19.

Bulmer, S. (2007). Theorizing Europeanization. In P. Graziano & M. Vink (Eds.), *Europeanization: New research agendas*. *Europeanization: New research agendas* (pp. 46–58). Basingstoke, England: Palgrave.

Currier, A. (2010). Political homophobia in postcolonial namibia. *Gender & Society, 24*(1), 110–129.

Elbasani, A. (Ed.) (2013). *European integration and transformation in the Western Balkans: Europeanization or business as usual?* Oxon, England: Routledge.

Freyburg, T., & Richter, S. (2010). National identity matters: The limited impact of EU political conditionality in the Western Balkans. *Journal of European Public Policy, 17*(2), 263–281.

Füle, Š. (2014). Statement of commissioner Füle on Belgrade Pride parade. *European Commission*. Retrieved September 28, 2014, from http://europa.eu/rapid/press-release_STATEMENT-14-289_en.htm.

Grabbe, H. (2006). *The EU transformative power: Europeanization through conditionality in Central and Eastern Europe*. New York: Palgrave Macmillan.

Graff, A. (2006). We are (not all) homophobes: A report from Poland. *Feminist Studies, 32*(2), 434–449.

Holmes, K. & Scott, E. (2015). Obama lectures Kenyan president on gay rights. *CNN* [Online], 25 July. Retrieved September 2, 2015, from http://www.cnn.com/2015/07/25/politics/obama-kenya-kenyatta/index.html.

Intergroup on LGBT Rights. (2014). LGBTI intergroup MEP heading to Belgrade Pride. *The European parliament intergroup on LGBT rights* [Online], 26 September. Retrieved September 3, 2015 http://www.lgbt-ep.eu/press-releases/lgbti-intergroup-mep-heading-to-belgrade-pride/.

Kahlina, K. (2015). Local histories, European LGBT designs: Sexual citizenship, nationalism, and "Europeanisation" in post-Yugoslav Croatia and Serbia. *Women's Studies International Forum, 49*, 73–83.

Kollman, K. (2009). European institutions, transnational networks and national same-sex unions policy: When soft law hits harder. *Contemporary Politics, 15*(1), 37–53.

Kristoffersson, M., van Roozendaal, B., & Poghosyan, L. (2016). European integration and LGBTI activism—partners in realizing change? In K. Slootmaeckers, H. Touquet, & P. Vermeersch (Eds.), *The EU enlargement and gay politics*. London: Palgrave Macmillan.

Kuhar, R. (2011). Resisting change: Same-sex partnership policy debates in Croatia and Slovenia. *Südosteuropa, 59*(1), 25–49.

Kuhar, R. (2012). Use of Europeanization frame in same-sex partnership issues across Europe. In E. Lombardo & M. Forest (Eds.), *The Europeanization of gender equality policies: A discursive-sociological approach* (pp. 168–191). Basingstoke, England: Palgrave Macmillan.

Kuhar, R., & Čeplak, M. M. (2016). Same-sex partnership debates in Slovenia: Between declarative support and lack of political will. In K. Slootmaeckers, H. Touquet, & P. Vermeersch (Eds.), *The EU enlargement and gay politics*. London: Palgrave Macmillan.

Kulpa, R. (2014). Western leveraged pedagogy of Central and Eastern Europe: Discourses of homophobia, tolerance, and nationhood. *Gender, Place Culture A Journal of Feminist Geography, 21*(4), 431–448.

Kulpa, R., & Mizielińska, J. (Eds.) (2011). *De-centring western sexualities: Central and Eastern European perspectives*. Surrey, England: Ashgate Publishing Company.

Kurkov, A. (2014). *Ukraine diaries: Dispatches from Kiev*. London: Harvill Secker.

Lennox, C., & Waites, M. (2013). Human Rights, Sexual Orientation and Gender Identity in the Commonwealth: From History and Law to Developing Activism and Transnational Dialogues. In C. Lennox, & M. Waites (Eds.), *Human Rights, Sexual Orientation and Gender Identity in the Commonwealth Struggles for Decriminalisation and Change* (pp. 1–59). London: School of Advanced Studies, University of London.

Makarychev, A., & Medvedev, S. (2015). Biopolitics and power in Putin's Russia. *Problems of Post-communism, 62*(1), 45–54.

Manners, I. (2002). Normative power Europe: A contradiction in terms? *Journal of Common Market Studies, 40*(2), 235–258.

Mole, R. (2011). Nationality and sexuality: Homophobic discourse and the "national threat" in contemporary Latvia. *Nations and Nationalism, 17*(3), 540–560.

Mole, R. C. M. (2016). Nationalism and homophobia in Central and Eastern Europe. In K. Slootmaeckers, H. Touquet, & P. Vermeersch (Eds.), *The EU enlargement and gay politics*. London: Palgrave Macmillan.

O'Dwyer, C. (2010). From conditionality to persuasion? Europeanization and the rights of sexual minorities in post-accession Poland. *Journal of European Integration, 32*(3), 229–247.

O'Dwyer, C. (2012). Does the EU help or hinder gay-rights movements in post-communist Europe? The case of Poland. *East European Politics, 28*(4), 332–352.

O'Dwyer, C., & Schwartz, K. Z. S. (2010). Minority rights after EU enlargement: A comparison of antigay politics in Poland and Latvia. *Comparative European politics, 8*(2), 220–243.

O'Dwyer, C., & Vermeersch, P. (2016). From pride to politics: Niche-party politics and LGBT rights in Poland. In K. Slootmaeckers, H. Touquet, &

P. Vermeersch (Eds.), *The EU enlargement and gay politics*. London: Palgrave Macmillan.

Paternotte, D., & Kollman, K. (2013). Regulating intimate relationships in the European polity: Same-sex unions and policy convergence. *Social Politics: International Studies in Gender, State & Society, 20*(4), 510–533.

Paternotte, D., & Tremblay, M. (2015). *The Ashgate Research Companion to Lesbian and Gay Activism*. Farnham: Routledge.

Puar, J. (2007). *Terrorist assemblages: Homonationalism in queer times*. London: Duke University Press.

Puar, J. (2013). Rethinking homonationalism. *International Journal of Middle East Studies, 45*(2), 336–339.

Radaelli, C. M. (2003). The Europeanization of public policy. In K. Featherstone & C. M. Radaelli (Eds.), *The politics of Europeanization* (pp. 27–56). Oxford: Oxford University Press.

Roth, K. (2014). Q&A: How to tackle the backlash against gay rights? *World Economic Forum* [Online], 10 November. Retrieved September 9, 2015, from https://agenda.weforum.org/2014/11/qa-how-to-tackle-the-backlash-against-gay-rights/.

Schimmelfennig, F., & Sedelmeier, U. (Eds.) (2005). *The Europeanization of Central and Eastern Europe*. Ithaca, NY: Cornell University Press.

Schütze, R. (2009). *From dual to cooperative federalism*. Oxford: Oxford University Press.

Subotic, J. (2010). Explaining Difficult States: the Problems of Europeanization in Serbia. *East European Politics & Societies, 24*(4), 595–616.

Subotic, J. (2011). Europe Is a State of Mind: Identity and Europeanization in the Balkans. *International Studies Quarterly, 55*(2), 309–330.

Swimelar, S. (2016). The struggle for visibility and equality: Bosnian LGBT rights developments. In K. Slootmaeckers, H. Touquet, & P. Vermeersch (Eds.), *The EU enlargement and gay politics*. London: Palgrave Macmillan.

Vermeersch, P. (2005). EU enlargement and immigration policy in Poland and Slovakia. *Communist and Post-Communist Studies, 38*(1), 71–88.

Weeks, J. (2015). Gay liberation and it legacies. In D. Paternotte & M. Tremblay (Eds.), *The Ashgate research companion to lesbian and gay activism*. Farnham, England: Ashgate.

Weiss, M. L., & Bosia, M. J. (Eds.) (2013). *Global homophobia: States, movements, and the politics of oppression*. Urbana: University of Illinois Press.

PART I

The Broader Picture: LGBT Issues in the EU

The Co-evolution of EU's Eastern Enlargement and LGBT Politics: An Ever Gayer Union?

Koen Slootmaeckers and Heleen Touquet

INTRODUCTION

The EU identifies and presents itself as an organisation founded on 'fundamental values' and as a defender and guardian of fundamental rights. The development of this 'fundamental rights myth'[1] (Smismans 2010) has taken place against the broader backdrop of a globalisation of human rights discourse (Smismans 2010; Stychin 2004). Fundamental values have also increasingly become the narrative driving EU foreign policy, including enlargement and neighbourhood policies. As Article 3(5) clarifies, 'In its relations with the wider world, the [European] Union shall uphold

K. Slootmaeckers (✉)
School of Politics and International Relations, Queen Mary University of London, London, UK
Leuven International and European Studies (LINES), KU Leuven — University of Leuven, Leuven, Belgium

H. Touquet
Leuven International and European Studies (LINES), KU Leuven — University of Leuven, Leuven, Belgium

© The Editor(s) (if applicable) and The Author(s) 2016   19
K. Slootmaeckers et al. (eds.), *The EU Enlargement and Gay Politics*, DOI 10.1057/978-1-137-48093-4_2

and promote its values and interests and contribute to the protection of its citizens. It shall contribute to […] the protection of human rights'. Article 49 sets forth respect for the so-called founding values—'respect for human dignity, freedom, democracy, equality, the rule of law and respect for human rights' (Art. 2 TEU)—as a precondition for EU membership.

In recent years, LGBT rights have become part and parcel of this fundamental rights myth (Ayoub and Paternotte 2014a, p. 3): being 'gay-friendly' has now become a symbol for what it means to be truly European and vice versa.[2] And with this evolution, the EU's enlargement policy has become an important mechanism for transforming candidate member states into countries ready (and worthy) to become a member of the EU and take up the responsibilities of such membership, including respect for LGBT rights. Whilst there is an expanding body of literature regarding the impact of EU accession on LGBT rights in new member states, little has been done to map the evolution of these rights within the context of enlargement policy. In this chapter, we aim to do exactly this.

Our focus here is tracing the position that LGBT rights has occupied within the EU enlargement from the 1990s onwards. In the first part of the chapter, we examine how fundamental rights—and LGBT rights in particular—have become an important element of the enlargement process over time. Our approach is institutional,[3] focusing on changes within the EU and its policies through the progression of the various iterations of the Eastern enlargement. The second part of the chapter focuses on what we identify as two turning points in this process: the fifth and sixth enlargements.[4] Here, we devote more attention to the case study of Croatia, as it presents valuable insights into the processes described earlier in the chapter. Lastly, we examine the Western Balkan countries that are still in the midst of the accession process, and evaluate the prospects for LGBT rights in these countries, given the EU's new focus on these rights.

THE GROWING IMPORTANCE OF LGBT RIGHTS IN THE ACCESSION PROCESS

In order to trace the evolution of the position of LGBT rights within the enlargement process, we have classified EU policy changes into two analytically different but interrelated categories, namely whether the changes have a *direct* or *indirect* effect (see Fig. 2.1).[5] We first discuss changes with an indirect impact, meaning increased importance of these fundamental rights within EU (foreign) policies. These changes are reflected in Fig. 2.1 by white diamonds and dotted lines. Next, we focus on changes that have had

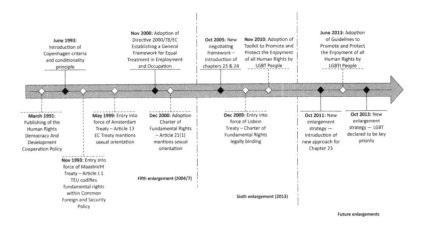

Fig. 2.1 The co-evolution of EU enlargement and the EU's fundamental and LGBT rights policies. Note: *Black diamonds* changes that had a direct effect on LGBT rights within the EU enlargement process. *White diamonds* indicators of a larger shift at the EU level towards an increased focus on fundamental and LGBT rights

a direct effect on the enlargement policy and the place that LGBT rights occupy within the policy (black diamonds and full lines in the figure).

The Larger Shift in the EU's Changing Fundamental Rights Policy

Although the concept of fundamental rights has occasionally been referenced with respect to the EU's relations with the wider world and candidate countries beginning in the 1970s (see Williams 2004, pp. 40–44, 54–58), an explicit narrative on fundamental rights specifically in external relations emerged only in the 1990s (Smismans 2010). After the fall of the Iron Curtain, and thus the prospect of EU enlargement to post-communist countries with a questionable track record in human rights protection, the European Commission[6] published the *Human Rights Democracy and Development Cooperation Policy* on 25 March 1991 (first change in Fig. 2.1). This was the first European developmental policy on democracy and human rights in the context of external relations (Smismans 2010). In response, in November 1991, the Council and the member states issued a joint resolution giving high priority to the promotion of human rights in the EU's relations with third (developing) countries. But more importantly, in the same month, the Maastricht Treaty (1991; entered into force 1993) was signed, which codified the goal to promote, develop and consolidate democracy, the rule of law and respect for human rights and fundamental freedoms via the EU's external relations. At this time, LGBT rights were not included in the EU's commitment to human rights, despite the fact that LGBT rights (particularly anti-discrimination) were part of the European Parliament's agenda in the 1980s and 1990s (see Mos 2014; Swiebel 2009).

It was not until the Treaty of Amsterdam (1997; entered into force 1999) that the concept of fundamental rights in the EU was further developed, and the EU was given legislative competences to defend both human rights and LGBT rights. The Treaty of Amsterdam, in addition to amending the Treaty on the European Union (TEU) to include language stating that the EU was 'founded on the principles of liberty, democracy, respect for human rights and fundamental freedoms, and the rule of law, principles which are common to the Member States' (Article 6(1), TEU),[7] expanded the legislative competences of the EU regarding anti-discrimination. Article 13 was introduced into the Treaty Establishing the European Community (EC Treaty),[8] creating the legal basis for EU institutions to combat discrimination based on, amongst other categories, sexual orientation. A year later, the EU consolidated its new competences by adopting the Employment Directive (2000/78/EC Directive) and the Charter of Fundamental Rights, both explicitly mentioning sexual orientation as a protected class within the principles of non-discrimination. While the newly created Article 13 of the EC Treaty has no direct effect on candidate member states, and the Charter of Fundamental Rights does not create new competences for the EU, both documents are important with regard to the impact of the enlargement process on LGBT rights, as their explicit reference to sexual orientation strengthens the idea that discrimination against LGBT people is not in accordance with 'European values' (Waaldijk 2006). The 2000/8/EC directive, on the other hand, did have a direct impact on the EU accession process, as it created EU *acquis* on LGBT rights (see section "Direct Changes to LGBT Rights in the Enlargement Process").

The next important change in the EU's fundamental rights policy occurred with the Treaty of Lisbon (2007; entered into force 2009). This treaty, and provision 8 in particular, changes Article 6 of the TEU, giving the Charter of Fundamental Rights the same legal status as the (founding) treaties, although without expanding the EU's competences. As the provisions of the charter are directed towards EU institutions, and apply only to member states when they are implementing EU legislation, the impact of the charter on the accession process is rather limited (Ficchi 2011). In this regard, the added value of a binding charter is more symbolic, in that it promotes and strengthens the perception that the EU is a legitimate political actor, founded on shared values that are codified in one document. The new character of the charter thus increases the legitimacy of the accession criteria for candidate countries, as the EU is now legally obliged to uphold the same values it demands from its candidate countries.

Lastly, in 2010, the *Toolkit to Promote and Protect the Enjoyment of all Human Rights by Lesbian, Gay, Bisexual and Transgender People* was issued to EU diplomats, with instructions to protect the human rights of LGBT people. This toolkit was designed to 'help the EU institutions, EU Member State capitals, EU Delegations, Representations and Embassies to react proactively to violations of the human rights of LGBT people, and to address structural causes behind these violations' (Council of the European Union 2010, p. 1). It was expanded in 2013 with a set of guidelines that are binding for EU delegations (the toolkit was not binding). The aim of these *Guidelines to Promote and Protect the Enjoyment of all Human Rights by Lesbian, Gay, Bisexual, Transgender and Intersex (LGBTI) Persons*[9] is to 'provide officials of EU institutions and EU Member States with guidance to be used in contacts with third countries and with international and civil society organisations [...] in order to promote and protect the human rights of LGBTI persons within its external action' (Council of the European Union 2013, p. 2). Although they were created with an eye toward (re-)affirming the place of LGBT rights within EU external relations, these documents only indirectly affect the EU enlargement process. This is because of the institutional division of labour within the EU and its external relations policies: whilst the Commission is in charge of the enlargement policy, the European External Action Service (EEAS) is responsible for the EU's relations with the rest of the world. Both the toolkit and the guidelines relate to the work of the EEAS and provide EU delegations around the world with a checklist to assess LGBT human rights issues. However, because the EU has limited *acquis* regarding LGBT rights,[10] the European Commission uses all existing tools, including the guidelines to promote the protection of sexual minorities in candidate countries.

These changes have all contributed to a greater focus on fundamental rights and LGBT rights in EU institutions. In the next section we will review the evolution of the enlargement policy (black diamonds in Fig. 2.1), highlighting its increasing focus on fundamental rights.

Direct Changes to LGBT Rights in the Enlargement Process

Apart from a more general shift in focus towards fundamental rights within the EU, several changes to the EU enlargement strategy have had a direct impact on how LGBT rights are addressed.

The 1993, the Copenhagen European Council summit adopted a set of criteria for EU accession, demanding that candidate countries (a) have stable institutions guaranteeing democracy, rule of law and human rights (political conditions); (b) have a functioning market economy (economic conditions); and (c) accept established EU law and practices (legal conditions) (Nenadović 2012). In addition to formalising the EU accession process, these criteria created much wider leverage on candidate countries (Grabbe 2006), enabling the European institutions 'to steer the pre-accession developments in the candidate countries' (Kochenov 2008, p. 34). Compliance with EU accession requirements has evolved from a simple statement of fact—either a country complies or it doesn't—to a dynamic process wherein progress is constantly monitored and (re-)evaluated. Although these Copenhagen criteria do not explicitly mention LGBT rights, they have brought LGBT rights within the scope of the accession process via the requirement that candidate countries must be members of the Council of Europe (CoE).[11] As a consequence, the decriminalisation of homosexual acts and the equalisation of the ages of consent became part of enlargement conditions (Kochenov 2007).

The adoption of the 2000/78/EC directive was a key turning point in the positioning of LGBT rights within the context of enlargement. It marked the first time that a document directly banning discrimination on sexual grounds became part of the *acquis*: candidate countries are required to adopt legislation protecting LGBT people from employment discrimination.

In 2005, the European Commission amended enlargement policy such that fundamental rights would become a key part of pre-accession negotiations. It introduced Chapter 23 (on judiciary and fundamental rights) to the negotiations, a chapter specifically dealing with fundamental rights (see Nozar 2012).[12] The creation of a separate chapter gave the EU the opportunity to focus on particularly critical areas (Neuman Stanivukovi 2012). Fundamental rights were no longer merely a 'precondition' to open accession negotiations, but became an integral part of the negotiation process. Progress in the areas of judiciary and fundamental rights became the keystone of the advancement of the accession process in general (Hillion 2013).[13] However, as Nozar (2012) points out, there is a limited amount of hard *acquis* in many of the areas covered by Chapter 23. The requirements are largely general principles and 'European standards'. To determine exact targets and to measure progress, a benchmarking system was introduced. Candidate countries were required to meet opening benchmarks in order to open negotiations on a particular chapter, and closing benchmarks to conclude negotiations. The European Commission describes these benchmarks in the 2006 enlargement strategy paper:

> Benchmarks are measurable and linked to key elements of the Acquis chapter. In general, opening benchmarks concern key preparatory steps for future alignment (such as strategies or action plans), and the fulfilment of contractual obligations that mirror Acquis requirements. Closing benchmarks primarily concern legislative measures, administrative or judicial bodies, and a track record of implementation of the Acquis. (COM 2006, 649, final, p. 6)

After the conclusion of the accession negotiations with Croatia in 2011, the Commission again amended the enlargement strategy to establish a new approach for Chapter 23 (COM 2011, 666, final; see also Hillion 2013). Its purpose was to 'invigorate the monitoring of the candidates' absorption of the EU fundamental rights *acquis* in the context of accession negotiations' (Hillion 2013, p. 6). This new approach is based on the principle that:

> [Issues related to the judiciary and fundamental rights and to justice and home affairs] should be tackled early in the accession process and the corresponding chapters [23 and 24] opened accordingly on the basis of action plans, as they require the establishment of convincing track records. The Commission would report regularly, at all stages of the process, on progress achieved in these areas along milestones defined in the action plans with, where appropriate, the necessary corrective measures. (COM 2011, 666, final, p. 5)

Finally, in 2013, LGBT issues were *explicitly* identified as a key issue in Chapter 23 of the *Enlargement Strategy and Main Challenges 2013–2014*

(COM 2013, 700, final).[14] From their observation that homophobia, discrimination and hate crimes based on sexual orientation were widespread in the Western Balkans and Turkey, partly due to an incomplete legislative framework and inconsistent implementation of legal provisions currently in place, the European Commission found that:

> There is an urgent need for *anti-discrimination legislation* to be extended to include sexual orientation and gender identity within its scope in Turkey and the former Yugoslav Republic of Macedonia. *Hate crime legislation* still needs to be introduced in most countries. Training of law enforcement, ombudsman institutions, judges and media professionals is needed to raise awareness of new legislation, *to ensure proper implementation* and contribute to increasing understanding. Countries must pursue a *zero-tolerance approach to hate speech, violence and intimidation* and take steps as a matter of priority to address cases from the past and be prepared to react robustly to new cases in the future. Countries need to take measures to *counter stereotypes and misinformation*, including in the education system. Religious or cultural values cannot be invoked to justify any form of discrimination. Freedom of assembly and expression should be protected, including through appropriate handling of pride parades [...]. (COM 2013, 700, final, p. 11, original emphasis)

This excerpt from the strategy paper shows that not only did the EU identify LGBT issues as a key priority, but the demands formulated by the Commission went beyond the hard *acquis*, as evidenced by their call for zero tolerance to homophobia, education and the proper handling of Pride parades. The emphasis on Pride parades in particular has garnered intense media attention, and has made the holding of Pride parades a litmus test for readiness for EU membership (for a critical view on Pride as a litmus test, see Bilić 2016).

THE EUROPEANISATION OF LGBT RIGHTS DURING THE FIFTH AND SIXTH ENLARGEMENT ROUNDS[15]

Tracking the Impact of the Enlargement on LGBT Rights in CEE

Our overview of the co-evolution of the EU enlargement policy and the EU's fundamental rights policies has shown that with every successive enlargement round, fundamental rights have become an increasingly prominent component of accession negotiations. These changes have resulted from the lessons learned through the various iterations of the Eastern enlargement. In this section we take a closer look at the enlargement rounds to identify the concrete impact of the increased focus on fundamental and LGBT rights in acceding countries. It is beyond the scope of this article, however, to provide a detailed overview of the impact of Europeanisation on LGBT issues in CEE, and we focus instead on three relevant aspects: the EU's top-down approach, the lack of public debate, and the post-accession backlash.

In line with the analysis presented above, it is said that LGBT issues were not a priority for the EU for the 2004 and 2007 enlargements (Ames 2004; Kochenov 2006). In the annual *Regular Reports* (now called *Progress Reports*, i.e. the annual reports monitoring candidate countries progress), LGBT rights were scarcely touched upon (Ames 2004). The EU considered the protection of ethnic minorities such as the Roma to be of greater importance for EU membership. Several of our interviewees maintained that the larger focus on ethnic minorities than on sexual minorities was a political decision by the EU.[16] LGBT rights were nearly absent from the negotiations: 'for those 10 accession countries, nobody spoke about LGBT. There was the human rights chapter, but LGBT was not really visible'.[17]

This was not the only factor limiting the impact of the EU accession on LGBT rights in CEE countries (Kochenov 2006). As a result of European pressure, new legislation was adopted in a very technocratic and top-down process, without public debate (Chetaille 2011; Roseneil and Stoilova 2011). The adoption of new laws was thus a 'chimera, in that formal [laws were being] put into place without any real chance of implementation' (Jacoby 2001, p. 175). Or, as one Lithuanian activist opined:

> I interpret it as a huge drawback, because the discussion was absent and you know the LGBT rights issue is still heavily sexualised. People first of all think that it is about sex and not about civil and political rights, and because the discussion is missing, because the legal reforms were forced upon the country by external pressures. I don't think it was the cleverest way to do it.[18]

Moreover, the lack of expertise regarding LGBT rights, the absence of standards, and the heterogeneity among member states created a space for political manoeuvring on the issue by candidate countries (Ames 2004; Kochenov 2006, 2007; O'Dwyer 2010, 2012; O'Dwyer and Schwartz 2010). 'Talking the talk' was enough to convince the EU of compliance

(Haughton 2007). This was largely due to the accession process itself, which was rather top-down and elite-driven, with only marginal involvement of civil society (Galbreath 2003; Kutter and Trappmann 2010) and with a relative lack of instruments to stimulate social learning processes. A representative of ILGA-Europe remarked that local activists had few opportunities to raise LGBT issues at the local level.[19] However, ILGA-Europe did create the opportunity to access EU institutions (see Kristoffersson et al. 2016).

After EU accession, social and public debate on LGBT issues became very lively among the acceding CEE countries (O'Dwyer 2010, 2012; O'Dwyer and Schwartz 2010). State-sponsored homophobia was evident in several countries, as politicians utilised homophobic (nationalist) rhetoric to gain political capital (Mole 2011). Some countries went so far as to turn back the clock on LGBT rights, banning gay Pride parades and introducing homophobic legislation.[20] The two clearest examples are Poland and Lithuania.[21] In Poland, the Kaczyński period[22] not only witnessed the banning of Prides (by Lech Kaczyński when he was mayor of Warsaw), but the government also attempted to implement anti-gay legislation (Boersema 2010; O'Dwyer and Schwartz 2010) by proposing a bill prohibiting homosexuals from becoming teachers. In Lithuania, four years after accession, the government passed the *Law on the Protection of Minors against the Detrimental Effects of Public Information*. In the initial draft of this bill, all information about homosexuality, whether sexual in nature or not, was defined as detrimental. After strong international pressure, the bill was amended. The word 'homosexuality' was removed, yet the nature of the law remained the same. 'In essence [the law] means, because [the Lithuanian] constitution defines marriage between a man and a woman, that […] any information regarding homosexuality as such can be qualified as having a detrimental effect [as all information undermining the constitutional conception of family is considered to be so]'.[23]

Lessons Learned? The Case of LGBT Rights in Croatia

The Croatian accession process was the first to include Chapter 23, which specifically addressed judiciary and fundamental rights (cf. section "Direct Changes to LGBT Rights in the Enlargement Process"). Croatia's accession process, however, suffered setbacks due to the country's lack of cooperation with the International Criminal Tribunal for the former Yugoslavia (ICTY), one of the preconditions for accession. These delays even led to the temporary closure of negotiations on Chapter 23 (Neuman Stanivukovi 2012).[24] As a consequence, the negotiation period for the chapter was short (less than 2 years), and EU officials acknowledged that some of the changes were rushed through,[25] as negotiations were governed by a dynamic oriented towards closure.[26]

In spite of this, the legislative impact of the process was quite substantial. The 2013 annual Rainbow Europe Index published by ILGA-Europe (2013) months before Croatia's accession showed that not only did the anti-discrimination legislation in the EU's latest member state exceed EU requirements, but the level of protection of most fifth enlargement countries and some older EU member states did as well. Apart from legislation, we note three important changes compared with the 2004 accessions: more involvement of civil society groups, greater public debate on LGBT rights, and the vocal support of LGBT rights by the political elite.

LGBT organisations in Croatia were much more involved in the accession process. Croatian LGBT NGOs (Non-Governmental Organizations) were able to exploit pressure from the EU in their advocacy work. Using the annual EU monitoring and the progress reports issued by the Commission as a tool and framework for their advocacy campaigns, LGBT activists were able to push for legislative change beyond EU membership requirements.[27] At the same time, however, our interviewees all mentioned that these laws lacked adequate implementation (see also Kahlina 2015).

Croatia also had much greater public and political debate on LGBT issues. For example, Pride parades have been happening in Zagreb since 2002. After the opening of Chapter 23 in the EU negotiations (2009), LGBT rights became a prominent political topic,[28] and it was no longer possible for those in power to ignore the rights of the LGBT community, as these issues became part of the public debate.[29] This was clearly in evidence in the events surrounding the gay Pride in Split (see also Moss 2014). After the first Split Pride in 2011 was met with violent counter-demonstrations, Prime Minister Zoran Milanović (Social Democratic Party [SDP]) in 2012 called on residents of Split to show tolerance and to accept the 'standard democratic practice of Western Europe' (quoted in msnbc.com news services 2012). Vesna Pusić, Minister of Foreign and European Affairs (SDP), and Ivo Baldasar, the newly elected mayor of Split (SDP), joined the 2013 Pride.[30] Both politicians referred to European values and standards in their speeches on the event, with Pusić (Media Servis 2013) declaring that because 'politically we have become Europe, it is time to begin to behave as such'. Further proof can be found in the election campaign of Ivo Baldasar weeks before the Split Pride parade, during which he openly showed his support for LGBT issues and actively advocated for LGBT rights.[31] At the time, Baldasar not only promised that he would attend the (2013) Pride, but also committed to supporting the creation of an LGBT centre in the city. Although activists have remained sceptical whether politicians actually believe in LGBT rights, they see it as a sign that times are changing, with politicians now beginning to use the advocacy of LGBT rights to gain political capital.[32] Wide cross-party consensus on the desirability of EU accession also prevented LGBT issues from becoming a politically contentious topic.[33] Croatia's accession process was partly a way of proving its Europeanness and distancing itself from the Balkans (Kahlina 2015). Support for LGBT rights positioned Croatia within 'LGBT-tolerant Europe' (Kahlina 2015; Moss 2014).

Croatia's accession in June 2013 was immediately followed by a backlash against LGBT rights in the form of a marriage referendum.[34] The citizen group *U Ime Obitelji* (In the Name of the Family) had begun collecting signatures in the spring of 2013 to demand a referendum on the constitutional definition of marriage, and succeeded in collecting almost twice the required number of signatures. The referendum was held, and Croatians voted in favour of introducing of a heterosexual definition of marriage in the constitution (37 % turnout, with 65 % voting for and 35 % against). Nevertheless, the political elite at the time remained committed to LGBT rights. After the referendum, the centre-left government continued to push for the Life Partnership Act [*Životnom Partnerstvu*],[35] disregarding the initiative's 'protect the family' rhetoric (the law was adopted in the summer of 2014). Even during the referendum campaign, high-level politicians, particularly Prime Minster Zoran Milanović, Deputy Prime Minister Vesna Pusić and President Ivo Josipović, argued against the referendum (Hina 2013; Pavelić 2013), as did many public figures and celebrities.[36]

The Croatian case suggests that the EU's increased attention on fundamental rights has paid off. The EU managed to push through actual legislative reform, and there is some evidence of social learning on the part of political elite as well (Slootmaeckers 2014). While these changes can be seen as effects of the new enlargement strategy and leverage tools (see section "Direct Changes to LGBT Rights in the Enlargement Process"), two other contributing factors should be taken into account. First, there is the global 'mainstreaming' of LGBT rights[37] that might have accelerated the changes in Croatia, especially the elite discourse on the issue. A second important factor is the increasing transnationalisation of civil society (see Ayoub 2013). LGBT rights groups in Croatia—and in other Western Balkan countries—have received considerable support from their counterparts in the West, who have shared their knowledge and tactics. Most of these groups are also members of various transnational networks.[38] Moreover, whilst European LGBT activism (especially ILGA-Europe) was still consolidating its position in Europe during the fifth enlargement, it has now become a high-capacity organisation with a great number of experiences it can share with local activists (see also Kristoffersson et al. 2016). Many of the CEE groups have also learned from their experience, and are in contact with the groups from the Balkans. This has resulted in growing LGBT activism and in civil society groups that have been more effective than those in CEE in 2004.

In Lieu of a Conclusion: Food for Thought on the Future of LGBT Rights in the Western Balkans

The previous sections have illustrated the co-evolution of the EU enlargement process and fundamental rights, including LGBT rights, policies and the impact on the new member states. With fundamental rights increasingly moving to the centre of the enlargement process, we have found that the impact of the EU accession process on candidate countries seems to be expanding with each iteration of the Eastern enlargement. However, the Croatian case has also shown that the EU does not work in isolation, and that to understand the impact of EU enlargement on LGBT rights in candidate countries, various processes must be taken into account. Consequently, despite the fact that LGBT rights have become even more central to the accession process since the Croatian experience, we cannot be sure about the impact on the countries currently in the EU 'waiting room'.

Instead of a traditional conclusion to this chapter, we want to make a brief reference to the future and the expected impact of EU accession on LGBT rights in the rest of the Western Balkan countries. While legal changes have already occurred in most countries, the continued impact of EU accession on LGBT politics in (potential) candidate countries will be dependent both on domestic factors that might limit EU influence and on the politics surrounding the enlargement, i.e. willingness of the EU to prioritise LGBT rights.

With regard to domestic factors, the chief issue is the limited statehood of several Western Balkan countries (see Börzel 2013; Elbasani 2013; Noutcheva and Aydin-Düzgit 2012). The status of Bosnia and Kosovo as semi-protectorates and the internal problems of the Former Yugoslav Republic of Macedonia (henceforth, Macedonia) make it unlikely that they will achieve member status very soon. Bosnia's EU integration process, for example, is being held up by the country's constitutional problems (cf. Sejdić and Finci ruling), whilst Kosovo's progress is slowed by its contested statehood (and nationhood). Similarly, despite being granted candidate status in 2005 and 2013, respectively, the progress of both Macedonia and Albania is stagnating. Although the European Commission recommended the opening of negotiations with Macedonia in 2009, Macedonia's progress seems deadlocked due to its naming dispute with Greece, and the accession process of Albania is hampered by its weak state capacity and the unwillingness of the political elite to introduce reforms beyond formal compliance (Börzel 2013; Elbasani 2013). Therefore, the incentive for reform and the ability of the EU to coerce these states will be much lower here than elsewhere.

This is particularly evident in the case of Macedonia. With regard to LGBT rights, the Macedonian government adopted anti-discrimination legislation in 2010 (SEC 2010, 1332, final), but the new law is 'still not in line with the *acquis* as it does not explicitly prohibit discrimination on grounds of sexual orientation in employment and occupation' (SWD 2013, 413, final, p. 37). Among countries where legislation is in place, problems with the rule of law limit the proper implementation of these laws. Attacks against LGBT activists occur regularly throughout the region (for a detailed overview see Pearce and Cooper 2013). For example, when the magazine *Kosovo 2.0* published its fourth edition, *Sex*, it included stories of LGBT activist offices as the target of repeated vandalism, violence and, at one point, even arson. Pearce and Cooper (2013) continue their overview with similar events in Albania, Bosnia and Herzegovina, and Serbia. In many cases, the perpetrators of these attacks have not been identified, tried, and convicted (see ILGA-Europe 2015). Activists have complained of a lack of cooperation by police and the limited capacity (and/or willingness) of the court system to deal with anti-discrimination and hate crime violations.

Another important domestic factor influencing the impact of EU accession on LGBT rights is the extent to which ruling political elites identify as 'European' or 'Western' (see also Freyburg and Richter 2010; Subotić

2010, 2011), which is highly dependent on the parties voted into office. A case in point is Serbia. The Serbian government comprises a majority of right-wing nationalist parties that exhibit no sense of a European identity. Although they claim to be in favour of EU membership, the Serbian government refuses to uncritically accept the EU demands. Especially with regard to Kosovo or the Belgrade Pride, the Serbian authorities are reluctant to give in to EU demands (for a more elaborate account on the political will regarding the Belgrade Pride, see Fagan and Slootmaeckers 2014).[39] The Montenegrin government, on the other hand, does have a distinct pro-European attitude, which has helped to improve the status of LGBT rights in Montenegro.[40] The government adopted the *Strategy for Improving the Quality of Life of LGBT Persons 2013–2018* (see LGBT Forum Progress 2013), provided protection for the first Pride events in the country (in Budva and Podgorica), and even announced that it would begin drafting a same-sex partnership law (Tomovic 2014). Local activists have also noted that some institutions (e.g. the police, the Office of the Ombudsman and the Ministry of Justice) have begun to recognise that the protection of human rights of LGBT persons is part of their professional responsibilities, and not simply something they are arbitrarily made to do.[41]

Finally, when considering the impact of the EU on LGBT rights in the Western Balkans, one must take into account that decisions regarding the enlargement have become increasingly politicised, rather than simply procedural as in previous rounds. First, some member states are suffering from 'enlargement fatigue' and are questioning the absorption capacity of the EU (Neuman Stanivukovi 2012). Second, what should be a technical process of aligning legislation has been tainted by political considerations. As a result, LGBT rights are often on the losing side when it comes to trade-offs with other issues the EU regards as more important, especially regional security. When Macedonia was negotiating the visa liberalisation agreements, anti-discrimination based on sexual orientation was one of the four EU requirements. However, because of pressure from conservative groups within the country, which resonated with the conservative agenda of the government, the explicit reference to sexual orientation was dropped from the language. According to the Minister of Labour and Social Policy, LGBT people would be protected under the 'other grounds' mentioned in the law (see also Fouéré 2016).[42] These groups framed the issue as a choice for or against same-sex marriage, an issue that has nothing to do with anti-discrimination. Despite the pressure by the EP LGBT

Intergroup and other actors, the visa liberalisation deal was approved. In Kosovo, the EU's leverage regarding LGBT rights is also through the visa liberalisation negotiations. It remains to be seen whether these conditions will be fulfilled and whether the process will be distorted by the normalisation of relations between Serbia and Kosovo.

The importance of this latter process for the EU and its impact on the EU enlargement has already been seen in the case of Serbian accession. The trade-off between regional security (and a solution to the 'Kosovo problem') and LGBT rights has not favoured the rights of the LGBT community, which has become evident in the debate surrounding the Pride parades in Serbia (see Fagan and Slootmaeckers 2014). At the time, the normalisation of relations between Serbia and Kosovo was a key priority for the EU. In fact, EU documents suggest that Serbia would not be sanctioned for banning the Pride parade as long as they made progress on the more important issue of Kosovo. For example, in 2012, EU officials stated that holding a Pride parade would help Serbia on its path to EU member status, but that the accession process would not be halted if the parade were not held (B92 2012). Furthermore, during his visit to Belgrade a week later, European Commissioner for Enlargement Štefan Füle did not discuss the Pride ban with Serbian authorities (Korica 2012). Despite expressing regret that the threats of radical groups were deemed serious enough to justify a ban, Füle's spokesperson suggested that there were more important issues to discuss (Korica 2012). Interestingly, it was only after the signing of the Brussels Agreement (Spring 2013) that the EU language on Pride parade bans was changed, and 'lack of political will' was first mentioned as a reason for the ban in the EU *2013 Progress Report*. Coincidence or not, LGBT issues were also identified that year as a key priority within the fundamental rights chapters of the enlargement strategy.[43] However, a Commission official admitted that although a new trend had been established in 2013, the prioritisation of LGBT issues within the enlargement process continued to be subject to the developments on the main driver of this enlargement round—regional stability.[44]

To summarise the overarching argument of the chapter, we have seen that since the formulation of the Copenhagen criteria (1993), the issue of fundamental rights has become an increasingly important component of the enlargement process. With the increased attention within the EU for LGBT rights (especially in its external relations), these rights have recently been declared a priority within the fundamental rights section of the EU enlargement. Although these changes at the EU level have contributed to positive changes in the new member states, especially in Croatia, we advocate caution when contemplating the potential impact of the EU on the current (potential) candidate countries. Not only is the potential impact of the EU contingent on domestic factors such as the countries' (limited) statehood and state identity—i.e. the orientation of politicians towards the EU—but it is also affected by the particular position of (potential) candidate countries within the EU's foreign policy—neither fully external nor internal policy, but still expected to adhere to EU rules—and the discrepancy between the comprehensive external and limited internal policy regarding LGBT rights, which limits the EU's leverage on the issue.[45] Consequently, the influence of the EU on LGBT rights is largely dependent on the EU's priorities and whether issues like regional stability will push LGBT rights into the background.

Notes

1. Smismans (2010) debunks the EU's idealised relationship with fundamental rights, highlighting that the EU was founded on ideas of economic cooperation, which sometimes threatened fundamental rights.
2. One must keep in mind that the EU's exceptionalism on LGBT rights is part of the fundamental rights myth, and does not necessarily reflect the reality. One mechanism keeping this myth alive consists in continually identifying a 'homophobic other' both within and outside the borders of the EU (often in the 'imagined East'). For more critical engagement with this East–West divide and LGBT issues, see Ammaturo (2015), Kulpa (2014), and Kulpa and Mizielińska (2011).
3. This chapter does not address the influence of local and regional LGBT activism on EU policy; for this perspective, see the chapter by Kristoffersson et al. (2016).
4. The fifth enlargement occurred in two waves. In the 2004 wave, the EU welcomed as new member states eight CEE countries (Czech Republic, Estonia, Hungary, Latvia, Lithuania, Poland, Slovakia, and Slovenia) and Cyprus and Malta. In the second wave (2007), two more CEE states joined: Bulgaria and Romania. The sixth enlargement round marked the accession of Croatia (2013).
5. For the sake of economy, we have opted to focus on changes made by the European Commission and the Council of the European Union. Although the European Parliament (EP) has played an important role in putting LGBT rights on the EU's political agenda, its role within the EU enlarge-

ment process remains rather limited. Furthermore, adding all the resolutions and reports drafted by the EP to our timeline would result in an overcrowded figure with reduced readability.

6. At the time, known as the Commission of the European Communities.
7. This statement was further expanded with the Treaty of Lisbon (2007), and now states: 'The Union is founded on the values of respect for human dignity, freedom, democracy, equality, the rule of law and respect for human rights, including the rights of persons belonging to minorities. These values are common to the Member States in a society in which pluralism, non-discrimination, tolerance, justice, solidarity and equality between women and men prevail' (Article 2, TEU).
8. The Treaty of Lisbon changed the name of the EC Treaty to the Treaty on the Functioning of the European Union (TFEU) and changed the numbering to Article 19, TFEU.
9. The 'I' in LGBTI stands for Intersex.
10. Two recent initiatives for change are worth mentioning here. The first is the horizontal *Equal Treatment Directive*, which would provide protection on all grounds mentioned in Article 19 of the TFEU (and Article 21 of the Charter of Fundamental Rights) in all areas akin to Directive 2000/43/EC on racial discrimination. This horizontal directive, however, has been blocked in the council since 2009, with financial issues regarding accessibility criteria being the main stumble block. Additionally, there is movement within the Juncker Commission to introduce an EU-wide action plan (or framework strategy) to protect LGBT people from discrimination (Intergroup LGBT Rights 2014, 2015).
11. Although it is a rather odd condition, and it is not mentioned in any of the treaties, the EU has explicitly demonstrated that membership in the CoE is considered a necessary step towards accession (Kochenov 2008).
12. See the approval of the negotiations framework for Croatia: http://ec.europa.eu/enlargement/pdf/croatia/st20004_05_hr_framedoc_en.pdf.
13. The importance of chapters 23 and 24 for the EU enlargement process is further acknowledged in the framework of the negotiationsfor Montenegro (CONF-ME 2012, 2) and Serbia (CONF-RS 2014, 1).
14. In recent years, the EU has started using the acronym 'LGBTI' instead of 'LGBT' in order to include intersex individuals in their policy. To avoid confusion, in this chapter we use only the LGBT acronym except when directly quoting EU documents.
15. This section is based on data for six countries among the new CEE member states from the fifth enlargement, i.e. Hungary, Latvia, Lithuania, Poland, Romania and Slovenia. We are aware that the experiences from other countries differ from the experiences presented here. However, the general trend described in this section can be applied to almost all CEE

new member states. For a more detailed analysis of the impact of EU accession on LGBT rights among the new member states, especially with regard to national differences, we refer to the work of Ayoub (2014, 2015).

16. Face-to-face interview with representative of Mozaika on 19 October 2012 in Dublin; face-to-face interview with representative of the Campaign Against Homophobia on 19 October 2012 in Dublin; personal communication with EU official (European Parliament) on 19 October 2012 in Dublin.

17. Face-to-face interview with representative of Mozaika on 17 October 2012 in Dublin.

18. Skype interview with representative of Lithuanian Gay League on 4 December 2012.

19. Face-to-face interview with representative of ILGA-Europe, on 30 August 2012 in Brussels.

20. These backlashes were due not only to the lack of social learning during the pre-accession period, but also to the lack of an infringement mechanism in the EU's legal framework to allow sanctioning of countries that breached the basic rules of democracy and human rights (Inotai 2012).

21. Backlashes also occurred in other countries. In Latvia (2006) and Hungary (2012), for example, the government amended the constitutional definition of marriage to that of a union between a man and a woman. In Romania, marriage has had a heterosexual definition, although this definition has never been codified in the constitution despite various attempts. While the Family Code remains outside EU competence, one interviewee remarked that 'without pressure from the EU, politicians do not care anymore, and now [in some countries] the situation is worse than before' (face-to-face interview with representative of the ACCEPT Association on 19 October 2012 in Dublin).

22. The Kaczyński brothers were in power from 2005 to 2010: Jarosław Kaczyński as prime minister (2005–2007) and Lech Kaczyński as president (2005–2010).

23. Skype interview with representative of Lithuanian Gay League on 4 December 2012.

24. For a discussion of Croatia's troublesome cooperation with the ICTY during the accession process, see Boduszyński (2013, pp. 48–50).

25. Face-to-face interview with EU official, European Commission (DG Enlargement), on 29 May 2013 in Brussels; phone interview with Ulrike Lunacek, Member of the European Parliament and co-president of LGBT Intergroup, on 15 May 2013.

26. Face-to-face interview with EU official, European Commission (DG Enlargement), on 24 October 2013 in Zagreb.

27. Face-to-face interview with a representative of Iskorak on 20 October 2012 in Dublin; face-to-face interview with representative of the Croatian

Labour Party (and founder of Iskorak) on 21 October 2013, Zagreb; face-to-face interview with representative of Zagreb Pride on 24 October 2013 in Zagreb.

28. Face-to-face interview with Representative of Zagreb Pride, on 24 October 2013 in Zagreb; Face-to-face interview with representative of Zagreb Pride on 29 October 2013 in Zagreb.

29. Face-to-face interview with independent Croatian activist on 12 June 2014 in Zagreb.

30. The right-wing party HDZ has never openly supported LGBT rights in Croatia. However, they have repeatedly told activists that their silence on the issue was a sign of their support, although they have publicly spoken against same-sex marriage(Vuletić 2013).

31. Informal conversation with LGBT activist from Split.

32. Face-to-face interview with representative of Zagreb Pride on 24 October 2013 in Zagreb; face-to-face interview with independent Croatian activist on 12 June 2014 in Zagreb.

33. The issue of state identity and the collective identity of the governing political elite was another factor that played a significant role during the fifth enlargement. In Poland, for example, LGBT rights were often discursively contrasted with the country's national identity. As O'Dwyer (2012, p. 342) has shown, the EU pressure for LGBT rights caused the issue to be 'framed as a question of national identity. Homosexuality mapped very easily onto a broader debate about Polish identity'.

34. Although the use of the word 'backlash' here is similar to that regarding the backlash that occurred in the fifth enlargement round, it is important to address one key difference between the Croatian and CEE cases. Whereas in CEE most of the backlash resulted from political (and state-sponsored) homophobia, the Croatian backlash was the result of a grass-roots initiative.

35. This piece of legislation would give same-sex couples the same rights as married couples except for adoption. However, it does regulate those who already live with children(Milekic 2014).

36. Face-to-face interview with representative of Zagreb Pride on 24 October 2013 in Zagreb.

37. See Pearce and Cooper (2013, p. 324) for a timeline of international instruments addressing LGBT rights.

38. E.g. ILGA-Europe, BABELNOR, and IGLYO.

39. Face-to-face interview with representative of Labris, on 20 October 2012 in Dublin.

40. Face-to-face interview with representative of LGBT Forum Progress on 15 October 2012 in Dublin.

41. Skype interview with representative of Queer Montenegro on 20 August 2014.

42. Interview with former EU official, Brussels, May 2013.
43. When Pride took place in 2014, Prime Minister Aleksandar Vučić did not attend, nor did he defend the event. On the contrary, in a press conference afterwards, he thanked the opponents of the Pride for their tolerance and for refraining from violence.
44. Face-to-face interview with EU official, European Commission (DG Enlargement), on 6 March 2014 in Brussels.
45. Face-to-face interview with EU official, European Commission (DG Near), on 26 May 2015 in Brussels.

REFERENCES

Ames, L. M. (2004). Beyond gay paree: What does the enlargement of the European Union mean for same-sex partners. *Emory International Law Review, 18*, 503–554.
Ammaturo, F. R. (2015). The 'Pink Agenda': Questioning and challenging European homonationalist sexual citizenship. *Sociology*, online first. Retrieved from http://soc.sagepub.com/cgi/doi/10.1177/0038038514559324.
Ayoub, P. M. (2013). Cooperative transnationalism in contemporary Europe: Europeanization and political opportunities for LGBT mobilization in the European Union. *European Political Science Review, 5*(2), 279–310.
Ayoub, P. M. (2014). With arms wide shut: Threat perception, norm reception, and mobilized resistance to LGBT rights. *Journal of Human Rights, 13*(3), 337–362.
Ayoub, P. M. (2015). Contested norms in new-adopter states: International determinants of LGBT rights legislation. *European Journal of International Relations, 21*(2), 293–322.
Ayoub, P. M., & Paternotte, D. (2014a). Introduction. In P. M. Ayoub & D. Paternotte (Eds.), *LGBT activism and the making of Europe: A rainbow Europe?* (pp. 1–25). Basingstoke, England: Palgrave Macmillan.
B92. (2012). Holding of gay pride parade still uncertain. [online] *B92*. Retrieved March 5, 2014, from http://www.b92.net/eng/news/society.php?yyyy=2012&mm=09&dd=29&nav_id=82413.
Bilić, B. (2016). Whose pride? LGBT 'Community' and the organisation of pride parades in Serbia. In K. Slootmaeckers, H. Touquet, & P. Vermeersch (Eds.), *The EU enlargement and gay politics*. London: Palgrave Macmillan.
Boduszyński, M. P. (2013). The trials and triumphs of Europeanization of Croatia: The unbearable weight of structure and state-building? In A. Elbasani (Ed.), (pp. 39–53). Oxon, England: Routledge.
Boersema, W. (2010). The tyranny of the majority. gays in Poland. In I. Dubel & A. Hielkema (Eds.), *Urgency required: Gay and lesbian rights are human rights* (pp. 280–283). Amsterdam: Humanist Institute for Cooperation with Developing Countries (Hivos).

Börzel, T. A. (2013). When Europeanization hits limited statehood: The Western Balkans as a test case for the transformative power of Europe. In A. Elbasani (Ed.), *European integration and transformation in the Western Balkans: Europeanization or business as usual?* (pp. 173–184). Oxon, England: Routledge.

Chetaille, A. (2011). Poland: Sovereignty and sexuality in post-socialist times. In M. Tremblay, D. Paternotte, & C. Johnson (Eds.), *The lesbian and gay movement and the state: Comparative insights into a transformed relationship.* Surrey, England: Ashgate Publishing Limited.

Council Directive. 2000/43/EC of 29 June 2000 implementing the principle of equal treatment between persons irrespective of racial or ethnic origin.

Council Directive. 2000/78/EC of 27 November 2000 establishing a general framework for equal treatment in employment and occupation.

Council of the European Union (2010). *Toolkit to promote and protect the enjoyment of all human rights by Lesbian, Gay, Bisexual and Transgender (LGBT) people.* Brussels, Belgium: European Union.

Council of the European Union (2013). *Guidelines to promote and protect the enjoyment of all human rights by Lesbian, Gay, Bisexual, Transgender and Intersex (LGBTI) persons.* Luxembourg: European Union.

Elbasani, A. (Ed.) (2013). *European integration and transformation in the Western Balkans: Europeanization or business as usual?* Oxon, England: Routledge.

Enlargement strategy and main challenges 2006–2007 including annexed special report on the EU's capacity to integrate new members, COM (2006) 649, final.

Enlargement strategy and main challenges 2011–2012, COM (2011) 666, final.

Enlargement strategy and main challenges 2013–2014, COM (2013) 700, final.

Fagan, A., & Slootmaeckers, K. 2014. Too proud to have pride? The EU's (in) ability to promote LGBT equality in Serbia. Paper presented at ECPR Joint Sessions. Salamanca.

Ficchi, L. (2011). Candidate countries facing a binding charter of fundamental rights: What's new. In G. Di Federico (Ed.), *The EU charter of fundamental rights: From declaration to binding instrument* (pp. 109–121). New York: Springer.

Fouéré, E. (2016). The curious case of Macedonia: A personal insight of a former head of the EU delegation in Macedonia. In K. Slootmaeckers, H. Touquet, & P. Vermeersch (Eds.), *The EU enlargement and gay politics.* London: Palgrave Macmillan.

Freyburg, T., & Richter, S. (2010). National identity matters: the limited impact of EU political conditionality in the Western Balkans. *Journal of European Public Policy, 17*(2), 263–281.

Galbreath, D. (2003). The politics of European integration and minority rights in Estonia and Latvia. *Perspectives on European Politics and Society, 4*(1), 35–53.

General EU Position: Ministerial Meeting Opening the Intergovernmental Conference on the Accession of Montenegro to the European Union. CONF-ME (2012) 2.

General EU Position: Ministerial Meeting Opening the Intergovernmental Conference on the Accession of Serbia to the European Union. CONF-RS (2014) 1.

Grabbe, H. (2006). *The EU transformative power: Europeanization through conditionality in Central and Eastern Europe.* New York: Palgrave Macmillan.

Haughton, T. (2007). When does the EU make a difference? Conditionality and the accession process in Central and Eastern Europe. *Political Studies Review, 5*(2), 233–246.

Hillion, C. (2013). *Enlarging the European Union and deepening its fundamental rights protection. European policy analysis.* Stockholm: Swedish Institute for European Policy Studies.

Hina. (2013). REFERENDUM O GAY BRAKU Pusić: 'Treba izići i glasati protiv, to je prvi korak prema diskriminaciji'. [online] Jutarnji. Retrieved November 18, 2013, from http://www.jutarnji.hr/pusic-o-referendumu-o-gay-braku–treba-izici-i-glasati-protiv–to-je-prvi-korak-prema-diskriminaciji-/1140304/.

ILGA-Europe. (2013). *ILGA-Europe Rainbow Map (Index).* [online] Retrieved May 29, 2015, from http://www.ilga-europe.org/sites/default/files/Attachments/side_b_-_rainbow_europe_index_may_20131.pdf.

ILGA-Europe (2015). *Annual review of the human rights situation of lesbian, gay, bisexual, trans and intersex people in Europe 2015.* Brussels, Belgium: ILGA-Europe.

Inotai, A. (2012). A Hungarian perspective. In H. Swoboda, E. Stetter, & J. M. Wiersma (Eds.), *EU enlargement anno 2012: A progressive engagement* (pp. 69–76). Brussels, Belgium: European Union.

Intergroup on LGBT Rights. (2014). Juncker I Commission—Jourová commits to LGBTI Action Plan; Navracsics rejected over fundamental rights. [online] The European Parliament Intergroup on LGBT Rights. Retrieved June 1, 2015,fromhttp://www.lgbt-ep.eu/press-releases/juncker-i-commission-jourova-commits-to-lgbti-action-plan-navracsics-rejected-over-fundamental-rights/.

Intergroup on LGBT Rights. (2015). Commissioner Jourová committed to LGBTI action plan in 2015. [online] The European Parliament Intergroup on LGBT Rights. Retrieved June 1, 2015, from http://www.lgbt-ep.eu/press-releases/commissioner-jourova-committed-to-lgbti-action-plan-in-2015/?utm_source=feedburner&utm_medium=feed&utm_campaign=Feed%3A+intergrouplgbt+%28The+European+Parliament%27s+Intergroup+on+LGBT+Rights%29.

Jacoby, W. (2001). Tutors and pupils: International organizations, Central European elites, and Western models. *Governance, 14*(2), 169–200.

Kahlina, K. (2015). Local histories, European LGBT designs: Sexual citizenship, nationalism, and 'Europeanisation' in post-Yugoslav Croatia and Serbia. *Women's Studies International Forum, 49*, 73–83.

Kochenov, D. (2006). Democracy and human rights-not for gay people: EU Eastern enlargement and its impact on the protection of the rights of sexual minorities. *Texas Wesleyan Law Review, 13*, 459–496.

Kochenov, D. (2007). Gay rights in the EU: A long way forward for the union of 27. *Croatian Yearbook of European Law and Policy, 3*(3), 469–490.

Kochenov, D. (2008). *EU enlargement and the failure of conditionality: Pre-accession conditionality in the fields of democracy and the rule of law.* Alphen aan den Rijn, The Netherlands: Kluwer Law International.

Korica, B. (2012). Banning of gay pride may damage Serbia's European Union chances. [online] *Gay Star News.* Retrieved April 9, 2015, from http://www.gaystarnews.com/article/banning-gay-pride-may-damage-serbia%E2%80%99s-european-union-chances051012.

Kristoffersson, M., van Roozendaal, B., & Poghosyan, L. (2016). European integration and LGBTI activism—partners in realizing change? In K. Slootmaeckers, H. Touquet, & P. Vermeersch (Eds.), *The EU enlargement and gay politics.* London: Palgrave Macmillan.

Kulpa, R. (2014). Western leveraged pedagogy of Central and Eastern Europe: Discourses of homophobia, tolerance, and nationhood. *Gender, Place Culture A Journal of Feminist Geography, 21*(4), 431–448.

Kulpa, R., & Mizielińska, J. (Eds.) (2011). *De-centring western sexualities: Central and Eastern European perspectives.* Surrey, England: Ashgate Publishing Company.

Kutter, A., & Trappmann, V. (2010). Civil society in Central and Eastern Europe: The ambivalent legacy of accession. *Acta Politica, 45*(1–2), 41–69.

LGBT Forum Progress. 2013. Adopted strategy for improvement of quality of life of the LGBT persons. [online] ILGA-Europe. Retrieved August 20, 2014, from http://www.ilga-europe.org/home/guide_europe/country_by_country/montenegro/adopted_strategy_for_improvement_of_quality_of_life_of_the_lgbt_persons.

Manners, I. (2010). Global Europa: Mythology of the European Union in world politics. *Journal of Common Market Studies, 48*(1), 67–87.

Media Servis. (2013). Split položio ispit tolerancije i demokracije: 'Vlado, poduzmite konkretne korake! Ljudska prava ne mogu čekati!'. *Index.* 8 Jun. Retrieved June 16, 2013, from http://www.index.hr/vijesti/clanak/split-polozio-ispit-tolerancije-i-demokracije-quotvlado-poduzmite-konkretne-korake-ljudska-prava-ne-mogu-cekatiquot/682267.aspx.

Milekic, S. (2014). Croatia to legalise same-sex partnerships. *Balkan insight.* [online] Retrieved from http://www.balkaninsight.com/en/article/croatia-to-legalise-same-sex-partnerships.

Mole, R. (2011). Nationality and sexuality: homophobic discourse and the 'national threat' in contemporary Latvia. *Nations and Nationalism, 17*(3), 540–560.

Mos, M. (2014). Of gay rights and Christmas ornaments: The political history of sexual orientation non-discrimination in the treaty of Amsterdam. *Journal of Common Market Studies, 52*(3), 632–649.

Moss, K. (2014). Split Europe: Homonationalism and homophobia in Croatia. In P. M. Ayoub & D. Paternotte (Eds.), *LGBT activism and the making of Europe: A rainbow Europe?* (pp. 212–232). Basingstoke, England: Palgrave Macmillan.

msnbc.com News Services. (2012). In unprecedented move, Croatian ministers to join disputed gay pride march. [online] Retrieved December 3, 2013, from http://worldnews.nbcnews.com/_news/2012/06/06/12085915-in-unprecedented-move-croatian-ministers-to-join-disputed-gay-pride-march.

Nenadović, M. (2012). Enlargement anno 2012. In H. Swoboda, E. Stetter, & J. M. Wiersma (Eds.), *EU enlargement anno 2012: A progressive engagement* (pp. 21–34). Brussels, Belgium: European Union.

Neuman Stanivukovi, S. (2012). Croatia as the 28th EU member state: How did we get here and where should we go from now? [online] Papiers d'actualité/Current Affairs in Perspective. Retrieved May 27, 2013, from http://www.fondation-pierredubois.ch/images/stories/papiers_dactualit/no1_2012_croatia.pdf.

Noutcheva, G., & Aydin-Düzgit, S. (2012). Lost in Europeanisation: The Western Balkans and Turkey. *West European Politics, 35*(1), 59–78.

Nozar, W. (2012). The 100% union: The rise of chapters 23 and 24. In H. Swoboda, E. Stetter, & J. M. Wiersma (Eds.), *EU enlargement anno 2012: A progressive engagement* (pp. 87–96). Brussels, Belgium: European Union.

O'Dwyer, C. (2010). From conditionality to persuasion? Europeanization and the rights of sexual minorities in post-accession Poland. *Journal of European Integration, 32*(3), 229–247.

O'Dwyer, C. (2012). Does the EU help or hinder gay-rights movements in post-communist Europe? The case of Poland. *East European Politics, 28*(4), 332–352.

O'Dwyer, C., & Schwartz, K. Z. S. (2010). Minority rights after EU enlargement: A comparison of antigay politics in Poland and Latvia. *Comparative European politics, 8*(2), 220–243.

Pavelić, B. (2013). Anti-gay marriage ballot has Croatian liberals worried. [online] *Balkan insight.* 28 Nov. Retrieved November 28, 2013, from http://www.balkaninsight.com/en/article/anti-gay-marriage-ballot-has-croatian-liberals-worried.

Pearce, S. C., & Cooper, A. (2013). LGBT movements in Southeast Europe: Violence, justice, and international intersections. In D. Peterson & V. R. Panfil

(Eds.), *Handbook of LGBT communities, crime, and justice* (pp. 311–338). New York: Springer.

Roseneil, S., & Stoilova, M. (2011). Heteronormativity, intimate citizenship and the regulation of same-sex sexualities in Bulgaria. In R. Kulpa & J. Mizielińska (Eds.), *De-centring western sexualities: Central and Eastern European perspectives* (pp. 167–190). Surrey, England: Ashgate Publishing Company.

Slootmaeckers, K. (2014). From EU-induced institutional change to normative change: When organizations matter. *Reviews & Critical Commentary.* Retrieved from http://councilforeuropeanstudies.org/critcom/from-eu-induced-institutional-change-to-normative-change-when-organizations-matter/.

Smismans, S. (2010). The European Union's fundamental rights myth. *Journal of Common Market Studies, 48*(1), 45–66.

Stychin, C. F. (2004). Same-sex sexualities and the globalization of human rights discourse. *McGill Law Journal, 49*(4), 951–968.

Subotić, J. (2010). Explaining difficult states: The problems of Europeanization in Serbia. *East European Politics & Societies, 24*(4), 595–616.

Subotić, J. (2011). Europe is a state of mind: Identity and Europeanization in the Balkans. *International Studies Quarterly, 55*(2), 309–330.

Swiebel, J. (2009). Lesbian, gay, bisexual and transgender human rights: The search for an international strategy. *Contemporary Politics, 15*(1), 19–35.

The Former Yugoslav Republic of Macedonia 2010 progress report, SEC (2010) 1332, final.

The Former Yugoslav Republic of Macedonia 2013 progress report, SWD (2013) 413, final.

Tomovic, D. (2014). Montenegro plans to legalize gay marriages. [online] *Balkan insight.* Retrieved August 19, 2014, from http://www.balkaninsight.com/en/article/monenegro-plans-to-legalize-gay-marriages.

Vuletić, D. (2013). Out of the homeland: The Croatian right and gay rights. *Southeastern Europe, 37*(1), 36–59.

Waaldijk, K. (2006). Legislation in fifteen EU member states against sexual orientation discrimination in employment: The implementation of Directive 2000/78/EC. In A. Weyembergh & S. Carstocea (Eds.), *The gays'and lesbians' rights in an enlarged European Union* (pp. 17–47). Brussels, Belgium: Institut d'Etudes Européennes.

Williams, A. (2004). *EU human rights policies: A study in irony.* Oxford: Oxford University Press.

CHAPTER 3

European Integration and LGBTI Activism: Partners in Realising Change?

Mattias Kristoffersson, Björn van Roozendaal,
and Lilit Poghosyan

INTRODUCTION

Today, there can no longer be any doubt that the promotion of LGBTI human rights is an important part of the EU's enlargement and foreign policy. The 2012 *EU Strategic Framework on Human Rights and Democracy* adopted by the European Council solidified the EU commitment to human rights by providing a clear path on how the EU wishes to promote human rights globally. Keeping with the commitments laid out in this strategic framework, in 2013 the Council adopted a comprehensive set of guidelines on the promotion of LGBTI human rights in foreign policy. This policy document, unanimously adopted by all member states, unequivocally placed LGBTI issues at the core of what the EU represents. Moreover, in 2013 and 2014, the European Commission made the promotion of LGBTI human rights a priority within the enlargement policy (see Slootmaeckers and Touquet 2016), and its annual strategies called in for 'a zero-tolerance approach to hate speech, violence and intimidation' and for 'strong leadership from the authorities to bring about a change

M. Kristoffersson (✉) • B. van Roozendaal • L. Poghosyan
ILGA-Europe, Brussels, Belgium

© The Editor(s) (if applicable) and The Author(s) 2016   45
K. Slootmaeckers et al. (eds.), *The EU Enlargement and Gay Politics*, DOI 10.1057/978-1-137-48093-4_3

in the frequently hostile societal attitudes towards lesbian, gay, bisexual, transgender and intersex (LGBTI) people' (COM 2014, Final, p. 15). It also urged accession countries 'to take measures to counter stereotypes and misinformation, including within the education system', reiterating that 'religious or cultural values cannot be invoked to justify any form of discrimination' (p. 15). These developments support the common notion that the promotion of LGBTI human rights has become increasingly connected with the EU (see also Ayoub and Paternotte 2014).

The embrace of LGBTI human rights as part of EU enlargement and foreign policy is largely the result of effective advocacy and mobilisation efforts by activists throughout the continent. It began with the advocacy for the inclusion of sexual orientation as grounds for non-discrimination in the Amsterdam Treaty, which, in becoming part of the EU *acquis*, created the opportunity to develop benchmarks for LGBTI human rights in relation to the EU enlargement agenda (cf. Slootmaeckers and Touquet 2016). Such leverage allowed activists to gain concrete advances during pre-accession periods, most notably around the protection of fundamental human rights such as the freedom of assembly and association and increasingly in relation to establishing anti-discrimination laws and policies as well.

The aim of this chapter is to provide activists' perspectives on how the gradual inclusion of sexual orientation and gender identity in the EU agenda has created opportunities to push for the advancement of LGBTI rights within accession countries.[1] First, we set out in general terms the process for including LGBTI issues in the EU agenda. Next, we provide insights into the opportunities this has brought for both the development of the European LGBTI movement and the (gradual) inclusion of LGBTI human rights issues in the accession agenda across the different iterations of the Eastern enlargement. Finally, we assess some of the shortcomings in relation to the implementation of standards derived from the EU *acquis* that have become apparent in many countries after EU accession.

BACKGROUND: LGBTI ISSUES GRADUALLY GAINING GROUND IN THE EU

Until the Treaty of Amsterdam (1997), the EU had made only tentative attempts at discussing the issue of LGBTI rights. During the 1980s, the European Parliament (EP) adopted two non-binding resolutions that highlighted sexual discrimination in the workplace (Squarcialupi report

1984)[2] and discrimination against transsexuals (1989),[3] but no policy proposals had been put forward by the Commission. In 1994, the groundbreaking Roth report (1994), which was drafted with considerable input from ILGA[4] (see Ayoub and Paternotte 2015), brought up the issue of widespread discrimination based on sexual orientation in the areas of employment, partnership rights, adoption, and privacy. The report is considered a cornerstone in the EP work on LGBT rights, and led the EP to call upon the Commission to draft anti-discrimination recommendations in relation to sexual orientation. The EP sought to end the practice of different and discriminatory ages of consent for heterosexual and homosexual acts, all forms of discrimination in labour law, and the barring of gay and lesbian couples from marriage (or equivalent legal framework) and adoption (Langenkamp 2003).

Beginning in the early 1990s, activists had begun lobbying the EU and its member states on the rights of gay and lesbians (Ayoub and Paternotte 2015; Bell 2001). In 1993, the book *Homosexuality: A European Community Issue*, edited by Andrew Clapham and Kees Waaldijk, was published with financial support from the European Commission. In this book, the rights of homosexuals were framed as an internal market issue, where differences in the treatment of homosexuals constituted an obstacle to the free movement of people within the community (Swiebel 2009). The EU later addressed this issue in the Amsterdam Treaty, which extended the EU's competences to combat discrimination based on sex, race or ethnicity, religion or belief, disability, age and sexual orientation (cf. Slootmaeckers and Touquet 2016). The treaty was the first such international agreement to explicitly include sexual orientation, and provided the legal foundation upon which new legislative proposals could be built (Bell 2001).

The historical importance of the treaty notwithstanding, the reactions from the European LGBT movement—which at the time was rather small and poorly funded—were not all positive. Many activists questioned whether the new treaty provisions would have any real meaning, as any action in the area required unanimity in the Council. Given some of the member states' track record on LGBT rights, a unanimous vote was not at all certain. Many also questioned whether the conservative Irish Commissioner for Social Affairs, Pádraig Flynn, would put forward any proposal to turn the new competence into policy. Hence, at the time, there was no real indication that Article 13 would be the huge breakthrough it turned out to be.

Nevertheless, in 1998, after it had published the report *Equality for Lesbians and Gay Men: A Relevant Issue in the Civil and Social Dialogue* (Beger et al. 1998), which documented the legal and social situation for lesbians and gay men in the 15 member states, ILGA-Europe called upon the Commission to act on turning Article 13 into concrete measures. In November 1999—sooner than expected—the Commission tabled an anti-discrimination package consisting of two directives, which were adopted by the Council in 2000 without 'many of the delays and controversies that had been predicted' (Swiebel 2009, p. 23). The swift process was partly the result of member states wanting to show a firm stance against racism after Jörg Haider's xenophobic Freedom Party had taken part of the coalition government in Austria (Swiebel 2009). The resulting Racial Equality Directive (2000/43/EC) obliged member states to adopt anti-discrimination legislation in the areas of employment, education, social protection including social security and healthcare, and access to and the supply of goods and services, including housing. Largely due to what Bell (2002, p. 104) called the 'bandwagon effect', the Framework Employment Directive (2000/78/EC), which dealt with discrimination on the grounds of disability, religion or belief, age and sexual orientation, was adopted a few months later. The Framework Employment Directive, however, was much narrower in scope than the Racial Equality Directive, as it prohibited discrimination only in the workplace. Consequently, LGBT people were not protected through EU legislation from discrimination in other areas: they could still be refused hospital visitation rights for partners, be denied social benefits reserved for married couples, or be forced to pay higher premiums on health insurance (Bakowski 2010). This two-tier hierarchy of EU anti-discrimination legislation remains to this day.[5] Notwithstanding its limited scope, the importance of the Framework Employment Directive should not be underestimated. Not only is it the first piece of international legislation prohibiting discrimination based on sexual orientation, but as a part of the *acquis*, it must also be implemented by both existing and aspiring member states (Bell 2001; Slootmaeckers and Touquet 2016).

Another development in 2000 was the proclamation of the EU Charter of Fundamental Rights (henceforth, 'Charter'). The Charter brings together in a single document the fundamental rights that are protected within the EU, thus making them more visible and anchoring them to EU law. ILGA-Europe and the European Parliament Intergroup on LGBT Rights actively lobbied the convention that drafted the charter. And their efforts were successful, as Article 21 of the charter explicitly prohibits discrimination on the grounds of sexual orientation. By including sexual orientation in its provisions, the Charter further reinforced the concept that LGBT rights are human rights. Initially, the Charter was not legally binding, but through the Lisbon Treaty (2007), it was given the same legal authority as the treaties. Thus to the document ensures that human rights are protected with the implementation of EU law.

Finally, along with the directives and the Charter, the Commission launched a funding programme (a so-called action programme) for promoting networking and knowledge in the member states and the civil society (Swiebel 2009). This had direct impact on the work of ILGA and ILGA-Europe, the regional offspring of ILGA created in 1996. With the new competences granted by the Amsterdam Treaty, the Commission addressed the need for a professionalised body representing the LGBT community in Brussels. Hence, in 2000, ILGA-Europe received its first core funding from the Commission, made possible by co-funding from a private foundation. The core funding vastly enhanced the influence of ILGA-Europe, as it was now able to set up a permanent office in Brussels and hire staff for the first time. Up to that point, all of ILGA-Europe's work had been done on a voluntary basis and with a very limited budget, largely derived from membership fees. The professionalisation of ILGA-Europe allowed the organisation to establish a permanent presence in Brussels, to work more efficiently in producing reports and to lobby the EU institutions for, inter alia, the inclusion of LGBTI human rights in the accession process.

THE EU ACCESSION PROCESS

The EU accession process would prove to be a useful conduit for establishing the concept that LGBTI rights are human rights. The conditions for accession to the European Union were laid out in the Copenhagen criteria in 1993. To join the EU, candidate countries were required to meet three criteria: a political criterion, an economic criterion, and acceptance of the full EU *acquis*. The political criterion required the country to fulfil conditions regarding the rule of law, democracy, human rights and respect for and protection of minorities. The Copenhagen criteria represent the first steps towards improving LGBT rights in aspiring member states (cf. Slootmaeckers and Touquet 2016). However, neither the criteria nor the EU treaty defined human rights or the concept of minorities. Whilst it is reasonable to assume that the protection of sexual minorities was part of the membership requirements (Langenkamp 2003), LGBT rights were rather absent from the accession process (Ames 2004).

An important break from this practice came in September 1998, when the EP adopted the so-called Frischi resolution, named after Austrian Member of Parliament (MEP) Friedhelm Frischenschlager, which confirmed that it 'will not give its consent to the accession of any country that, through its legislation or policies, violates the human rights of lesbians and gay men', and called 'on all applicant countries to repeal all legislation violating the human rights of lesbians and gay men, in particular discriminatory age of consent laws' (European Parliament 1998). The resolution further called for the European Commission to 'take into consideration respect and observance of the human rights of gays and lesbians when negotiating the accession of applicant countries'. The resolution was drafted and lobbied for by ILGA-Europe and the then European Parliament Gay and Lesbian Intergroup, and would become the basis for future advocacy efforts to make EU membership conditional upon the protection of sexual minorities (ILGA-Europe 1998; Vadstrup and Krickler 2002). However, the impact of the resolution remained limited, as the EP had no co-decision powers in this area. Moreover, double standards were applied. For example, whilst Austria still had a discriminatory age of consent—an issue addressed in the Frischi resolution (Bell 2001)— candidate countries were required to abolish such provisions before becoming member states.

It soon became apparent, however, that despite the EP's request to the Commission, the emphasis of minority protection was on national and ethnic minorities—not least the Roma population (Ames 2004; Schimmelfennig 2006)—whereas LGBT rights received scant attention in the Commission's progress reports (Ames 2004). Discriminatory provisions in the penal codes had only been mentioned briefly in some of the reports on Romania and Cyprus, even though similar provisions were also in force in Bulgaria, Estonia, Hungary and Lithuania (Langenkamp 2003; Bell 2001). In contrast, the general societal discrimination against the Roma minority had been acknowledged more widely. Seeing the progress made in the case of the Roma, ILGA-Europe strove to achieve the same for the LGBT movement by convincing the Commission to acknowledge that the general societal discrimination against LGBT people was also a legitimate issue for the accession process. To this end, ILGA-Europe, together with its member organisations, embarked on a project to gather information on the legal and social situation of gays and lesbians in the candidate countries. The project resulted in the 2001 report, *Equality for Lesbians and Gay Men. A Relevant Issue in the EU Accession Process* (ILGA-Europe 2001). Moreover, in June 2001, the Gay and Lesbian Intergroup organised a hearing in the European Parliament—hosted by MEPs Joke Swiebel, Michael Cashman and Patsy Sörensen—on the situation of gays and lesbians in the candidate countries, and ILGA-Europe was given the opportunity to present the results from the report to MEPs and Commission representatives. Following the hearing, ILGA-Europe received a letter from the Commissioner for Enlargement, expressing his assurance that the issues brought forward in the report would receive the Commission's full attention. From this point on, LGBT rights were on the accession agenda, and future progress reports included references to issues regarding sexual orientation (Langenkamp 2003). However, it is only since 2008 that the Commission has progressively and meaningfully increased the number of references to LGBT issues in the progress reports. By this time, ILGA-Europe had greater capacities and was engaging systematically with member organisations in candidate countries in order to collect evidence of discrimination, and with that evidence, advocating for the inclusion of LGBT rights in the Commission's reports and strategy. ILGA-Europe's feedback to the Commission's 2008 progress reports reads:

> In general there is a clearly positive development in the progress reports as the human rights issues of LGBT people are covered more extensively and in a larger number of reports than last year (seven out of eight reports had several explicit references to the LGBT issues). Also, the reports for this year cover wider scope of discrimination against LGBT people and give more concrete recommendation to the states to introduce anti-discrimination laws and policies that are in line with EU acquis. It is especially positive to notice that some reports refer to the discrimination faced by LGBT people in various spheres of social and economic life. There are also more explicit references to the human rights of transgender people in most of the reports when comparing with the previous year. (ILGA-Europe 2008, p. 1)

Notwithstanding the above-mentioned success with regard to the Commission reports and candidate state adoption of comprehensive anti-discriminations laws, the acknowledgment of the importance of societal attitude change and the role of political leadership in instigating that change was lacking. In 2013, the ILGA-Europe reached out to the Director-General of the Directorate-General for Enlargement, Stefano Sannino, who agreed to meet with ILGA-Europe staff and activists from current candidate countries. During that meeting, Mr. Sannino committed to prioritisation of LGBTI issues in the 2013 enlargement strategy. Indeed, in this year, the Commission for the first time referred to LGBTI in its strategy paper, emphasising a zero-tolerance approach to hate speech, violence and intimidation against LGBTI people, and calling for more robust measures to tackle violence and discrimination against the LGBTI community as well as measures to counter stereotypes and misinformation. Also in 2013, 'I' (for 'Intersex') was added to the LGBT acronym, following the reference to intersex in the LGBTI guidelines adopted earlier that year. The 2014 Commission enlargement strategy used similarly strong language.

To conclude, we note that the Amsterdam Treaty was a turning point in the EU's commitment to LGBT rights, as it placed sexual orientation issues within EU competence and on the enlargement agenda. It would take another decade, however, before the Commission would firmly commit to full LGBTI equality in the accession process. The increasing commitment to LGBTI issues in the accession process was thus in no small part the result of the lobbying efforts of ILGA-Europe in collaboration with the LGBT Intergroup (now LGBTI Intergroup) and member organisations.

This section has shown that the important developments around the turn of the century created a European political opportunity structure that would have a substantial impact on the work of LGBTI activists in Central and Eastern Europe, and even more so in the Western Balkans, as they could now use a European route to put forward their demands. Additionally, EU funding had strengthened a transnational network of LGBTI organisations such as ILGA-Europe, which allowed it to serve as both a conduit of knowledge and best practices for national LGBTI groups and to continue its work as a professional advocacy organisation in Brussels. In the following section, we will elaborate on the impact of this new opportunity structure on activism on the ground in candidate countries.

Effects on Activism

The Accession Process as Leverage for Change

Many of the activists interviewed for this article stressed the importance of the political support from the EU as a result of the accession process. This commitment and support created a feeling among activists that they were 'no longer alone', that they were 'more secure and respected [by state authorities]' and that 'the doors of the state institutions were opening to them'. Continuous agenda-setting on the part of ILGA-Europe helped to ensure that the EU used its political leverage to advance the human rights of LGBTI people in candidate countries, and local activists received political support through the accession process.

From the fifth enlargement onwards, the EU consolidated its commitment to LGBT human rights by placing the importance of non-discrimination on the grounds of sexual orientation in a more central position in its agenda for candidate countries (cf. Slootmaeckers and Touquet 2016). With the new approach to Chapter 23, the EU became more consistent in its insistence on respect for LGBTI rights from candidate countries, opening the door for the inclusion of LGBTI rights in political discussions. This provided activists with a new means to ensure that their demands were heard by their governments. In the words of an Albanian activist, 'Our government really wanted to be part of the European family and was ready to do everything for that. We both [activists and the government] used the accession process for our goals. It became a win-win situation when the politicians would "score in front of the EU" for protecting LGBTI rights—at least on paper—while we as activists would get our demands met'. ILGA-Europe contributed to this situation by raising LGBTI human rights concerns when meeting with governments, EU diplomats and delegations. The EU also provided support through public statements, meetings with LGBTI activists, and participation in Pride events,[6] all of which contributed to political and public debate, increasing the visibility and legitimacy of LGBTI issues. By approaching the issue from the perspective of accession, LGBTI groups found increasing political support.

The legitimacy offered by the EU and the strong European aspirations of candidate countries created an opportunity for LGBTI activists to frame their demands within the EU norms of diversity and non-discrimination. In the words of a Slovenian activist, 'before the accession, "EU values" or

"EU standards" was the magic word we could use, and politicians were pretty much willing to accept it'. The EU reference was important in the public debate, where the human rights of LGBT people were presented as an important reflection of European values. European aspirations (or state identity: see Subotić 2010, 2011) proved to be important leverage for LGBT activists in many accession countries.

This opportunity, however, was not without limitations. EU leverage was instrumental in most candidate countries in achieving important legal and policy reforms concerning LGBT human rights, but this leverage weakened dramatically after accession (see e.g. O'Dwyer 2012; Slootmaeckers and Touquet 2016). The new legislation consequently existed only on paper, as implementation was limited, and further change was hampered by a lack of political leadership in realising the goal of equality for LGBT people. The European framing of LGBT issues, which for Central and Eastern European (CEE) countries proved to be highly successful before accession, at times came to be used in a negative way. In new and current candidate member states, opponents to gay rights also framed the debate in EU terms: the EU norms in terms of LGBTI rights were a threat to the national and cultural identity of the country (see Mole 2011, 2016). Euroscepticism became value-based (see Leconte 2008), and in this case tainted with homophobia. With the increased connection between EU and LGBTI-friendliness, Eurosceptic players have argued that becoming part of the EU will force the country to become gay, or that gays will be 'imported'.

When faced with this kind of opposition, activists must reframe their message such that it continues to resonate in a local context. For example, in Macedonia, where EU aspiration is waning, this EU framing no longer resonates with the ruling coalition (cf. Fouéré 2016). Consequently, activists have turned towards a more general human rights and diversity approach. They have also used 'coming out' strategies to argue that LGBT people are already part of society. A Macedonian activist, for example, stated, 'I came out publically to show that I am not imported, that I am part of this country'. In Albania, activists have relied on a 'tradition and history' framing. In an exhibition in the Albanian National History Museum, they have displayed objects with sentimental value to LGBTI Albanians, accompanied by stories; in other sections they have featured works from other museums in different countries showing LGBTI people in different domains of life.[7] The message was twofold: we are part of the history and tradition of this country, and LGBTI is an important part of world history and humanity. In short, the accession process has been a very useful tool for activists. By providing a form of external justification and legitimacy, it has helped local activists achieve their goals, although this leverage decreases substantially after accession. In addition to obliging governments to provide some form of LGBTI rights protection, the accession process has contributed to a gradual shift in the framing of LGBTI issues as a matter of human rights, rather than as a question of morality and acceptance. It also provided a framework of 'European values' that LGBTI organisations and activists have used effectively in their advocacy efforts with state authorities (see also Ayoub 2013; Kuhar 2011). However, this European perspective does not always resonate at a local level, forcing activists to be creative and to balance this framing with others dealing with local history and tradition.

The Emerging Transnational Network: ILGA-Europe
One of the most significant results of the new political opportunity structure was the allocation of EU funds to ILGA-Europe (cf. supra), which strengthened the transnational network of LGBTI organisations. As the umbrella organisation of national LGBTI groups, ILGA-Europe also serves as a conduit of knowledge and best practices for the national groups, and a platform upon which the organisations in the network can meet and share knowledge and experiences. ILGA-Europe's annual conferences are an important venue for this knowledge sharing. All of the activists interviewed stressed the importance of the conferences in bringing activists together. In the years prior to the 2004 enlargement, the conferences largely gathered activists from the EU member states and the CEE candidate countries, and were primarily devoted to EU accession issues. Participants could attend (capacity-building) workshops, meet with invited politicians and experts, and most importantly, meet activists from other countries to share knowledge and experiences. One of the advantages of the conferences was that they provided an opportunity for activists from accession countries to meet their Western European counterparts and to learn from the advances that had been made in the Western LGBTI movement. Some of the conferences were held in the CEE candidate countries, which further strengthened the connections between ILGA-Europe and the national LGBTI organisations in these countries. It also provided an important venue for activists from candidate countries to

meet with invited MEPs and other politicians, and to directly discuss their concerns and the situations for LGBTI people in the countries.

Apart from the conferences, ILGA-Europe had several projects aimed at bringing together activists from accession countries, which always included elements of capacity-building, such as strengthening the organisations' advocacy capacity or providing financial training to manage and attract funding. Moreover, ILGA-Europe established a network comprising one representative from each country, who met twice a year to share best practices and experiences, and to support each other in the accession process.[8] Additionally, ILGA-Europe organised study visits to Brussels for activists so they could meet with representatives of the Commission and have direct access to the EU institutions to report on their issues. The increased interaction between activists from candidate countries and those from the EU member states allowed for additional pressure on the EU to confront LGBT issues, in that activists from member states could lobby their governments to pressure EU institutions to include LGBTI issues in the accession processes.

A large part of ILGA-Europe's work with activists from candidate countries has been aimed at providing knowledge of the European institutions and raising awareness of how the accession process can be used as a tool to promote LGBTI rights. The EU is a complicated system, and successful advocacy thus requires knowledge of its functions: activists need to 'learn the EU language', so to speak. Based in Brussels, ILGA-Europe has been able to provide this knowledge by organising the study visits mentioned above. One activist expressed the importance of these visits:

> If my country is about to become a member of the EU, and this is my biggest leverage to bring about legislative change and ensure freedom of assembly and association, then of course, the best way for me to fully understand what leverage that leverage really is, is to touch it, to talk to it, to be close to it.

To a large extent, the EU accession process has provided an opportunity for the European LGBTI movement to deconstruct the EU and learn its mechanisms, processes and structure. For both national-level groups and ILGA-Europe, the fifth enlargement was a 'learning decade', a process through which the movement was able to discover how best to exploit EU support in terms of LGBTI equality. The impact of this period is still felt today, as ILGA-Europe's member organisations generally have a good knowledge of EU institutions.

The dual function of ILGA-Europe as both a member-based and professional advocacy organisation is best illustrated by its contribution to the Commission's progress reports on candidate countries. Because it is based in Brussels and has a very close relationship with the European institutions, ILGA-Europe can bring their member organisations to Brussels to meet directly with decision-makers. This allows activists to provide the Commission with first-hand information on LGBTI rights violations within their countries, information that may be included in the progress reports. The national LGBTI organisations have thus made good use of the 'European route' to put forward their concerns and demands to their governments by directly lobbying the EU to put pressure on their governments regarding LGBTI rights. Together with annual submissions coordinated by ILGA-Europe for the Commission's progress reports, this has become the main lobbying approach. ILGA-Europe has become an important partner to the Commission in providing information on discrimination based on sexual orientation and, increasingly, on gender identity as well for the annual progress reports.

This illustrates well how ILGA-Europe and its member organisations have worked in symbiosis to monitor the situation for the LGBTI community in candidate countries and any shortcomings in the implementation of EU standards (most notably the 2000/78/EC directive). Neither one could be successful without the other. With ILGA-Europe, much of the work has been about opening doors, creating opportunities and providing training and advice on the information needed to successfully lobby the Commission. In other words, it was about building the national LGBTI organisations' capacity to work with the EU institutions to ensure that all shortfalls in the implementation of anti-discrimination laws were documented in the progress reports.[9] In the words of an Estonian activist:

[The accession process] certainly gave us a lot of contacts, and gave us access to the European level lobbying. [...] So it did provide a spark for activists on a different level, as we realised that if we don't have the proper cooperation partners in terms of politicians and policy-makers in our home country yet, then what we can do is to go to the European level and influence the policies from there.

Last but not least, several mainstream EU programmes have helped to strengthen the transnational network of activists and youth groups. Through the European Voluntary Service, a programme helping young people to volunteer abroad, an Estonian LGBTI activist was able to travel to Poland to work with an LGBTI organisation there. Various youth programmes have provided funding and training that has empowered the Estonian LGBTI movement, as all of the existing organisations have ties with individuals with experience from these programmes.

In conclusion, the enlargement process contributed to the strengthening of ILGA-Europe as a European transnational LGBTI network, which in turn enhanced the ability of national LGBTI organisations to use the political opportunities provided by EU accession in advancing the human rights of LGBTI people in their countries. This provided the national organisations with increased resources and helped them mature into an impactful movement. Having a professional body in Brussels further helped to disseminate the best practices and knowledge of the EU institutions to its member organisations, while also advocating for the expansion of LGBTI rights policies at a European level.

Funding
The EU accession process also influenced LGBTI rights and activism in candidate countries via its funding schemes. Whilst we will address some examples of how funding contributed to the cause, we are unable to present a full picture of how EU funding affected the LGBTI movement and equality in candidate countries, as EU funding was not obtained by LGBTI organisations in all candidate countries. In particular, it was not available or accessible to small LGBTI organisations, as they lacked absorption and management capacity needed for such substantial funding. Hence, it became common practice for mainstream NGOs to be granted funds to work on LGBTI issues. ILGA-Europe, however, has continuously advocated increased financial support—coupled with political support—for LGBTI organisations, as well as for a change in EU financial regulations to make funding more flexible and more accessible for smaller organisations.

Three funding avenues were available. First, the Commission's PHARE and TACIS Democracy Programme, a pre-accession assistance scheme, involved in the funding of micro-projects that were chosen and supervised by the European Commission delegations (Braithwaite et al. 1998). For the sixth enlargement and the current candidate member states, this is the Instruments for Pre-Accession Assistance (IPA).[10] Second, as part of the anti-discrimination package, in 2000 the European Council adopted the Anti-Discrimination Action Programme (2001–2006), which was designed to promote, through non-legislative avenues, measures to prevent and combat discrimination on the grounds mentioned in Article 13. The Action Programme aimed to support organisations taking part in combating discrimination and to enable them to gain experience from other parts of the EU in order to compare and contrast their different approaches. The programme places special emphasis on the exchange of ideas and good practice across different parts of the Union. Most importantly, the initiative was open not only to the member states, but also to the candidate states (Bell 2001). Third, some EU member states offered funding to the accession countries. Most notable among these was the MaTra programme by the Dutch government that has provided funding to many groups in the candidate countries since the early 2000s.

The EU funding had a huge effect on LGBTI organisations in candidate countries. The following example from Romania indicates that there was also a level of political will on the part of the Commission to use these funds to support the LGBTI movement. In 2000, the Commission had received a written question from an MEP asking whether the EU funded any LGBT initiatives in Romania, and the answer had been that no LGBT initiatives had received any EU funding. Shortly thereafter, Adrian Coman, director of the Romanian LGBT organisation *Asociatia ACCEPT*, asked for a meeting with the head of the EU delegation in order to discuss how to put pressure on the government to repeal the criminal law. During the meeting, the head of the delegation brought up the issue of funding, and encouraged Coman to apply. These funds allowed *Asociatia ACCEPT* to hire staff and to expand their work and visibility (for more on *ACCEPT*, see also Belavusau and Kochenov 2016). At the time, although some funds had been provided from private donors and EU member state governments, the EU funding was particularly important, as it was representative of a regulated agreement between Romania and the EU, and thus viewed in a positive light, unlike funds from private donors, which were often interpreted as 'meddling in Romania's private business'.

By providing financial support to organisations working on LGBTI issues, the EU also helped elevate the discussion of LGBTI issues to political and public debate in accession countries. For example, the EU-funded project in Montenegro, which was co-funded by ILGA-Europe, ushered in debate on LGBTI issues. Before the beginning of the project, activists who had contacted the institutions typically received no response, but when they began sending letters with the EU logo, the response was almost immediate. It 'opened doors to institutions', noted a Montenegrin activist. He further added, 'Everything that is done [in terms of legal and policy advances] in this country for LGBTI rights is connected with EU integration processes'.

However, EU funding for LGBTI equality has not always been viewed positively by candidate country governments. In Poland, for example, the political climate changed dramatically for the LGBT community in 2005 when the Kaczyński government gained power (see O'Dwyer 2012). The new minister of education declared that he would scrutinise every project under the PHARE programme, threatening to interfere with youth projects that had an LGBT element. Whilst the minister initially followed through on his threat, the Polish LGBT movement managed, via EU pressure, to stop him from interfering in the regulation of the European youth programmes.

Legislative Change—But Not Attitudes
We want to conclude by focusing on issues concerning aspects that have not been strongly affected by the EU accession process—most importantly, the public's attitude towards LGBTI people. The greatest impact of the accession process and EU leverage on candidate countries by far has been in the legislative arena. The process has led to the fastest and largest wave of adoption of LGBT-friendly legislation in Europe, the value of which should not be underestimated. In 2001, six of the ten accession countries (Bulgaria, Cyprus, Estonia, Hungary, Lithuania and Romania) still had discriminatory provisions in their penal codes, mainly different age of consent for same-sex and opposite-sex sexual activities. In Romania, homosexuality was still criminalised, under the vagueness of the term 'public scandal'. By 2004, all countries had abolished these provisions (Swiebel 2009; Bell 2001), and all of the current candidate member states except for Turkey adopted anti-discrimination legislation in the area of employment. Moreover, with the exception of Macedonia, all Western Balkan countries went beyond the EU minimum standards, and banned discrimination in other areas of life—some even banning discrimination on the basis of gender identity.

However, while these rapid developments must undoubtedly be considered as a large success—from the perspective that good legislation will affect society—one must also acknowledge that this success has not necessarily been accompanied by a comparable change in public attitudes. The EU leverage during the accession process is a strong mechanism for achieving legal change, but legal change alone is not enough to create real social change; changing hearts and minds often takes more time and effort than changing laws. Moreover, activists in Europe also learned that success achieved during the accession period provides no safeguards for continued support from their governments post-accession. Whilst strong political leverage mechanisms are in place in the period leading to accession, there are no strong human rights enforcement mechanisms in place for countries within the EU. In practice, this has often meant that political leadership on LGBTI issues pre-accession would not be maintained after accession. National equality bodies often proved to be incapable of effectively implementing laws and policies. Hungary, Lithuania and Poland are good examples of countries where the progress made pre-accession was not maintained post-accession. On the contrary, political leaders have often gained political capital by publically displaying homo- and transphobia (cf. state-sponsored homophobia). The adoption of anti-discrimination legislation in itself does not necessarily mean that real progress is achieved towards the realisation of the human rights of LGBTI people. Legislation must thus go hand in hand with effective implementation mechanisms, as well as with public awareness-raising and educational activities targeting policymakers, law enforcement personnel and the general public.

This was recently acknowledged by the EU. Although it missed an opportunity to outline the broader picture of LGBTI rights during the fifth enlargement, the EU has now tried to address this gap in current accession processes with the 'fundamental first approach', for example, by ensuring that awareness campaigns are developed within candidate countries.

Another criticism has been the discrepancy between the EU's internal and external policies. Whilst the EU has increasingly presented itself as a pioneer in LGBTI issues outside its territories, these ideals in many cases are not reflected within its borders. Internally, the EU is lacking the leadership to champion the LGBTI agenda. Existing enforcement mechanisms, notably the infringement procedure, are rarely applied. Another illustrative example is the fact that the European Commission still does not have an internal strategy to improve the situation of LGBTI people within its territories, whereas the 2013 guidelines for supporting LGBTI people's human rights are considered the EU's strategy on LGBTI issues in its foreign policy. This situation creates double standards, which have been identified by civil society organisations as a weakening factor in the EU's impact in third countries. To address this issue, in 2014, ILGA-Europe recommended that the EU External Action Service discuss the implementation of the EU guidelines supporting LGBTI human rights in a joint meeting of the Council Working Group on Human Rights (COHOM) and the Council Working Group on Fundamental Rights and Freedom of Movement (FREMP), with the goal of ensuring coherence in LGBTI human rights issues in internal and external policy. Whilst an increasing number of member states have raised similar concerns, it remains to be seen whether the EU and its member states are willing to address this concern.

Conclusion

The EU enlargement process has had a considerable effect on LGBTI activism in new EU member states and in candidate countries. The requirement to implement the EU *acquis*, including anti-discrimination provisions regarding sexual orientation, placed LGBTI rights within the framework of the accession process and changed the political opportunity structure for activists in Central and Eastern Europe, the Western Balkans and Turkey. Through these developments, the discriminatory mechanisms targeting LGBTI people were slowly dismantled in countries that were to become EU members. The fifth enlargement pre-accession process can also be regarded as paving the way for the gradual ascension of LGBTI rights as a centrepiece of EU foreign policy, something that would come to have significant implications both in Europe and elsewhere.

With help from an emerging transnational network of LGBTI organisations, national activists could now use a European route via Brussels to advance their cause at the local level. LGBT issues in these countries gained visibility through which the movement could grow. The accession process allowed the movement to engage in the development and realisation of a human rights agenda, work that included documentation and advocacy activities.

At a European level, through the adoption of the Amsterdam Treaty and the development of a framework programme to combat discrimination, ILGA-Europe was transformed into a professional advocacy organisation in Brussels, while remaining a platform for activists to meet and to strategically choose advocacy goals. In this way, the accession process significantly influenced the structure of ILGA-Europe's work. After a somewhat rocky start, the EU has provided both political and financial support for LGBTI activists in the candidate countries. Thus, the route to EU integration, which specifically required the adoption of sexual orientation-inclusive anti-discrimination legislation and improved human rights situations in general, provided an effective argument for the advancement of public debate. Through the development of a pan-European network, a European advocacy agenda was developed, and an infrastructure was created that helped to strengthen the capacity of LGBTI organisations in the accession countries and beyond.

However, it became clear after the fifth enlargement that the legislative changes regarding LGBTI rights did not necessarily lead to further social change. With backlashes occurring in various CEE countries, the limitations of the enlargement process became apparent. In order to address the problem, the Commission announced in 2013 that it would 'increase political support and visibility by inter alia ensuring these issues are systematically addressed in the appropriate fora with enlargement countries as well as in the accession negotiations, setting clearer policy priorities and improving monitoring and follow-up' (COM 2013, 700 final, p. 12). The Commission also announced a conference on LGBTI rights, the improvement of strategic relations with stakeholders and programmatic support to substantiate its political commitment. In 2014, this strategy translated into concrete actions that included a high-level regional conference with a focus on LGBTI rights, as well as increased technical support to train government bodies.

The mixed reality of increased EU attention on LGBTI rights and an increased Euroscepticism in countries like Macedonia, Serbia and Turkey leaves activists with a greater challenge in the effective use of EU accession. In other countries, notably Albania and Montenegro, where there is far greater pro-EU sentiment, activists manage to harvest their successes on the EU accession agenda. Activists in all countries, however, have a considerable challenge ahead. Because geopolitical developments have put LGBTI issues in the spotlight, support for or opposition to the LGBTI agenda has for many people become a symbolic way to express their world view. Consequently, the challenge for LGBTI rights supporters has expanded from a focus on politicians and policymakers, to include general society. The coming years will reveal how EU political leaders will stand up to this challenge.

NOTES

1. The chapter is based on interviews with LGBT activists from Albania, Estonia, the Former Yugoslav Republic (FYR) of Macedonia, Montenegro, Poland, Romania and Slovenia, as well as former members of the ILGA-Europe executive board and staff. Thus the chapter does not necessarily provide a comprehensive overview of the impact of the accession process on all countries, as interviews were held with a limited number of activists.
2. Squarcialupi, Vera (1984) *Report drawn up on behalf of the Committee on Social Affairs and Employment on sexual discrimination at the workplace. Working Documents 1983–1984, Document 1-1358/83, 13 February 1984.*
3. Official journal of the European Communities No C 256/33-37 of 9.10.1989.
4. ILGA-Europe was formally established only in 1996.
5. Gender identity and gender expression are not included in the 2000/78/EC directive. Transgender people are protected under the EU's provisions on equal treatment between men and women. The 2006 Recast Directive (2006/54/EC)—aimed at consolidating the existing EU provisions on equal treatment between men and women—is the first directive to explicitly reference discrimination based on 'gender reassignment'.
6. ILGA-Europe mobilised this support.
7. For information on the exhibition see: https://evsbeyondbarriers.wordpress.com/2013/05/24/art-1-exhibition-in-the-national-historical-museum-tirana/ and see http://archive.globalgayz.com/europe/albania/love-stories-and-forbidden-objects-at-the-national-museum-of-albania/.
8. It is important to note that even though these meetings provided an opportunity for ILGA-Europe to share their knowledge and expertise and to provide practical input on how activists could organise their advocacy on the national level, the main function of the network was to provide a framework for activists to meet and to enable peer-learning and support. These networks also contributed to bringing consistency to the movement, as there were at times high rotations among the groups, with new groups emerging and older groups being less active.
9. In addition to this work on the accession process, ILGA-Europe continued to lobby the European institutions to expand the scope and the definition of Article 13 of the Amsterdam Treatybeyond the area of employment.
10. In November 2014, DG NEAR's Civil Society Facility approved financial support for the establishment of the Regional LGBTI Association for the Western Balkans and Turkey. The project started in January 2015. The association was to have been formally registered by October 2015 and currently includes 27 LGBTI organisations from the region.

EUROPEAN INTEGRATION AND LGBTI ACTIVISM... 65

REFERENCES

Ames, L. M. (2004). Beyond gay paree: What does the enlargement of the European Union mean for same-sex partners. *Emory International Law Review, 18*, 503–554.

Ayoub, P. M. (2013). Cooperative transnationalism in contemporary Europe: Europeanization and political opportunities for LGBT mobilization in the European Union. *European Political Science Review, 5*(2), 279–310.

Ayoub, P. M., & Paternotte, D. (Eds.) (2014). *LGBT activism and the making of Europe: A rainbow Europe?* Basingstoke, England: Palgrave Macmillan.

Ayoub, P. M., & Paternotte, D. (2015). Challenging borders, imagining Europe: Transnational LGBT activism in a new Europe. In N. A. Naples & J. Bickham Mendez (Eds.), *Border politics: Social movements, collective identitites, and globalization* (pp. 230–259). New York: New York University Press.

Bakowski, P. (2010). The European Union and right of LGBT people. Brussels, Belgium: Library of European Parliament. Retrieved August 26, 2015, from http://www.europarl.europa.eu/RegData/bibliotheque/briefing/2010/100048/LDM_BRI(2010)100048_REV2_EN.pdf.

Beger, N. J., Krickler, K., Lewis, J., & Wuch, M. (Eds.) (1998). *Equality for lesbians an gay men: a relevant issue in the civil and social dialogue.* Brussels, Belgium: ILGA-Europe.

Belavusau, U., & Kochenov, D. (2016). Federalizing legal opportunities for LGBT movements in the growing EU. In K. Slootmaeckers, H. Touquet, & P. Vermeersch (Eds.), *The EU enlargement and gay politics.* London: Palgrave Macmillan.

Bell, M. (2001). The European Union—A new source for rights for citizens in the accession countries? In ILGA-Europe (Ed.), *Equality for lesbians and gay men. A relevant issue in the EU accession process* (pp. 80–89). Brussels, Belgium: ILGA-Europe.

Bell, M. (2002). *Anti-discrimination law and the European Union.* Oxford: Oxford University Press.

Braithwaite, M., Eberhardt, E., & Johnson, T. (1998). *The European union's phare and tacis democracy programme. Compendium of Ad-hoc projects 1993–1997.* [Online] Retrieved August 26, 2015, from http://ec.europa.eu/europeaid/how/evaluation/evaluation_reports/evinfo/1997/951432_ev_en.pdf.

Clapham, A., & Waaldijk, K. (Eds.) (1993). *Homosexuality: A European Community issue—Essays on lesbian and gay rights in European law and policy.* Dordrecht, Netherlands: Nijhoff.

Enlargement Strategy and Main Challenges 2013–2014, COM(2013) 700 final.

Enlargement Strategy and Main Challenges 2014–2015, COM(2014) 700 final.

European Parliament Resolution of 17 September 1998 *on equal rights for gays and lesbians in the EC,* B4-0824 & 0852/98.

Fouéré, E. (2016). The curious case of Macedonia: A personal insight of a former head of the EU delegation in Macedonia. In K. Slootmaeckers, H. Touquet, & P. Vermeersch (Eds.), *The EU enlargement and gay politics*. London: Palgrave Macmillan.

ILGA-Europe (1998). *Report of the ILGA-Europe executive board 1997–1998.* Brussels, Belgium: ILGA-Europe.

ILGA-Europe (2001). *Equality for lesbians and gay men. A relevant issue in the EU accession process.* Brussels, Belgium: ILGA-Europe.

ILGA-Europe (2008). *Feedback on the European Commission's 2008 progress reports.* Brussels, Belgium: ILGA-Europe.

Kuhar, R. (2011). Resisting change: same-sex partnership policy debates in Croatia and Slovenia. *Südosteuropa, 59*(1), 25–49.

Langenkamp, T. J. (2003). Finding fundamental fairness: Protecting the rights of homosexuals under European Union accession law. *San Diego International Law Journal, 4,* 437–466.

Leconte, C. (2008). Opposing integration on matters of social and normative preferences: A new dimension of political contestation in the EU. *Journal of Common Market Studies, 46*(5), 1071–1091.

Mole, R. (2011). Nationality and sexuality: Homophobic discourse and the "national threat" in contemporary Latvia. *Nations and Nationalism, 17*(3), 540–560.

Mole, R. C. M. (2016). Nationalism and homophobia in Central and Eastern Europe. In K. Slootmaeckers, H. Touquet, & P. Vermeersch (Eds.), *The EU enlargement and gay politics*. London: Palgrave Macmillan.

O'Dwyer, C. (2012). Does the EU help or hinder gay-rights movements in post-communist Europe? The case of Poland. *East European Politics, 28*(4), 332–352.

Schimmelfennig, F. (2006). Enlargement and Central and Eastern Europe. In F. Carr & A. Massey (Eds.), *Public Policy and the New European Agendas* (pp. 81–98). Northampton, MA: Edward Elgar.

Slootmaeckers, K., & Touquet, H. (2016). The Co-evolution of EU's Eastern enlargement and LGBT politics: An ever gayer union? In K. Slootmaeckers, H. Touquet, & P. Vermeersch (Eds.), *The EU enlargement and gay politics*. London: Palgrave Macmillan.

Subotić, J. (2010). Explaining difficult states: The problems of Europeanization in Serbia. *East European Politics & Societies, 24*(4), 595–616.

Subotić, J. (2011). Europe is a state of mind: Identity and Europeanization in the Balkans. *International Studies Quarterly, 55*(2), 309–330.

Swiebel, J. (2009). Lesbian, gay, bisexual and transgender human rights: The search for an international strategy. *Contemporary Politics, 15*(1), 19–35.

Vadstrup, M., & Krickler, K. (Eds.) (2002). *Activity report 2001–2002*. Brussels, Belgium: ILGA-Europe.

LIST OF INTERVIEWS

Maxim Anmeghichean. Executive Director of GenderDoc-M (Moldova), Programmes Director ILGA-Europe 2005–2012 and member of ILGA-Europe Executive Board 2003–2005. Skype interview 2014-02-27.

Adrian Coman. Director of Asociatia ACCEPT (Romania) 1997–2002 and member of ILGA-Europe Executive Board 1998–2002. Telephone interview 2014-02-19.

Beth Fernandez. Programmes Officer ILGA-Europe 2008–2011. Skype interview 2014-02-27.

Danijel Kalezić. President of Queer Montenegro (Montenegro). Skype interview 2015-03-20.

Kocho Andonovski. Programme Director of LGBTI Support Centre (fyr Macedonia) and director of MASSO, Skype interview 2015-03-20

Lisette Kampus. Campaign Against Homophobia (Poland) and Estonian LGBT activist. Member of ILGA-Europe Executive Board 2006–2008. Skype interview 2014-03-05.

Nigel Warner. ILGA-Europe Council of Europe advisor and former member of ILGA-Europe Executive Board. Skype interview 2013-12-17.

Roman Kuhar. Researcher at The Peace Institute and former member of Legibitra (Slovenia). Skype interview 2014-02-19.

Xheni Karaj. Director of Alliance against discrimination of LGBT (Albania). Skype interview 2014-03-20.

CHAPTER 4

Federalizing Legal Opportunities for LGBT Movements in the Growing EU

Uladzislau Belavusau and Dimitry Kochenov

INTRODUCTION

European Union (EU) citizenship is not only a unique space for 'overcoming' nationality, often imagined in terms of the dominant ethnicity of member states (Kochenov 2010a). EU citizenship equally offers an activist arena for challenging sexual identities and inequalities embedded in those national citizenships, transnationalizing discourse on rights and gay emancipation in Central and Eastern Europe as a matter of EU law. *European*, in this context, becomes a language of rights and entitlements, which can be turned, *inter alia*, against their own states of nationality. On the one hand, transnational forms of citizenship facilitate the very dialogue on sexual rights among member states and problematize the construction of fixed identities (Belavusau 2015a, in press). On the other hand, EU citizenship is equally a realm of disciplining humiliation of member states (Davies 2010). The rhetoric of 'socially unfruitful' homosexuality and the prescription of women's reproductive role have been particularly visible in nationalist projects with ethno-centric views on group boundaries and longevity (Yuval-Davis 1997). The Union instead offers value models for anti-discrimination developments beyond the 'popula-

U. Belavusau (✉)
Department of European Studies, Universiteit van Amsterdam, The Netherlands

D. Kochenov
Faculty of Law, Rijksuniversiteit Groningen, The Netherlands

© The Editor(s) (if applicable) and The Author(s) 2016   69
K. Slootmaeckers et al. (eds.), *The EU Enlargement and Gay Politics*, DOI 10.1057/978-1-137-48093-4_4

tion' narrative of—largely patriarchal and heteronormative—national citizen-ships. Although not always legally enforceable due to the limited possibilities for harmonization and Union action, transnational and national lesbian, gay, bisexual, and transgender (LGBT) movements can capitalize on value models as a matter of EU federalism for lobbying just causes. The recent judgment of the US Supreme Court in *Obergefell v. Hodges* (2015) is an example of a federal opportunity for gays and lesbians—a legal track that sooner or later will be explored by the cause lawyers in Europe.

This contribution will highlight the progress of 'gay rights' litigation from the early 1990s before the Court of Justice. It will show how quasi-federal elements embedded in the ever-evolving EU law (Beaud 2007; Schütze 2009) on the one hand have created mobilizing opportunities for transnational LGBT litigation, and, on the other hand, have steadily Europeanized the discourse on gay rights as part and parcel of the Union's values (see also Kochenov 2009a).[1] Citizenship, anti-discrimination and fundamental rights developments have all contributed to the minimum 'European' standards of LGBT rights' protection. Likewise, we shall explore avenues for future LGBT litigation capitalizing on the opportunities embedded in EU law as it stands now.

To these ends, we first revisit the potential of LGBT rights in EU law through the looking glass of the theoretical discussion on Kreimer's (2001, pp. 72–73) vision of federalism and Karst's (1980, pp. 624–625) analysis of the 'freedom of intimate association': the basic idea that any authority should be as cautious as possible in regulating human intimacy and love. Following Karst (1980), we shall inquire whether we face the nascent 'right to love' translated into the less fortunate (i.e. with a due simplification, intolerant, homophobic, archaic) member states via the federalizing impact of EU law. While the presence of an exit option is indisputably inherent in the nature of virtually any federal system, the legal specificity of the supra-national Union in Europe, with its goal-oriented reading of competences and the growing awareness of possible implications of its actions for human rights protection, potentially also opens a way to an 'entry option' that would oblige member states to recognize less restrictive or simply different moral choices made by other states. Outside of the ideologically charged areas of sexuality, gender identity, and family law, such an 'entry option' is already a day-to-day reality in the EU: Europeans can thus bring their own law with them, as they move from one member state to another.

The second part will outline the genesis and evolution of LGBT rights in Europe: from stringent boundaries of sex discrimination to free movement of sex couples via the EU's citizenship regime. This part will high-light two major periods in the history of LGBT litigation at the Court of Justice: before the Amsterdam Treaty when sexual minorities explored the limits of the sex equality clause, and after the introduction of the special anti-discrimination provision into the Treaty on the Functioning of the European Union.

The third part will consequently unpack the necessity of and the ways to capitalize on the EU's values discourse along with novel anti-discrimination developments for the emancipation of LGBT rights, espe-cially in the context of the Eastward enlargement. It will highlight the most recent case law of the Court of Justice as supplying a box of litiga-tion opportunities for LGBT movements. That box, although it is still limited and imperfect, is apparently available even in Central and Eastern European (CEE) parts of the Union, where coming-outs remain rela-tively uncommon and public life is often infected with social homophobia and religious intolerance (BBC 2013; Turcescu and Stan 2005; for other examples in CEE, see Kochenov 2007).

FEDERAL OUTLOOK ON GAY RIGHTS IN THE UNION

Federalism contributes to freedom in at least two ways: by providing a minimal rights denominator at the federal level that is to be followed by all the states and—in the issues where such denominator is either not avail-able, or not sufficient—by providing an exit option for those who are unhappy in their native state.[2]

The Council of Europe (CoE) can be viewed in this context as the provider of the most general common denominator of rights available in Europe, while the European Union is the guarantor of the 'exit option' that it has granted to its citizens.[3] Wherever you move in the EU, you are always covered by important CoE rules,[4] especially including the European Convention on Human Rights (ECHR) as interpreted by the European Court of Human Rights.[5] All in all, however, the exit option becomes the most important in terms of empowering European citizens, since the EU, by its very nature, is not empowered to act in the majority of fields,[6] and given that rules of the Council of Europe are just as basic as they are important.

It is clear that when a federal system is integrated to such an extent that the local differences are negligible, the ability of such a system to enhance liberty is likely to be negligible too. Indeed, 'removing borders loses much of its value if what is on the other side is the same' (Davies 2008, p. 18). This point can also be proven with a simple use of numbers:

For example, assume that there are only two states, with equal populations of 100 each. Assume further that 70 percent of State A, and only 40 percent of State B, wish to outlaw smoking in public buildings. The others are opposed. If the decision is made on a supranational basis by a majority rule, 110 people will be pleased, and 90 displeased. If majorities in each state make a separate decision, 130 will be pleased and only 70 displeased. The level of satisfaction will be even greater if the smokers in State A decide to move to State B, and some anti-smokers in State B decide to move to State A (see McConnell 1987, p. 1494).

Thus, when the political or legal regimes across an internal border differ, federalism turns into an asset for the promotion of liberty. Such liberty is not an apodictic ideal of the totalitarian states, but results from diversity and mobility. Extreme interpretations of this dimension of federalism give the exit option more importance than political participation: 'a sufficiently decentralized regime with full mobility could perfectly satisfy each person's preferences even with no voting at all' (McConnell 1987, p. 1494). Practically, individual freedoms of citizens moving freely are potentially amplified since 'state-by state variation leaves open the possibility to each individual of choosing to avoid repression by leaving the repressive jurisdiction' (Kreimer 2001, p. 71). This is an effective way to deal with what Madison saw as the greatest potential threat to individual liberty, i.e. the tyranny of the majority. Although not a panacea, the exit option provided by federalism should not be underestimated.

The ability of the EU to advance liberty through federalism is extremely rich, as the member states vary greatly. Only a marginal part of legal regulation has been harmonized, allowing citizens to benefit from the existing variations from one member state to another. These variations are particularly important with regard to the positions the member states take on moral issues, such as abortion, same-sex marriage, divorce, and the like. By moving from one member state to another, citizens of the EU gain the possibility to choose the legal regime that suits them best; they are therefore in a better position than in unified systems, where by moving they can find little more than a change in weather. The situation of EU citizens thus approaches that of their US counterparts. 'Today, the lesbian who finds herself in Utah, like the gun lover who lives in Washington, D.C., and the gambler in Pennsylvania, need only cross the state border to be free of constraining rules' (Kreimer 2001, p. 72).

The inter-state situation activated by cause lawyers before the US Supreme Court is, to a vast degree, emblematic for EU law as well (*Obergefell v. Hodges* 2015). Although widely streamlined in media as the judgement about same-sex marriages, *de jure* the decision is more about recognition of rights derived from marriage than status, which ironically makes the recognition of status all over the American states only a matter of time. The case was launched after a same-sex couple, James Obergefell and John Arthur, married in Maryland. Their state of residence—Ohio—did not recognize their marriage license, which enabled them to file a lawsuit about discrimination. John Arthur was terminally ill and suffering from amyotrophic lateral sclerosis. For this reason, they wanted the other partner, James Obergefell, to be identified as his surviving spouse on his death certificate, based on their marriage in Maryland. Through this paradigm of rights based on free movement between the states, the Supreme Court delivered a truly landmark judgement establishing that a fundamental right to marry is apparently guaranteed to same-sex couples by the Due Process Clause and the Equal Protection Clause of the Fourteenth Amendment to the United States Constitution.

Besides an assumption that the states are self-governing and that there are important differences between them in terms of regulation of some issues of potential moral disagreement, in order to provide citizens with an 'exit option' that can have far-reaching effects on their freedom, three features of the federal system that would limit the states themselves are absolutely crucial. Agreeing with Kreimer (2001, p. 73), these should include the free movement right granted to citizens, equality between newcomers and native citizens in the new state of residence, and territorially limited state jurisdictions. Only when all the three elements are in place is it possible to talk about an exit option within a federal system that provides opportunities to safeguard liberty for all citizens. All three are now to be found in the EU.

EU citizenship is a *ius tractum* status, i.e. found in the EU primary treaties: it builds on the nationalities of the member states (Kochenov 2009b, p. 181), which are at the same time 'autonomous' and grounded in EU law (*Rottmann v. Freistaat Bayern* 2010, para. 5), bringing with it a set of rights specific to the EU legal order (Kochenov and Plender 2012). The most important of these have traditionally been considered non-discrimination on the basis of nationality[7]—in the words of Davies (2005, p. 55), *de facto* 'abolishing' the nationalities of the member states—and free movement in the territory of the Union.[8] The latter not only includes a right to travel around the EU, but also a right to settle anywhere you like with your family, to take up employment and to be treated exactly the same way as the natives of your new member state of residence are treated.[9] Changing member state and non-discrimination on the basis of nationality are thus the core rights of European citizenship stemming from the supranational legal order. Additionally, the member states are prohibited from creating obstacles to the free movement of citizens that would discourage their own nationals from moving to other member states (see Jacobs 2007, pp. 596–598). In addition, the member states cannot undermine the status of EU citizenship (*Rottmann v. Freistaat Bayern* 2010; see also Kochenov 2010b), or deprive citizens of the possibility to enjoy the 'substance of rights'[10] stemming from this status (Kochenov 2011; Iglesias Sánchez 2011), including unwritten rights (Kochenov 2013).

The first two of Kreimer's (2001) components of federalism necessary to enable an effective exit option are thus in place. The third is part of the EU system too: the member states are also sovereign states under international law, so their jurisdiction is most often limited to their own territory.[11] Applied to the situation of gay communities in member states, the exit option of European federalism already provides a viable alternative to life in potentially less 'gay-friendly' societies, such as Poland, Greece, or Slovakia, as moving to the Netherlands or Sweden is a protected EU citizenship right.

Having said all this, it is as clear as day that 'the exit option is no panacea' (Kreimer 2001, p. 72): the majority of people will only consider moving under exceptionally harsh circumstances. Moreover, a guarantee of a viable degree of legal unity of the Union is an indispensable consideration. Member states cannot specialize in accepting only citizens adhering to certain ideologies and rules of morality. Should this be the case, it would unquestionably result in the denial of the very idea of the Union, leading to its legal fragmentation.[12] Above all, moving between cultures, from one society to another, is difficult. In the EU, where citizenship rights are unquestionably connected to the personal and financial situation of the citizen concerned (see e.g. Kochenov 2009b, pp. 234–237), not merely the status of citizenship, it can even be impossible in some cases (Schiek in press).

Given that the exit option is unable to solve all the problems and is even not always available in practice, a certain degree of legal convergence with regard to the most important issues, particularly related to human rights, is needed. Such convergence can theoretically come in three ways:

via full harmonization, via partial supranational alignment, i.e. through terminology to be applied within the material scope of Union law, or via the federal requirement of recognition of national rules even outside the Member States in which such rules were initially adopted (Poiares Maduro 2007): the crucial pillars of EU law. In all these cases, deviations from the rules are to be strictly checked against the principles of EU law. Yet another way stems directly from the availability of the pan-European human rights minimum introduced by the CoE, reinforcing the overall framework of human rights protection. In this regard, it is remarkable, albeit completely unexpected, that the European Court of Human Rights has mostly recently followed the logic of the US Supreme Court in the settings of the Council of Europe, that is—unlike the EU, which is the 'exclusive club' of liberal democracies—covering countries as different as Iceland and Azerbaijan. In its judgement in the case *Oliari & Others v. Italy* (21 July 2015), the Court all of sudden established that Italy should offer some form of registered partnership or marriage to gay couples. It is remarkable that in this case, the judgement refers to comparative jurisprudence, giving the example of the decision in the US Supreme Court that precedes Strasbourg by just a couple of weeks (*Oliary & Others v. Italy* 2015, para. 56). This judgement also captures the growing consensus in the member states, noting that 11 countries of the Council of Europe recognize same-sex marriages, while 18 offer recognition of various forms of same-sex partnerships (*Oliary & Others v. Italy* 2015, para. 54).

While harmonization is always an option, notwithstanding the fact that applying this tool in a number of fields would imply a treaty change, mutual recognition enforced by EU institutions—one of the most successfully deployed ways of developing integration—can be more attractive in the European legal setting. This is particularly true in areas dealing with issues of deep moral disagreement between the member states. Consequently, the treaties currently in force need to be optimally used in order to bring about change without full harmonization. This can be done using two avenues that have already been mentioned: either via the formulation of European legal notions for some ambiguous terms to be used within the scope *ratione materiae* of Union law (i.e. 'family'),[13] or through the formulation of the principle of unconditional recognition of the national understanding of such terms even outside the borders of the member states where they were formulated. The second could be preferable, since it implies full respect of the national-level solutions and does not require the European Court of Justice (ECJ) to 'legislate'. Moreover, it is unquestionably in line with the mutual recognition approach.[14] This being said, the ECJ is clearly in the position to choose either way. Consequently, the EU legal system is likely to offer more than a simple 'exit option', but also what can be characterized as an 'entry option', i.e. a legal possibility to enter a member state other than your own and carry the rules of your old member state with you. The 'entry option' thus constitutes a clear deviation from Kreimer's (2001) third principle, limiting the territorial jurisdictions of the member states. This is so, since a number of EU citizens who exercise their rights to move to another member state can be better off in their new member state of residence, because the laws of the first member state would still apply to them (Davies 2007; Tryfonidou 2009, p. 43; Kochenov 2010c). Such situations, when mandated by Union law, would be outside the realm of private law: the functioning of the 'entry option' is a direct consequence of the way that Union law functions vis-à-vis national law of the member states. Such an entry option is the emanation of the specific nature of European federalism. As will be further exemplified with the Citizenship Directive, if a same-sex married couple moves to a Union state where same-sex marriage is still unrecognized, that latter member state will nevertheless be obliged to treat them as a married couple. In line with the recent US Supreme Court pattern of reasoning on rights recognized in another state (*Obergefell v. Hodges* 2015), this strategy of activating EU law in litigations could in a long perspective spill over the recognition of various forms of legal unions for lesbian and gay couples all over the Union.

EU law is, then, double-empowering: those who escape the substandard law of their own member state that does not respond to the needs of their life, enjoy additional protection having moved (and also upon return home, following the *Singh* principle).[15] Those who move to the member states whose political choices do not suit them well are empowered to bring the law of their member state of origin with them via mutual recognition, thus escaping local regulation in the new member state of residence. In both cases, EU law serves as a vehicle to shield citizens from the legitimate democratic outcomes in their jurisdiction of residence, protecting them from the localized majoritarian perceptions of morality and acceptability (Somek 2014). This double empowerment unquestionably implies a subtle (and sometimes not so subtle) pressure on the member states' democracies, thus improving their operation in the interests of all strata of society through welcoming an additional avenue of Socratic contestation (Kumm 2010).

BUMPY ROAD FOR GAY RIGHTS IN THE UNION: GENESIS, EVOLUTION AND CURRENT STATE OF ART

Since the initial Treaty of Rome, the legal constructs of sex(uality) have experienced an impressive proliferation, despite the fact that the primary integration process was essentially driven by pure economic rationales. A tiny and fairly toothless provision in Article 119 EEC (now Article 157 of the Treaty on the Functioning of the European Union [TFEU]) introduced the seminal wording of gender equality between men and women, the equal pay principle. Few scholars could have imagined in the 1950s that this brief provision would pave the way to the far-reaching and evolving set of sexual rights in EU law. All the principal EU institutions (the European Court of Justice [ECJ], the Council, the Commission and the Parliament) have been involved at various times and to varying degrees in the issues of gender mainstreaming, women's labor and social rights, pregnancy and positive discrimination, gay liberation and sexual identity, prostitution, pornography and the fight against pedophilia and sexual trafficking (Belavusau 2010).

Perhaps the culmination of gender rights (drawn out of the tiny gender equality clause) was the ECJ's rulings on transsexuals. In its 1996 judgement in *P. v. S.*,[16] the Court interpreted the provision on the equality of men and women to apply to cases of gender reassignment.[17] The EU citizenship project has, therefore, broken with the idea of exclusively biologically born women being timid and delicate subjects of patriarchal familial relations, whose main purpose is the procreation of community, and, ultimately, of the mythical nation.

While early national citizenship systematically shut women out, it also excluded gays unless they kept their identity hidden.[18] As nationalist rhetoric on citizenship was used to position women as subjects of procreation, non-heterosexual individuals were conceived as 'pathological', 'immoral' and 'foreign' to imagined domestic communities (Nagel 2003). Duties parlance was classically used to justify exclusion: not good enough to fight—not good enough to reap the fruits of citizenship (Kochenov 2014). This particularly cynical way of construing citizenship rights is now passé (but see Bellamy 2015).[19]

Quite characteristically, the homophobic narrative in the new member states of the Union, for example, is often framed as an 'imposition of hostile Western values' on blissfully prudish and moral 'national citizens' (see e.g. Kahlina 2015). The parallel discourse on the imagined pathology of homosexuality (a concept largely shaped by psychiatrists and criminologists)[20] gained sustenance from the HIV/AIDS epidemic (Belavusau and Isailović 2015).[21] Western countries had brought homosexuality into the vocabulary of active citizenship during the sexual revolution of the 1960s and the AIDS breakout in the 1980s. Dennis Altman predicted that economic growth and development would facilitate the integration of homosexuals into modern society (Altman 1982). Homosexuals do not map to any particular economic class and are therefore not easily reducible to an economically disadvantaged group. Nonetheless, economic development and globalization are incompatible with exclusion based on sexual orientation (Posner 1992). Likewise, the EU project based on internal market rationale is hardly compatible with discrimination on the basis of sexuality, as it could exclude large sections of the population from providing and receiving services, consuming goods and fostering economic growth on an inter-state basis.

As has been shown above, the ECJ has stretched the tiny sex equality clause to cover cases on gender reassignment and to protect the rights of transsexuals. However, it was the absolute maximum the Court was able to achieve to foster emancipation causes for LGBT individuals in the 1990s (von Toggenburg 2008; Waaldijk and Bonini-Baraldi 2006). Similar cases for gay and lesbian couples based on Article 157 TFEU have all failed.[22] The heteronormativity of the EU legal order is additionally sustained by the *de jure* exclusion—often wrongly relied upon—of family matters from the scope of EU regulation, although it would perhaps have been more correct to state that currently, national and EU law co-regulate family matters to a certain degree.[23] The ECJ has not had a chance to demand either absolute mutual recognition or clarify the meaning of a 'spouse' under Directive 2004/38—the two options open for changing the current practice of national-level non-compliance in a number of member states outlined above in detail. The 1996 case on transsexuals was already a huge achievement for LGBT rights, considering that back in the 1950s (when the European Economic Community [EEC] was established), judges all over Europe (including the European Court of Human Rights) employed the language of crime, pathology and deviation when describing any alternative sexuality (Grigolo 2013). Furthermore, it remained criminalized in many member states until the 1970s, with Romania becoming the last EU member state to decriminalize homosexuality in the 2000s (before its accession to the EU).[24]

The perceived limitations on EU action written into primary law (the ECJ simply refused to follow other jurisdictions around the world, including the United Nations Human Rights Committee,[25] in refusing to approach sexual orientation discrimination as sex discrimination) prompted the inclusion of a provision on anti-discrimination that would be self-standing and extend the emancipation potential beyond the ever-expanded yet proclaimed finite gender equality clause. Such a provision was negotiated into the Treaty of Amsterdam, which introduced Article 13 into the EC Treaty (today Article 19 TFEU). The new clause stands apart from the gender clause (the latter has acquired a richer harmonization scope) and lists sexual orientation among the additional grounds of prohibited discrimination (along with race and ethnicity, age, disability and religion). The clause does not straightforwardly impose, for example, the necessity of full legal recognition of same-sex marriages, but it enables EU harmonization powers to challenge discrimination based on sexual orientation.

Although not without caveats, Article 19 TFEU has already contributed to the rise of EU secondary law protecting LGBT rights in the employment context,[26] with several important judgements in this field.[27] Furthermore, Article 19 TFEU was inserted into the second part of the TFEU, entitled 'Non-Discrimination and Citizenship of the Union',[28] thus consolidating the project of EU citizenship with anti-discrimination ethos. Like most of the cases brought on the basis of Article 157 TFEU, the recent line of case law based on Article 19 TFEU primarily involves preliminary rulings at the Court of Justice. The biggest achievement so far is recognizing equal pay rights in various labor contexts (earlier acknowledged for women and transsexuals) for lesbian and gay couples, as soon as a state acknowledges a minimum legal status for the homosexual union (be it a partnership or a marriage)(see Borillo 2011; Kochenov 2009a; Möschel 2009).

In addition to Article 19 TFEU and a brief non-discrimination provision in the Charter of Fundamental Rights,[29] the next substantial EU basis for claiming gay rights is based on the so-called Citizenship Directive.[30] This instrument of secondary EU law employs a gender-neutral language for family unions and partners.[31] The Directive establishes several regimes for married, registered and unregistered partners. If a same-sex couple is married in a home state then EU law unquestionably requires the host state to recognize the marriage, as the wording of the Directive is crystal clear (Kochenov 2009a). In other words, mutual recognition has to do its job—no ECJ intervention at the level of definitions is required. In practice, host states not recognizing same-sex marriages often obstruct the practical enjoyment of the right of a spouse to join their partner—an issue which no doubt needs to be clarified in the case law of the ECJ. Given that if not asked what the law is, the ECJ will not tell—the eternal logic of Article 267 TFEU—activist litigation here is absolutely indispensable.

Two situations are possible in the case of a registered partnership. Should the host member state treat registered partnerships as equivalent to marriage, an individual then has the right to join their partner as if they were spouses. If the host state does not treat registered partnerships as equal to marriage, then the couple falls into the category of unregistered partners in a 'durable relationship'. However, EU law creates no obligation to recognize registered partnerships. Unregistered partners do not enjoy the same right as a spouse to join their partner. Instead, the Directive obliges member states to 'facilitate entry and residence' to unregistered partners who are in a 'durable relationship'. This unclear rule applies equally to same-sex couples and to couples of the opposite sex.[32] Such situations cover same-sex couples where one is a EU citizen. In addition, the Family Reunification Directive allows spouses who are third-country nationals to be united with third-country nationals residing lawfully in the territory of a member state. However, member states are not explicitly obliged to extend this right to same-sex registered (or unregistered) partnerships.[33] The evident limitation is that some EU countries—albeit in ever-decreasing numbers— do not recognize any form of same-sex unions. Furthermore, Poland and the UK negotiated a specific protocol to the Charter, which has been presented as opt-out of these countries from substantial parts of the Charter.[34] In addition, Poland has adopted a specific declaration on morality and family law.[35] In practice, this acclaimed opt-out from the Charter is meaningless: technically, non-discrimination matters can always be handled by reference to Article 19 TFEU, the general principle of equality and fundamental rights (Barnard 2008).

The federal elements embedded in the ever-evolving EU law discussed above have created mobilizing opportunities for transnational LGBT litigation, and, on the other hand, have steadily Europeanized the discourse on gay rights as part-and-parcel of Union values. EU citizenship, non-discrimination and fundamental rights' developments have all contributed to the minimum 'European' standards of sexual rights. The ultimate question is whether we face the nascent 'right to love', translated into conservative states through the vertical distribution of EU law. With this overwhelming EU federalization, the discourse on LGBT rights can no longer be silenced in the moralistic socio-political narratives of the homophobic elites, prevalent in some member states. As has been demonstrated in recent studies, the 'Europeanization of LGBT rights begins primarily as a vertical process in which the EU imposes formal rules on Member States and builds the capacities of civil society [...] to lobby domestic institutions. This engenders new domestic discourses and generates media attention around the LGBT issue, which domestic groups then use to draw attention from outside' (Ayoub 2013, p. 280). Yet the borders of the homo-space (an indispensable aspect of EU sexual citizenship; see Belavusau in press) are continuously being negotiated with the public universal hetero-counterpart. In this respect, fairly progressive discourse on EU sexual rights also consolidates views on same-sex relations, as based on an act of copy-paste from heterosexual family relations. However, the current scope of protection incorporated into the primary law and the neutral language of family 'partners' in the Citizenship Directive leaves the Union with an open project for sexual rights, which could further accommodate less typical (beyond heteronormative and patriarchal) forms of intimacy—including networks of friends, lovers and partners—as spaces for socialization.[36] A relationship is no longer a procreative prerequisite of 'good citizenship', but an end in itself, developing into *the right to love*.

EU LITIGATION BOX FOR CEE: EXAMPLE OF *ACCEPT*

The previous parts first revealed the theoretical implications of EU federalism for LGBT rights in Europe and then traced evolution of LGBT rights protected by EU law. This part will exemplify how cause lawyers and other interested litigators can use the available instruments in the box of EU law to further advance gay rights throughout Europe, especially in Central and Eastern Europe, where national legal opportunities to challenge discrimination seem shallow at times. Thus, part 4 will demonstrate how the EU non-discrimination clause (Article 19 TFEU) can be switched on even in the absence of LGBT plaintiffs, while part 5 will unpack how the Citizenship Directive can in the long term be activated to spill over recognition of various forms of same-sex unions in all member states.

At the vertical level, EU sexual citizenship distributes sexual rights to member states through several channels. Before accession, future member states are obliged to adopt governance of sexual rights through the Copenhagen criteria on the rule of law and fundamental rights (that is, for example, to decriminalize adult same-sex relations). After accession, EU institutions contribute to the minimum level of emancipation of sexual standards across member states (for example, non-discrimination in employment and asylum). Furthermore, the EU offers a litigation space for active citizens and social movements to advance their sexual causes at the Court of Justice (Heffer and Voeten 2014). The ECJ has bolstered the proliferation of gender equality and taken a moral-neutral position to adjudications on sexual services. Finally, sexual rights find their way vertically to member states through the federal discourse of EU citizenship. The rhetoric of gender and sexual emancipation is strongly associated with idealistic perceptions of European politics and law (Ayoub and Paternotte 2014). EU federalization fosters the social imagination of EU citizens and social movements who, in turn, rely on EU sexual standards as a strategy for humiliating member states. *European* becomes the language of rights and entitlements. EU sexual citizenship thus turns into a realm for disciplining embarrassment in the Union. Dictating gender roles, sexual choices and lifestyles is not yet fully precluded. Yet, thanks to the EU, it is finally a cause for shame and yields less cash (Kulpa 2014).

One recent case from Luxembourg that stands out from the rest as particularly promising in litigation terms is the judgement in *Asociaţia ACCEPT*.[37] This case, which put homophobia under the spotlight of EU law, illustrates the value of pragmatic cause litigation (similar to the *Defrenne* saga in the 1970s) for the benefit of a disempowered minority and the rise of an active form of citizenship mobilizing EU sexual rights. A Romanian football club was found to be performing direct discrimination by not distancing itself from the words of its patron. The patron announced that he would never hire a gay player. A non-discrimination organization managed to bring this case in the absence of a single plaintiff. The *locus standi* for organizations is undoubtedly a huge achievement of EU non-discrimination law in that it encourages the litigious potential of active citizenship.[38] This tactic, based on civil litigants and social movements, gives a true boost to otherwise 'desperate' cases that lack individual plaintiffs. The latter factor is particularly emblematic for the LGBT community, especially in member states with more socially prevalent homophobia and religious obscurantism. In such societies, where coming out is still uncommon, revealing alternative sexuality often leads to social ostracism and numerous employment difficulties. As convincingly demonstrated by Foucault, heteronormativity is not exclusively a matter of repression (Rabinow 1984, p. 294). Instead, it is often sustained by keeping the sexual as a most cherished secret of Western society. The 'closet' (that is, the concealment of sexuality) serves as an asylum for many gays and lesbians. Hence, a deafening and embarrassing silence remains the stigma of queer citizens.

These scenarios for strategic litigation either by a strong and genuinely independent equality body or by an autonomous human rights organization essentially revolutionize perspectives for future development of non-discrimination law in Europe. They give a veritable boost to otherwise 'desperate' cases with no individual plaintiffs available. There are a number of factors in various segments of non-discrimination protection preventing individual plaintiffs from launching a case, including *inter alia*:

- Low awareness about legal possibilities to seek judicial redress, frequently combined with imperfect knowledge of the official language of procedures (very often affecting migrants);
- Serious physical or mental handicaps (in the case of disabled people);
- Age of affected victims (in the cases of both youngsters and elderly people);
- Religious considerations and subordinated status (e.g. women in some traditional Islamic families);
- A fear of public disgrace and considerations of privacy, etc.

Various fact-finding missions initiated by ACCEPT indicate that LGBT persons are commonly intimidated and harassed by police forces. Under the threat of getting outed, victims pay bribes and rarely initiate legal action.[39] It is therefore ever important to promote this tool of cause lawyering[40] by both the equality bodies (in the sense of the equality Directives) and independent NGOs, in addition to the traditional focus on individual plaintiffs. This new wave of strategic litigation may yield its precious fruits for the mobilization of social movements representing protected minorities (see Hilson 2002). The litigation track of ACCEPT (essentially *actio populis*) creates a new legal opportunity for gay and lesbian organizations in Luxembourg after their substantial defeat in the 'gay cases' in the 1990s and 2000s (Beger 2000). The initial political opportunity in the member states and EU level—where gay organizations started their lobbying not earlier than in the 1990s, compared to the feminist organizations effectively exploring both legal and political EU opportunities[41]—was equally low.[42] Enabled with sufficient financial and information resources (a task that should be duly understood as an objective of EU investments), this focus on social movements is capable of strengthening equal opportunities in Europe under the double vigilance of EU institutions and civil society.[43]

Right to Love as the Proper Framework for Analysis

Given the political climate in some member states, as well as anti-gay public opinion, it is clear that once the entry option for the gay families, coupled with a more effective deployment of Article 19 TFEU principles, begins to function as it should within the European Union, the less liberal member states will do their best to block the application of free movement to gay citizens' family members. Different exceptions are likely to be invoked in order to justify discrimination. A similar situation occurred in the American case, with a gay couple legally married in Maryland seeking recognition of rights derived from their marriage in Ohio. Obviously, Ohioan authorities did their best to prevent that recognition. At which point, the cause lawyers used this legal opportunity to foster equality in the US Supreme Court (*Obergefell v. Hodges* 2015; see also Tryfonidou 2015b).

As far as potential morality exceptions are concerned, Karst's logic can be employed in the analysis of their potential reach. In his fundamental essay on the *Freedom of Intimate Association*, Karst (1980, p. 627) defended the point that 'freedom does not imply that the state is wholly disabled from promoting majoritarian views of morality. What the freedom does demand is a serious search for justifications by the state for any significant impairment of values of intimate association'.[44] In other words, 'we must search for a state interest of very great importance' (p. 672). The states should not only be allowed to hide behind the screen of 'morality'; serious justifications for any limitation need to be provided. Once stricter scrutiny in such a context becomes a dominating standard, the states will start losing overwhelmingly and systematically, as the majority of anti-gay policies are essentially entirely deprived of any sense and largely aim at the perpetuation of prejudice,[45] being 'the product of folklore and fantasy rather than evidence of real risk of harm' (Karst 1980, pp. 684–685). The potential dangers of such new standard for the states' ability to regulate marriage are evident.[46] Restricting marriage and non-marital intimate association will be extremely difficult, which is a good thing, as 'where marriage is involved the state does not have a contracting party's choice to accept or reject a compact' (Karst 1980, p. 652).

There is no room, in the European legal context, for the imposition of Karst's vision on the member states willing to suppress certain forms of intimate association at the national level following the perceived interests of the majority of their citizens. However, the Union can apply Karst's reasoning when the law of such a member state is forming an obstacle for a couple exercising free movement rights in the EU, i.e. once the operability of the entry option is at stake. In a situation when the achievement of the goals of the EU Treaties is threatened, the strictest scrutiny is to be required.

Unlike in the free movement of goods,[47] public morality is not included among the treaty grounds on which a member state willing to justify a restriction can rely. While Article 21 (1) (TFEU) allows for 'limitations and conditions laid down in the Treaties and by measures adopted to give it effect the most commonly used *lex specialis* instrument, Article 45 (3) only includes 'public policy, public security and public health' among the possible grounds. It seems that deviating using these exceptions in order to justify non-recognition of same-sex partnerships or marriages is virtually impossible, since, in the situation when the usability of health and security arguments can be dismissed right away, public policy cannot possibly consist in discriminating on the basis of sex.[48]

While it is ultimately up to the Court to establish the possible extent of exceptions from the application of the entry option, the text of the relevant provisions as well as the position usually taken by the Court in cases involving deviations from the main treaty rule make it clear that any exceptions are to be interpreted restrictively and do not entitle the member states to discriminate. This means that Union law is unlikely to be of assistance for any member state in CEE seeking exceptions from general application of the law of free movement of persons in order to respect the homophobic opinion of the majority.[49]

Conclusions

EU citizenship provides vertical opportunities for claiming sexual rights, in addition to horizontal developments occurring in certain member states (Alter and Vargas 2000).[50] The federal structure of the EU boasting unique exit and entry options unquestionably broadens the horizon of rights enjoyed by minority communities. Moreover, the current multilevel system of fundamental rights protection in Europe (EU, Council of Europe, national states and a relatively vast number of actors such as the media and NGOs) equally boosts political opportunities for advocacy groups to mobilize around the social issues of gender and sexual equality. As studies by political scientists demonstrate, such groups continuously frame their demands as 'European'; in effect, they make issues of equality and acceptance matters of human rights, and thus they become domestic responsibilities of the EU community (Ayoub 2013; Cichowski 2013; Zippel 2004; Heffer and Voeten 2014).

While the presence of an exit option is indisputably inherent to the nature of virtually any federal system, the legal specificity of the supranational community in Europe, with its goal-oriented reading of competences and the growing awareness of the possible implications of its actions for human rights protection potentially also opens a way to an 'entry option' that would oblige member states to recognize less restrictive or simply different moral choices made by other states.

This chapter has demonstrated that outside the ideologically charged areas of sexuality, gender identity and family law, such an 'entry option' is already a day-to-day reality in the EU. The careful analysis of the EU harmonization developments in primary and secondary law, as well as of the case law of the Court of Justice through the looking glass of Kreimer's (2001) 'federalism' and Karst's (1980) 'freedom of intimate association', reveal multiple opportunities for mobilizing EU law as a strong shield against homophobia, in particular in Central and Eastern Europe. In the future, European LGBT movements will have to further capitalize on the available yet not entirely explored paradigm of EU citizenship—with its entry and exist options for mobile couples—as well as on the *actio popularis* litigation schemes innovatively embedded in EU anti-discrimination law.

Notes

1. Part of this chapter is based on the argument substantially developed in this earlier article.
2. Federalism as referred to here should be understood as operating on the level of national member states, the European Union, and the Council of Europe.
3. Arts 20 and 21 TFEU. The concept of the exit option will be further detailed below.

4. All EU Member States are also Members of the Council of Europe. Art. 6 TEU stipulates that the Union is bound by fundamental rights as reflected in the European Convention of Human Rights and undertakes to accede this Convention. This creates a unique symbiosis of the two organizations: EU and CoE.

5. For an overview of numerous cases on gay rights at the Court in Strasbourg, see Johnson (2014).

6. According to Art. 5 TEU, the EU can only act 'within the limits of the powers conferred upon it by the Treaties'.

7. Art. 18 TFEU. See generally Davies (2003), highlighting the relationship between the principle of non-discrimination based on nationality and the right to free movement, Boeles (2005) and Epiney (2007, p. 612).

8. Art. 21 TFEU.

9. See Council Directive No. 2004/38, Art. 24.

10. Case C-34/09 *Ruiz Zambrano v Office national de l'emploi* (*ONEm*) [2011]; for the annotation of the case, see M. van den Brink (in press).

11. There exist examples to the contrary, which are not easily accepted by the member states. See e.g. Fichera (2009) and Scott (2014).

12. This loosely compares to the US principle that the states are not free to choose their citizens. The same does not apply to the instances when the Member States apply EU and their own law in admitting new immigrants, which also affects third country nationals residing in the EU: the Union as a single working-living space does not exist for them (Kochenov and van den Brink 2015).

13. The ECJ has a rich history of articulating EU legal terminology, e.g. 'worker' or 'the court or tribunal of the Member States', as much broader than the national definitions available in the legal systems of the Member States.

14. The latest addition to the fine-tuning of mutual recognition is the clarity with which the ECJ spelled out the obligation, lying on the Member States not to check the presumption that their peers adhere to fundamental rights: for a critical analysis, see Kochenov (in press).

15. The principle established by the *Singh* case (1992) is that a person who moves with a Union citizen from one Member State to another also has a right to return; otherwise, a person would be deterred from moving in the first place. Therefore, it is EU law and not the domestic rules of your own Member State that also applies to family members, even if such family members are not Union citizens themselves.

16. Case C-13/94, *P. v. S. and Cornwall County Council*, EU:C:1996:170, [1996] ECR I-2143. Another pertinent case in this context is Case C-117/01, *K. B. v. National Health Service Pensions Agency and Secretary of State for Health*, EU:C:2004:7, [2004] ECR I-541.

17. Discrimination of transsexuals since then has been treated as an aspect of gender equality, as incorporated into Directive 2006/54/EC on equal opportunities and equal treatment of men and women in matters of employment and occupation. In June 2010, the European Parliament adopted a resolution (the 'Figueiredo report') calling for an inclusive EU gender equality strategy, specifically addressing issues linked to gender identity: European Parliament, 'Report on the assessment of the results of the 2006–2010 Roadmap for Equality between women and men, and forward-looking recommendations', 2009/2242(INI) (Committee on Women's Rights and Gender Equality, Rapporteur: Ilda Figueiredo, 12 May 2010).

18. Obviously, this statement is subject to a disclaimer about the liquidity of the concept of homosexuality, as introduced not earlier than the nineteenth century. Ancient Greek citizenship, in contrast, fostered an alternative view on sexuality and the role of man-to-man relations that could hardly be regarded as discriminatory in contemporary terms. See Cohen (2004).

19. Also see a soon-to-appear Kochenov reply in the same journal.

20. See the classic work of Foucault (1979), but see also Greenberg (1990).

21. In this regard, see the recent ECJ Case on blood donation by men who have sex with men, C-528/13 *Léger* [2015], echoing the most outdated perceptions of homosexuality as a health-threatening issue. For a commentary, see Belavusau and Isailović (2015).

22. Case 249/96, *Lisa Jacqueline Grant* v. *South-West Trains Ltd.*, EU:C:1998:63, [1998] ECR I-621; Case 122/99, *D. and Kingdom of Sweden v. Council of the European Union*, EU:C:2001, [2001] ECR I-4319; Case 117/01, *K.B. v. National Health Service Pensions Agency and Secretary of State for Health*, EU:C:2004, [2004] ECR I-541. About the defeat of the earlier cases, see Beger (2000). For a convincing argument that there is no logical reason to distinguish sex discrimination from discrimination on the basis of sexual orientation, see Koppelman (2001).

23. As will be demonstrated below in the context of the 'Citizenship Directive' and the case law of the ECJ, it is quite wrong to keep assuming that EU law does not regulate family matters. For a convincing rebuttal of this erroneous claim, see Stalford (2012, p. 223). The idea that family matters are completely excluded from EU regulation is often drawn from Rec. 22 of the Preamble to Council Directive 2000/78/EC of 27 November 2000 establishing a general framework for equal treatment in employment and occupation, OJ 2000 No. L303/16, as well as from the ECJ cases, like the recent Case C-147/08, *Jürgen Römer* v. *Freie und Hansestadt Hamburg*, EU:C:2011:286, [2011] ECR I-3591, para 38: 'As a preliminary point, it

should be observed that, as EU law stands at present, legislation on the marital status of persons falls within the competence of the Member States'.

24. For multiple (including Romanian) examples, see Kochenov (2006) and Belavusau (2015b).
25. E.g. *Toonen v. Australia*, Communication No. 488/1992, UN Doc CCPR/C/50/D/488/1992 (1994); *Young v. Australia*, Merits, Communication No 941/2000, UN Doc CCPR/C/78/D/941/2000, (2003) 5 IHRR 747, IHRL 1921 (UNHRC 2003), 6 August 2003, Human Rights Committee [UNHRC].
26. Council Directive 2000/78/EC establishing a general framework for equal treatment in employment and occupation.
27. Case C-267/06, *Tadao Maruko v. Versorgungstanstalt der deutschen Bühnen*, EU:C:2008:179, [2008] ECR I-1757.
28. Arts 20–24 TFEU.
29. Art. 21 of the CFR stipulates a general prohibition of discrimination, based on sexual orientation. Its Arts. 7 (respect for private and family life) and 9 (right to marry and right to found a family) both employ gender-neutral language for 'family', unlike some outdated national constitutions specifying that family is a union of a man and a woman, e.g. the current interpretation of Art. 6 in the German *Grundgesetz*. For discussion, see Sanders (2012).
30. Directive 2004/38/EC of the European Parliament and of the Council of 29 April 2004 on the right of citizens of the Union and their family members to move and reside freely within the territory of the Member States amending Regulation (EEC) No 1612/68 and repealing Directives 64/221/EEC, 68/360/EEC, 72/194/EEC, 73/148/EEC, 75/34/EEC, 75/35/EEC, 90/364/EEC, 90/365/EEC and 93/96/EEC, OJ 2004 No. L158/77.
31. Art. 2(2) Directive 2004/38 on the right of citizens of the Union, OJ 2004 No. L158/77 states: '"*family member*" means the spouse'. Rec. 3 of the Preamble to the Directive is even more explicit: 'Member States should implement this Directive without discrimination between the beneficiaries of this Directive on grounds such as [...] sexual orientation'.
32. For a broad discussion of the Directive with regard to same-sex couples, see Bell (2005). For a summary, see FRA (2009). For a recent academic study, see Tryfonidou (2015a).
33. Wider aspects of residence are regulated in Council Directive 2003/86/EC of 22 September 2003 on the right to family reunification, OJ 2003 No. L251/12.
34. Protocol 30 on the Application of the Charter of Fundamental Rights of the European Union to Poland and to the United Kingdom 2007, OJ 2012 No. C326/313.

35. Declaration No. 61 by the Republic of Poland on the Charter of Fundamental Rights of the European Union, OJ 2012 No. C326/360: 'The Charter does not affect in any way the right of Member States to legislate in the sphere of public morality, family law, as well as the protection of human dignity and respect for human physical and moral integrity'.

36. The concept of alternative forms of intimacy (especially among gays and lesbians), which is often missing in the heteronormative vision of equality, was advanced by Giddens (1992).

37. Case C-81/12, *Asociaţia ACCEPT* v. *Consiliul Naţional pentru Combaterea Discriminării*, EU:C:2013:275. For an extensive comment on the case, see Belavusau (2015b).

38. Art. 9(2) Council Directive 2000/78/EC establishing a general framework for equal treatment in employment and occupation, OJ 2000 No. L303/16.

39. For reports of ACCEPT, see http://accept-romania.ro/publicatii/.

40. In the literature, a vast number of alternative terminology is used to address cause lawyers, including social justice lawyers, public interest lawyers, rebellious lawyers, progressive lawyers, equal justice lawyers, critical lawyers, etc. Driven by altruism, empathy, self-interest, mixed motives, such lawyers advocate for a social cause rather than for a corporate interest or protection of individual concerns. For various accounts, see Sarat and Scheingold (1990). In the context of LGBT activism, see Cummings and NeJaime (2010).

41. Currently, European Women's Lobby (EWL) is the largest umbrella organization of women's associations in the EU. EWL membership extends to all 28 Member States.

42. Regarding the low legal and political EU-opportunities for gay activists in the 1990s, see Hilson (2002, pp. 248–249).

43. For the concept of double vigilance in EU law in the context of Roma protection, see Dawson and Muir (2011); on social movements and legal opportunity, see McCann (2006).

44. Or, put differently, '[m]easured against the freedom of intimate association, any governmental intrusion on personal choice of living arrangements demands substantial justification, in proportion to its likely influence in forcing people out of one form of intimate association and into another' (Karst 1980, p. 687).

45. The need for the state of Hawaii to justify its policy of exclusion of same-sex couples from access to marriage was at the bottom-line the Hawaii Supreme Court case of *Baehr v. Lewin*, 852 P.2d 44, 74 (Haw. 1993). The Hawaii Circuit Court then held that the State failed to meet the strict standard with the policy justifications it provided. See *Baehr v. Miike*, No.

91–1394, 1996 WL 694235, at *21 (Haw. Cir. Ct. Dec. 3, 1996). For the analysis of other relevant cases decided by the US state courts; see for example, *Inching Down the Aisle* (Anon 2003).
46. See *Zablocki v. Redhail*, 434 U.S. 374, 399 (1978) (Powell, J., concurring); see also Karst (1980, pp. 670–671).
47. Article 36 TFEU; see e.g. Case C-121/85 *Conegate Ltd. v. Her Majesty's Custom and Excise* [1986] E.C.R. 1007, §3 (interpreting Article 36 strictly). For a detailed analysis, see Belavusau (2010) and De Witte (2013).
48. Such public policy would be in manifest disagreement with the principles on which the Union is founded and used to limit free movement of persons, will amount to the violation of the duty of loyalty. Moreover, rather than disqualifying classes of citizens from moving into a particular Member State, public policy exceptions are to be grounded in personal conduct. See e.g. Council Directive No. 2004/38, Art. 27(20).
49. The Polish Declaration on family is manifestly useless in this context, since it cannot possibly justify derogations from EU citizenship and internal market provisions in the Treaties and in secondary law.
50. In citizenship studies, 'vertical' is sometimes understood as relationship between citizen and state, while 'horizontal' absorbs relationship among citizens developing a community with shared loyalties and character. For the purposes of this chapter, 'vertical opportunities' refer to EU claims while 'horizontal opportunities' describe cause lawyering based on national legal system(s).

REFERENCES

Alter, K., & Vargas, J. (2000). Explaining variation in the use of European litigation strategies: European community law and British gender equality policy. *Comparative Political Studies, 33*(4), 452–482.
Altman, D. (1982). *The homosexualization of America: The Americanization of the homosexual.* New York: St Martin's Press.
Anon (2003). Inching down the aisle: Differing paths toward the legalization of same-sex marriage in the United States and Europe. *Harvard Law Review, 116*(7), 2004–2028.
Ayoub, P. M. (2013). Cooperative transnationalism in contemporary Europe: Europeanization and political opportunities for LGBT mobilization in the European Union. *European Political Science Review, 5*(2), 279–310.
Ayoub, P. M., & Paternotte, D. (Eds.) (2014). *LGBT activism and the making of Europe: A rainbow Europe?* Basingstoke, England: Palgrave MacMillan.
Barnard, C. (2008). The "opt-out" for the UK and Poland from the charter of fundamental rights: Triumph of rhetoric over reading. In S. Griller & J. Ziller (Eds.), *Lisbon treaty: EU constitutionalism without a constitutional treaty?* (pp. 257–283). Vienna: Springer.

BBC. (2013). EU LGBT survey: Poll on homophobia sparks concern. *BBC News*, [Online] 17 May. Retrieved August 24, 2015, from http://www.bbc.co.uk/news/world-europe-22563843.

Beaud, O. (2007). *Théorie de la federation*. Paris: Presses Universitaires de France.

Beger, N. J. (2000). Queer readings of Europe: Gender identity, sexual orientation and the (Im)potence of rights politics at the European court of justice. *Social & Legal Studies, 9*(2), 249–270.

Belavusau, U. (2010). Sex in the union: EU law, taxation and the adult industry. *European Law Reporter, 4*, 144–150.

Belavusau, U. (2015a). Sex beyond the internal market: Towards EU sexual citizenship. *EUI Law Working Paper 6*. Florence, European University Institute.

Belavusau, U. (2015b). A penalty card for homophobia from EU non-discrimination law. *Columbia Journal of European Law, 21*(2), 237–259.

Belavusau, U. (in press). EU sexual citizenship: Sex beyond the internal market. In: D. Kochenov, ed. *EU citizenship and federalism: The role of rights*. Cambridge: Cambridge University Press.

Belavusau, U., & Isailović. (2015, August 26). Gay blood: Bad blood? A brief analysis of Léger Case [2015] C-528/13, *European Law Blog*, www.europeanlawblog.eu.

Bell, M. (2005). *EU directive on free movement and same-sex families: Guidelines on the implementation process*. Brussels, Belgium: ILGA-Europe.

Bellamy, R. (2015). A duty-free Europe? What's wrong with Kochenov's account of EU citizenship rights. *European Law Journal, 21*(4), 558–565.

Boeles, P. (2005). Europese burgers en derdelanders: wat betekent het verbod van discriminatie naar nationaliteit sinds Amsterdam? *Sociaal-economische wetgeving, 53*(12), 500–213.

Borillo, D. (2011). Pluralisme conjugal ou hiérarchie des sexualiatés. La reconnaissance juridique des couples homosexuelles dans l'Union européenne. *McGill Law Review, 46*, 875–922.

van den Brink, M., (in press). The origins and the potential federalising effects of the substance of rights test. In D. Kochenov, ed. *EU citizenship and federalism: The role of rights*. Cambridge: Cambridge University Press.

Cichowski, R. A. (2013). Legal mobilization, transnational activism and gender equality in the EU. *Canadian Journal of Law & Society, 28*(2), 209–227.

Cohen, D. (2004). *Law, sexuality, and society: The enforcement of morals in classical athens*. Cambridge: Cambridge University Press.

Cummings, S. L., & NeJaime, D. (2010). Lawyering for marriage equality. *UCLA Law Review, 57*(5), 1235–1331.

Davies, G. T. (2003). *Nationality discrimination in the European internal market*. The Hague, The Netherlands: Kluwer Law International.

Davies, G. T. (2005). "Any place I hang my hat?" or: Residence is the new nationality. *European Law Journal, 11*(1), 43–56.

Davies, G. T. (2007). Services, citizenship and the country of origin principle. *Europa Institute: Mitchell Working Paper Series 2*. Edinburgh: Europa Institute.

Davies, G. T. (2008). *A time to mourn—how I learned to stop worrying and quite like the European Union*. [Inaugural Lecture] 26 June. Amsterdam: Vrije Universiteit Amsterdam. Retrieved August 24, 2015, from http://dspace. ubvu.vu.nl/bitstream/handle/1871/13104/inauguraldavies.pdf?sequence=1.

Davies, G. T. (2010). The humiliation of the state as a constitutional tactic. In F. Amtenbrink & P. A. J. van den Bergh (Eds.), *The constitutional integrity of the European Union* (pp. 147–174). The Hague, The Netherlands: T. M. C. Asser Press.

Dawson, M., & Muir, E. (2011). Individual, institutional and collective vigilance in protecting fundamental rights in the EU: Lessons from the Roma. *Common Market Law Review, 48*(3), 751–775.

De Witte, F. (2013). Sex, drugs and EU law: The recognition of moral and ethical diversity in EU law. *Common Market Law Review, 50*(6), 1545–1478.

Epiney, A. (2007). The scope of Article 12 EC: Some remarks on the influence of European citizenship. *European Law Journal, 13*(5), 611–622.

European Agency for Fundamental Rights (FRA) (2009). *Same-sex couples, free movement of EU citizens, migration and asylum*. Vienna: European Agency for Fundamental Rights.

Fichera, M. (2009). The European arrest warrant and the sovereign state: A marriage of convenience? *European Law Journal, 15*(1), 70–97.

Foucault, M. (1979). *Histoire de la sexualité*. Paris: Éditions Gallimard.

Giddens, A. (1992). *The transformation of intimacy: Sexuality, love and eroticism in modern societies*. Cambridge, MA: Polity Press.

Greenberg, D. F. (1990). *The construction of homosexuality*. Chicago: Chicago University Press.

Grigolo, M. (2013). Sexualities and the ECHR: Introducing the universal sexual legal subject. *European Journal of International Law, 14*(5), 1023–1044.

Heffer, L. R., & Voeten, E. (2014). International courts as agents of legal change: Evidence from LGBT rights in Europe. *International Organization, 68*(1), 77–110.

Hilson, C. (2002). New social movements: The role of legal opportunity. *Journal of European Public Policy, 9*(2), 238–255.

Iglesias Sánchez, S. (2011). El asunto Ruiz Zambrano: una nueva aproximación del Tribunal de Justicia de la Unión Europea a la ciudadanía de la Unión. *Revista General de Derecho Europeo, 24*.

Jacobs, F. G. (2007). Citizenship of the European Union—A legal analysis. *European Law Journal, 13*(5), 591–610.

Johnson, P. (2014). *Homosexuality and the European court of human rights*. London: Routledge.

Kahlina, K. (2015). Local histories, European LGBT designs: Sexual citizenship, nationalism, and "Europeanisation" in post-Yugoslav Croatia and Serbia. *Women's Studies International Forum, 49*, 73–83.

Karst, K. L. (1980). The Freedom of Intimate Association. *Yale Law Journal, 89*(4), 624–692.

Kochenov, D. (2006). Democracy and human rights-not for gay people: EU eastern enlargement and its impact on the protection of the rights of sexual minorities. *Texas Wesleyan Law Review, 13*, 459–496.

Kochenov, D. (2007). Gay rights in the EU: A long way forward for the Union of 27. *Croatian Yearbook of European Law & Policy, 3*(3), 469–490.

Kochenov, D. (2009a). On options of citizens and moral choices of states: Gays and European federalism. *Fordham International Law Journal, 33*(1), 156–205.

Kochenov, D. (2009b). *Ius Tractum* of many faces: European citizenship and the difficult relationship between status and rights. *Columbia Journal of European Law, 15*(2), 169–237.

Kochenov, D. (2010a). Rounding up the circle: The mutation of member states' nationalities under pressure from EU citizenship. *EUI RSCAS Paper 23*. Florence, European University Institute.

Kochenov, D. (2010b). Case C-135/08 Janko Rottmann v. Freistaat Bayern, Judgement of the Court (Grand Chamber) of 2 March 2010. *Common Market Law Review, 47*(6), 1831–1846.

Kochenov, D. (2010c). Citizenship without respect: The EU's troubled equality ideal. *NYU Jean Monnet Working Paper 8*. New York: NYU School of Law.

Kochenov, D. (2011). A real European citizenship. *Columbia Journal of European Law, 18*, 56–109.

Kochenov, D. (2013). The right to have *what* rights? EU citizenship in need of clarification. *European Law Journal, 19*(4), 502–516.

Kochenov, D. (2014). EU citizenship without duties. *European Law Journal, 20*(4), 482–498.

Kochenov, D. (in press). The missing EU rule of law. In C Closa & D Kochenov, eds. Reinforcing the rule of law oversight in the European Union. Cambridge: Cambridge University Press.

Kochenov, D., & van den Brink, M. (2015). Pretending there is no union: Non-derivative quasi-citizenship rights of third-country nationals in the EU. *EUI Law Working Paper Law 5*. Florence: European University Institute.

Kochenov, D., & Plender, R. (2012). EU citizenship: From an incipient form to an incipient substance: The discovery of the treaty text. *European Law Review, 37*, 369–396.

Koppelman, A. (2001). The miscegenation analogy in Europe, or, Lisa Grant meets Adolph Hitler. In R. Wintermute & M. Andenaes (Eds.), *Legal recognition of same-sex partnerships: A study of national, European and international law* (pp. 623–633). Oxford, England: Hart Publishing.

Kreimer, S. F. (2001). Federalism and freedom. *Annals of the American Academy of Political and Social Science, 574*, 66–80.

Kulpa, R. (2014). Western leveraged pedagogy of Central and Eastern Europe: Discourses of homophobia, tolerance, and nationhood. *Gender, Place Culture A Journal of Feminist Geography, 21*(4), 431–448.

Kumm, M. (2010). The idea of Socratic contestation and the right to justification. *Law and Ethics of Human Rights, 4*(2), 142–175.

McCann, M. (2006). Law and social movements: Contemporary perspectives. *Annual Review of Law and Social Science, 2*, 17–38.

McConnell, M. (1987). Federalism: Evaluating the founders' design. *University of Chicago Law Review, 54*, 1484–1512.

Möschel, M. (2009). Life partnerships in Germany: Separate and unequal? *Columbia Journal of European Law, 16*(1), 37–65.

Nagel, J. (2003). *Race, ethnicity, and sexuality: Intimate intersections, forbidden frontiers.* Oxford: Oxford University Press.

Obergefell v. Hodges. (2015). 576_U.S.

Oliary, & Al. v. Italy. (2015). App. nos. 18766/11 and 36030/11.

Poiares Maduro, M. (2007). So close and yet so far: The paradoxes of mutual recognition. *Journal of European Public Policy, 14*(5), 814–825.

Posner, R. A. (1992). *Sex and reason.* Cambridge, MA: Harvard University Press.

Rabinow, P. (Ed.) (1984). *The Foucault reader.* New York: Pantheon Books.

Rottmann v. Freistaat Bayern. (2010). C-135/08 ECJ.

Ruiz Zambrano v. Office national de l'emploi (ONEm). (2011). C-34/09 ECJ.

Sanders, A. (2012). Marriage, same-sex partnership, and the German constitution. *German Law Journal, 13*(8), 911–940.

Sarat, A., & Scheingold, S. (Eds.) (1990). *Cause lawyering: Political commitments and professional responsibilities.* Oxford: Oxford University Press.

Schiek, D., (in press). Perspectives on social citizenship in the EU. In D. Kochenov, ed. *EU citizenship and federalism: The role of rights.* Cambridge: Cambridge University Press.

Schütze, R. (2009). *From dual to cooperative federalism.* Oxford: Oxford University Press.

Scott, J. (2014). The new EU "Extraterritoriality". *Common Market Law Review, 51*, 1343–1380.

Singh. (1992). C-370/90 ECJ.

Somek, A. (2014). Europe: Political, not cosmopolitan. *European Law Journal, 20*(2), 142–163.

Stalford, H. (2012). For better, for worse: The relationship between the EU citizenship and the development of cross-border family law. In M. Dougan, N. Nic Shuibhne, & E. Spaventa (Eds.), *Empowerment and disempowerment of European citizens* (pp. 225–252). Oxford, England: Hart Publishing.

von Toggenburg, G.N.. (2008). "LGBT" go Luxembourg: On the stance of lesbian gay bisexual and transgender rights before the European court of justice. *European Law Reporter*, pp. 174–185.

Tryfonidou, A. (2009). *Reverse discrimination in EU law*. The Hague, The Netherlands: Kluwer Law International.

Tryfonidou, A. (2015a). Free movement law and the cross-border legal recognition of same-sex relationships: The case for mutual recognition. *Columbia Journal of European Law, 21*(2), 195–248.

Tryfonidou, A. (2015b). Same-sex marriage: The EU is lagging behind. *EU Law Analysis*, [Online] 29 June. Retrieved August 24, 2015, from http://eulawanalysis.blogspot.nl/2015/06/same-sex-marriage-eu-is-lagging-behind.html.

Turcescu, L., & Stan, L. (2005). Religion, politics and sexuality in Romania. *Europe-Asia Studies, 57*(2), 291–310.

Waaldijk, K., & Bonini-Baraldi, M. (2006). *Sexual orientation discrimination in the European Union: National laws and the employment equality directive*. The Hague, The Netherlands: T. M. C. Asser Press.

Yuval-Davis, N. (1997). *Gender and nations*. London: Sage Publications.

Zippel, K. (2004). Transnational advocacy networks and policy cycles in the European Union: The case of sexual harassment. *Social Politics, 11*(1), 57–85.

PART II

Zooming in: Central and Eastern Europe

CHAPTER 5

Nationalism and Homophobia in Central and Eastern Europe

Richard C.M. Mole

INTRODUCTION

In terms of lesbian, gay, bisexual and transgender (LGBT) rights, few organizations have done as much to promote the legal equality of sexual minorities as the European Union (EU). Especially since the inclusion of sexual orientation in the equalities agenda through Article 19 of Treaty on the Functioning of the European Union (TFEU; formerly Article 13 TEC), there has been increased pressure at the European level for existing members and accession states to promote the equal rights of their LGBT citizens (Slootmaeckers and Touquet 2016). Despite similar top-down pressure, however, the degree of legal equality for LGBT individuals—not to mention social attitudes towards homosexuality—differs markedly across the region, with the situation particularly difficult in the states of the EU's Eastern Partnership. The aim of this chapter is to suggest that the failure of Europeanization—understood here as the adoption of EU laws and values—to liberalize attitudes towards sexual minorities in Central and Eastern Europe can be explained in large part with reference to the nation. In line with the conclusions of Freyburg and Richter (2010) and Schimmelfennig and Sedelmeier (2005) on the need to move beyond

R.C.M. Mole
School of Slavonic and East European, Studies, University College London, London, UK

© The Editor(s) (if applicable) and The Author(s) 2016
K. Slootmaeckers et al. (eds.), *The EU Enlargement and Gay Politics*, DOI 10.1057/978-1-137-48093-4_5

rationalist arguments and incorporate ideational factors to explain the relative success or failure of Europeanization, I argue that in many Central and East European member states and accession countries, homosexuality clashes with discourses of national identity, which have greater resonance among the population. This chapter will also demonstrate that EU support for LGBT equality can also have a negative impact on attitudes towards non-heteronormative individuals in states that are neither EU member states nor candidate countries, in that nationalist politicians use the EU's more liberal position towards LGBT rights to draw a boundary between the 'decadent West' and 'traditional East' for their own social and political purposes. The analysis will focus in particular on the case studies of Latvia, Serbia and Russia to show that in each case, the marginalization of LGBT individuals is legitimized with calls to 'the defence of the nation'.

The first part of the chapter will examine the nature of nationalism in Central and Eastern Europe, and why nationalism emerged as such a major component of the post-communist transition in much of the region, before going on to examine the perceived relationship between nationality and homosexuality from the perspective of various actors at different levels of analysis. The main body of the article will focus on the supposed threat posed by homosexuality to the continued existence of the nation and to national norms and values, as well as the politicization of homophobia by nationalist politicians to scapegoat LGBT citizens in the name of the nation.

NATIONALISM IN CENTRAL AND EASTERN EUROPE

Unlike in Western Europe, where nations emerged out of largely centralized states, the proto-nations of Central and Eastern Europe were usually subject communities of large multi-ethnic empires, where 'the frontiers of an existing state and of a rising nationality rarely coincided' (Kohn 1967, p. 457). As the local intelligentsias in Central and Eastern Europe who took up the nationalist ideals were often isolated from the ethnically heterogeneous aristocratic elites on the one hand, and the illiterate peasantry on the other, they mobilized popular support by appealing to shared culture, myths of common descent and common ancestry, infusing the idea of the nation as a political community with ethnocultural characteristics and thereby making a shared identity a political imperative (Smith 1996, pp. 140–141). While the division of Western and Eastern Europe into civic and ethnic nations is useful to understand how European nations emerged, such a clear division is no longer credible from an academic perspective. While it would be wrong, therefore, to suggest that ethnicity plays no role in the national identities of Western nations, the idea of nations as natural communities united by shared biology, culture and history is, however, particularly dominant in political discourse in Central and Eastern Europe, as Franjo Tudman, former President of Croatia, demonstrates quite clearly:

> Nations [...] grow up in a natural manner, in the objective and complex historical process, as a result of the development of all those material and spiritual forces which in a given area shape the national being of individual nations on the basis of blood, linguistic and cultural identity, and the common vital interests and links of fate between the ethnic community and the common homeland and the common historical traditions and aims. [...] Nations are the irreplaceable cells of the human community or of the whole of mankind's being. This fact cannot be disputed in any way. (in Spencer and Wollman 2002, p. 27)

This understanding of nations is not restricted to nationalists such as President Tudman, but is a view shared by most everyday citizens. Among academics, the prevailing view is that nations are socially constructed (Suny 2001; Gellner 1996; Hobsbawm 1995; Breuilly 1993). Even theorists who emphasize the pre-modern roots of contemporary national identities, such as Anthony Smith (1996, p. 179), admit that '[t]here is, at least in the case of historically well-preserved *ethnie*, a choice of motifs and myths from which different interest groups and classes can fashion their own readings of the communal past to which they belong'. Of course, the success of a social construction is that it seems natural. And, outside of academia, the dominant view is that nations are natural communities, united by shared biology, culture and history, stretching back centuries if not millennia and marching forward towards a common future (Gil-White 2001). Before we go on to discuss the impact of nationalism on perceptions of homosexuality in Central and Eastern Europe, we must first understand why nationalism became such a key component of social and political life after 1989.

The collapse of communism led simultaneously to dramatic new gains for liberal democracy and a resurgence of nationalism. The antipathy of communism towards both democracy and nationality ensured that both were embraced as the legitimating principles on which the new sovereign states of Central and Eastern Europe would rebuild their societies

(Linz and Stepan 1996). Although democracy and nationalism do share some of the same aims, their conflicting logics soon became apparent, and the commitment of many former communist states to the principles of democracy was frequently undermined by an upsurge in nationalist feeling, with ethnic politics emerging as a major component of the post-communist transition throughout much of Central and Eastern Europe. So why was this?

The nationalist forces that emerged after 1989 did not appear *ex nihilo*. To understand the resurgence of nationalism in the post-communist period, we must first examine the factors which (inadvertently) fuelled nationalist feelings during the communist era—even if such feelings could not be freely manifested. Firstly, we have to remember that the communist modernization programs encouraged urbanization, industrialization, mass education, increased literacy and social mobility—all factors which, according to the leading theories of nationalism, promote national awareness (Gellner 1996; Hobsbawm 1995; Smith 1996). This was particularly evident in the USSR, where, through the establishment of 15 Soviet Socialist Republics, the regime created quasi nation-states with their own territories, names, constitutions, administrations, legislatures and cultural and scientific institutions. Furthermore, the system of personal nationality meant that everyone had an official ethnicity. Individuals were unable to choose their own nationality, based on their language, residence or identity, but had to take that of their parents (Brubaker 1999). Everyone knew their ethnic identity. There were no grey areas; the boundaries were clear. Therefore, as Brubaker (1999, p. 17) explains, 'the Soviet regime pervasively institutionalized [...] territorial nationhood and ethnic nationality as fundamental social categories. In so doing, it inadvertently created a political field supremely conducive to nationalism'. Moreover, the nationalism that emerged was specifically ethnic in nature. Basing nationality on descent and not residence or language precluded the development of civic identities.

Despite Marxism's antipathy towards nationality and its characterization as 'false consciousness', communist citizens did define themselves primarily in national terms, an unintended consequence of the regimes' attempts to do away with civil society (Suny 1993). Communist parties throughout the region banned or tried to ban all intermediary associations, as they did not want any challengers to their power and as it was far easier to control an atomized society of individuals than organized collectivities (Schöpflin 1993). The resultant absence of collectivities such as classes, status groups or professional associations meant that national affiliation provided the only seemingly 'natural' bond between individuals that was available. Over the years, therefore, the relative 'dominance of the national discourse defined its constituents almost exclusively as subjects of the nation, effacing the multiplicity of possible identities' (Brubaker 1999, p. 160).

While during state socialism, it was communist ideology that helped the state and its citizens make sense of the world, the discrediting of Marxism-Leninism in the late 1980s and the early 1990s meant that the people of Central and Eastern Europe had no cognitive, ideological or organizational patterns to interpret the world around them or guide their decisions about whom to trust or with whom to cooperate (Mole 2013). And it was particularly during the period of unprecedented social, economic and political upheaval triggered by the collapse of state socialism that the people of Central and Eastern Europe sought stability, cohesion and 'familiar norms in an attempt to maximize predictability in an uncertain world' (Inglehart and Baker 2000, p. 28). However, as the absence of firmly established political and legal institutions meant that the newly sovereign states were unable to provide social cohesion on the basis of shared citizenship rights for all members of the state, aspiring political leaders sought instead to generate solidarity and at the same time to legitimate their claims to power by appealing to ethnicity and 'historical rights'. In the absence of civil society, they were left unchallenged to do so. Ethnicity could be sold to the electorate as a response to the universalism and artificial cosmopolitanism associated with the externally imposed communist system. In the context of the economic and political uncertainty characterizing the post-communist period, nationalist politicians argued that shared ethnic identity granted the titular nationalities of the states of Central and Eastern Europe the right to the state's political, economic and material resources and entitled them to exclude members of the out-group. Where no shared identity existed, members of the titular nationality questioned 'why people who define themselves differently but live side by side with them and whose solidarities they cannot rely on should be politically or economically or culturally favoured' (Schöpflin 2000, p. 39). While difference was largely defined in ethnic terms, non-normative sexuality was also seen as a dangerous marker of non-conformity, as we shall see later.

NATIONALITY/HOMOSEXUALITY

The first thing to make clear when discussing the relationship between nationality and homosexuality is that there is, of course, no *a priori* relationship between nationality and homosexuality (Weeks 1992). The relationship between sexual categories and the meaning ascribed to them is culturally and historically contingent. As Jeffrey Weeks (1992, p. xi) explains, 'homosexuality, like all forms of sexuality, has different meanings in different cultures—so much so that it becomes difficult to find any common essence which links the different ways it is lived'. The fact that certain societies are more supportive of LGBT equality than others, for example, shows that it is impossible to find a meta-level explanation for the meanings ascribed to homosexuality that holds across space and time; sexual categories and the meanings assigned to them are constructed by institutions such as the Church, the family and secular institutions, including parliaments, but also the law and especially medicine.[1] Institutions such as these 'produce and/or reproduce ideologies and norms, which define social expectations' with regard to acceptable sexual mores and behaviours (Štulhofer and Sandfort 2005, p. 5). Attaching specific meanings to homosexuality and excluding others is achieved through the establishment of a specific discourse that 'constitutes and organizes social relations around a particular structure of meanings' (Doty 1996, p. 239). With a focus on the discursive construction of the relationship between nationality and homosexuality, I will show how specific meaning is attached to non-heteronormative sexualities by nationalist political subjects for social and political purposes. While my main argument is that homophobia is manipulated by nationalist politicians (see section on 'Political homophobia' below), I acknowledge that the latter draw on non-subjective discourses of nationality and homosexuality to ensure greater resonance; here I am using non-subjective discourse in the Foucauldian sense of a discourse, the first usage of which cannot be traced to a specific subject, but which over the years has become common knowledge, a taken-for-granted 'truth' (see Foucault 1978). It is non-subjective discourses of nationality and homosexuality that I shall discuss first.

To return to the nature of national collectivities in Central and Eastern Europe, the belief in the nation as an extended kin group, united by shared biology, culture and history, can be maintained only by naturalizing the patriarchal family and associated public and private roles of men and women to ensure ethnic continuity as well as internal homogeneity and a clear demarcation from the Other (Yuval-Davis 1997).[2] Analysing the above tropes in turn, we will see how the presence of individuals performing non-heteronormative sexualities is perceived as a threat to the continued existence of the nation.

Continued Existence of the Nation

Given their emphasis on a shared bloodline and common descent, ethnic nations are more likely to have a patriarchal gender order and absolute rules on sexuality (Nagel 2000, 2003). The ethnic continuity of the nation is maintained by means of the patriarchal family, underpinned by heteronormative and patriarchal conceptions of masculinity and femininity. The most important role that women can play in the nation is that of the mother, producing sons (and daughters) for the nation and inculcating in them the ethnic language and culture, while men act as defenders and decision makers. While this hierarchical relationship first emerged in the private sphere, it has then been used to justify men's control of the public sphere and the articulation of the public as superior to the private (Pateman 1988, pp. 91–92). The nuclear family with its naturalized hierarchy between masculine and feminine and public and private is thus felt to be essential for the nation's past, present and continued future (Yuval-Davis and Anthias 1989, p. 7).

Regarding the reproduction of the nation, it is not just about women having babies, but having the *right kind* of babies (Pryke 1998, p. 542). To ensure that the nation is reproduced in its desired form, the 'ethnosexual frontier', to use Joane Nagel's (2000, p. 113) term, is 'surveilled and supervised, patrolled and policed, regulated and restricted'. As Anthias and Yuval-Davis argue (1989, p. 10):

> Often the distinction between one ethnic group and another is constituted centrally by the sexual behaviour of women. For example, a 'true' Sikh or Cypriot girl should behave in sexually appropriate ways. If she does not then neither her children nor herself may be constituted part of the 'community'.

While in reality the ethnosexual frontier is porous and elastic, considerable effort is put into ensuring that the purity of the national community remains unadulterated (Yuval-Davis 1997, p. 23). Responsibility for maintaining cultural boundaries lies almost exclusively with women, who are expected to perform traditional gender roles and cultural practices as a means of 'establishing markers of difference in the family and for the nation' (Novikova 2002, p. 330). In extreme cases, women who cross this frontier are at risk of being branded traitors (Nagel 2003, p. 141).

As the focus on the biological reproduction of the nation presupposes it to be heterosexual, gays and lesbians—by not having children—undermine the idea of the nation as a unified collectivity with a communal future, a view taken to extremes by Lech Kaczyński (who in 2005 would go on to become President of Poland), arguing that 'widespread homosexuality would lead to the disappearance of the human race' (Gal 1994, p. 269; see also Brenman and Byrne 2007). Moreover, the fact that homosexual sex is not procreative also means that it is seen as purely for pleasure and thus decadent—a very selfish, un-national value, one often ascribed to the threatening Other (Healey 2001). The construction of gay men as weak and effeminate and lesbians as strong and masculine thus confuses the patriarchal gender order and the public and private roles of men and women central to most ethnonational discourses. As such, lesbians often face considerable hostility, as they do not reproduce the role of mother in the heterosexual nuclear family and thus fail to pass on the traditions and cultural norms vital to the myth of the historicized national collective (Yuval-Davis and Anthias 1989, p. 7). To nationalists, any woman thought to be putting her sexual interests before the priority of national biological and cultural reproduction is considered an outrage (Gal 1994, p. 262).

Even if lesbians do have children, their contribution to the reproduction of the nation is unacknowledged, as the children born are not the result of the traditional nuclear family, thereby weakening one of the key pillars of the nation. In addition, producing 'fatherless' children challenges the national norm of patrilineal naming convention. As Connor (1992, p. 52) explains, 'the sense of kinship among members of a nation explains why surnames often serve as the principal marker of national identity', identifying those babies who are legitimate members of the national community.[3] In parts of Central and Eastern Europe, children are given not just the father's surname, but also a patronymic derived from his first name. By removing men from the equation, lesbians problematize the need for this patrilineal signifier of national continuity and thereby threaten the stability of the nation.

National Norms and Values

To maintain a clear boundary and hierarchical relationship between the Self and Other, nationalism works to convey the idea of internal homogeneity through shared norms and values, creating positive distinctiveness vis-à-vis other nations and thereby enhancing the self-esteem of the national Self (Tajfel and Turner 1986). According to social psychologists, the perception of internal homogeneity is achieved by categorizing the world into distinct nations, accentuating the differences among and similarities within nations and internalizing these categories (Tajfel and Turner 1986; Turner 1987). To enhance one's self-esteem through membership of the nation requires individual members to align their beliefs and behaviours with the positive norms and values of the nation and reject those that challenge them. This behavioural conformity furthers the idea of acceptable and unacceptable beliefs and conduct. In his seminal work *Nationalism and Sexuality*, Mosse shows how 'nationalist ideologies which arose in late eighteenth- and early nineteenth-century Europe were associated with attempts on the part of national bourgeoisies to create national collectivities in their own image. This image was grounded in a specific gender division of labour, sexual orientation and ethnicity which involved notions of respectability and appropriate sexual behaviour' (in Charles and Hintjens 1998, p. 2). Heterosexuality thus became a taken-for-granted attribute of the nation and dominant group norm (Peterson 1999), against which actions and beliefs were judged.

Homosexuality is seen not just as deviating from, but as actually threating the norms on which the nation is built. In terms of nation-building, the presence of gay men threatens the homosocial male bonding required to forge the nation and defend it militarily, while homosexuals are also perceived as not possessing the typically masculine virtues of 'willpower, honour, courage' needed to inspire action in the name of the nation (Nagel 1998, p. 245). As Mosse (1996, p. 4) argues, the 'ideal of masculinity [...] as a symbol of personal and national regeneration' requires a countertype, an Other lacking in masculinity, against which the normative masculine ideal is strengthened and legitimized. These countertypes, of which homosexuals are a key group, do not just represent different types of masculinity but are constructed as 'enemies', whereby the 'line between modern masculinity and its enemies had to be sharply drawn in order that manliness as the symbol of a healthy society might gain strength from this contrast' (Mosse 1996, pp. 67–68).[4] Nations therefore need to distinguish '"proper" homosociality from more explicitly sexualised male-male relations, a compulsion that requires the identification, isolation and containment of male homosexuality' (Parker et al. 1992, p. 6). While one could argue, according to Mosse, that normative masculinity could not exist without its homosexual countertype, violence towards public manifestations of (what are perceived to be) effeminacy and unmanliness of homosexual men is therefore legitimized with reference to their 'enemy' status.

Furthermore, expressions of non-heteronormative sexuality demonstrate heterogeneity within the nation, challenging the belief in the internal homogeneity of the Self vis-à-vis the Other. By deviating from the norm, gays and lesbians are often branded deviant and abnormal. In Latvia, parliamentary deputy Pēteris Tabūns's repeatedly emphasized Latvians' 'normal principles of morality', which he contrasted with the behavioural norms of homosexual men and lesbians, who are 'abnormally oriented', while former government minister Ainars Baštiks deemed Riga Pride to be offensive because 'an abnormality' was 'proclaimed as a normal occurrence' (Mozaīka 2007, pp. 25,27). Homosexuality is thus dangerous because it blurs the clearly defined and stoutly maintained 'distinction between normality and abnormality' (Mozaīka 2007, p. 30), which, according to George Mosse (1985, p. 10), has always 'provided the mechanism that enforced control and ensured security'.

In Central and Eastern Europe, one of the powerful national norms is religious adherence, a factor that explains opposition to LGBT equality in a number of states in the region. Throughout the centuries, the words of St Paul (Romans I: 26–28) and narrative of Sodom and Gomorrah (Genesis: 18–19) have been used to condemn same-sex practices. Indeed, the main branches of the Christian Church in Central and Eastern Europe have certainly been highly vocal in their condemnation of non-heteronormative sexuality. The current position of the Catholic Church to homosexuality is closely tied to procreation. Same-sex acts are considered sinful in that sexuality is presented as being 'naturally ordered to the good of spouses and the generation and education of children' (Catechism of the Catholic Church 2353). Homosexual acts thus 'close the sexual act to the gift of life. They do not proceed from a genuine affective and sexual complementarity. Under no circumstances can they be approved' (Catechism of the Catholic Church 2357). The position of the Orthodox Church is equally unequivocal. At the August 2000 Sacred Bishop's Council, the Russian Orthodox Church adopted *The Basis of the Social Concept*, setting out the Church's position on a range of social issues. The chapter entitled 'Problems of Bioethics' makes it clear that:

> The Orthodox Church proceeds from the invariable conviction that the divinely established marital union of man and woman cannot be compared

to the perverted manifestations of sexuality. She believes homosexuality to be a sinful distortion of human nature. … While treating people with homosexual inclinations with pastoral responsibility, the Church is resolutely against the attempts to present this sinful tendency as a "norm" and even something to be proud of and emulate.

In general, social science research confirms that strength of religious belief is the strongest predictor of negative attitudes to homosexuality. Rowatt et al. (2009) and Whitley (2009) explain the link between religious belief and intolerance towards gays and lesbians with reference to conservatism, i.e. there is a strong correlation between religiosity and conservatism and between conservatism and homophobia. Plugge-Foust and Strickland (2000) see the relationship between religiosity and homophobia somewhat differently, arguing that homophobia is an irrational thought process and that Christians are more likely to believe what others would consider irrational. In general, Herek and Glunt found that 'the more often that their subjects went to church, the more hostile those subjects were towards homosexuality' (in Plugge-Foust and Strickland 2000, p. 241). Even in nations with low levels of religiosity, such as Latvia, religion is used to legitimize the banning of gay pride marches. Aigars Kalvītis, Prime Minister, insisted that Latvia is a state based on Christian values and Riga should 'not promote things like that. For sexual minorities to parade in the very heart of Riga, next to the Dome Church, is unacceptable' (BBC 2005). What the Latvian case shows is that negative attitudes towards homosexuality are not always conditioned by religion per se, but rather by discourses of religion in identity narratives, constructed as a norm to legitimize a particular understanding of national community (see Ayoub 2014; Hall 2015; Pavasović Trošt and Slootmaeckers 2015).

What the above analysis shows is that the nation is understood as a natural phenomenon, growing out of extended kin groups, united by shared biology, culture, history, norms and values, stretching back centuries if not millennia and marching forward towards a common future. The continuity of the nation as well as its internal homogeneity and clear demarcation from the Other are ensured by means of endogenous biological reproduction, a myth that can be maintained only by naturalizing the patriarchal family and associated public and private roles of men and women and, in particular, by controlling women's sexuality. Individuals performing non-normative sexualities are thought to threaten this national narrative by undermining the patriarchal family, failing to adhere to national stereotypes of masculinity and femininity, confusing the public/private roles of men and women, undermining the nation's internal homogeneity and deviating from its shared norms, especially those derived from religious teaching. As a result, homosexuality and nationality in some parts of Central and Eastern Europe are seen as not just conflicting but mutually exclusive, a belief reflected in a banner held by a protester at Riga gay pride in the summer of 2009, which read 'More gays, less Latvians [*sic.*]' (Hilpern 2009). However, the greatest threat that gays and lesbians are believed to pose to the continued existence of the nation is that they fail to reproduce. While this appears to be a genuinely held belief and has real effects on the lives of LGBT individuals, analytically, it is, of course, absolute nonsense. If the birth rate is falling, it is to the heterosexual majority that the nation's opprobrium should be directed. Indeed, the danger that homosexuality is supposed to pose to the nation is challenged by the very national myth that non-normative sexualities are supposed to threaten. If nations have existed for millennia, as nationalists would have us believe, their continued existence throughout the centuries can hardly be said to have been hampered by homosexuality, which has been recorded since the times of the Ancient Greeks.

From an academic perspective, we can see that the meanings attached to the relationship between nationality and homosexuality discussed above were not the result of a specific political project, but should rather be understood as a non-subjective discourse. The threat to the nation posed by homosexuality is perceived as 'common knowledge', a taken-for-granted 'truth', and it is this 'truth' that nationalist politicians are able to manipulate to further their own particular ends, as we shall see below.

POLITICAL HOMOPHOBIA

I will now turn to subjective discourses of nationality/sexuality to demonstrate how specific meanings are attached to non-heteronormative sexualities by individual subjects in order to create moral leadership and social and political hierarchies, and to legitimate particular truth-regimes. Russian President Vladimir Putin's instrumental use of homophobic discourse with the declared aim of defending Russian national values will be particularly illustrative here, as will similar debates in Latvia and Serbia.

As the track records of nationalist politicians demonstrate, attacking homosexuality can be a very useful strategy for discrediting opponents and shoring up support among nationalist and conservative voters, a sizeable proportion of the electorate in many Central and East European states (Rohrschneider and Whitefield 2012). It is the alienness of homosexuality and its association with Western values that proves particularly useful to nationalists, allowing them to construct gays and lesbians as disloyal enemies of the state and reinforcing the idea that homosexuality is a foreign import; in Latvia, it was even claimed that homosexuality did not exist until the country joined the EU (Greenwood 2007). And it is especially when their political positions are felt to be under threat that nationalists will resort to attacking sexual minorities.

In Latvia, it was the parliamentary debate in 2006 over the EU's Employment Equality Directive, banning sexual orientation discrimination in employment, that prompted Members of Parliament (MPs) to publicly reject EU norms on LGBT equality. Although, as an EU member state, Latvia was obliged to implement the legislation, the parliament initially voted it down; indeed, Latvia was the last member state of the EU to transpose the directive. The opposition to the law was framed as an attempt to safeguard the continued existence of the nation. During the debate, Janis Smits, Chairman of the Parliamentary Human Rights Commission, all but likened homosexuality to an act of genocide and warned that any MP who voted in favour of the Employment Equality Directive 'should no longer go and place flowers by the Monument to Freedom, because with his vote he will be the same as those people who once tried to annihilate our people' (Mozaīka 2007, p. 30).

The perceived 'national threat' in Latvia was a consequence of 50 years of Soviet occupation, as a result of which the desired ethnic conceptualization of Latvian-ness was threatened by the presence of hundreds of thousands of Russian-speaking, Soviet-era immigrants. To counter this threat, politicians sought to exclude phenomena that would undermine the ethnic reproduction of the nation, and any behaviour perceived to discourage procreation was presented as a threat to the future of the national collectivity. In addition to 'limiting women's reproductive options by working symbolically to delegitimise abortion and empirically to cripple the work of newly established family planning organisations and sex educators', MPs also sought to demonize sexual practices that failed to produce children, with gays and lesbians a popular target (Rivkin-Fish 2006, p. 152). In view of the fact that the nation was presented as being in danger of dying out due to the low birth rate in Latvia, the issues of procreation and motherhood shifted from the private to the public sphere, while the resultant emphasis on women's roles as mothers gave 'traditionalist claims

legitimacy among broad sectors of the populations' and allowed discrimination against gay men and lesbians to be legitimated in the name of the
future of the Latvian ethnic nation (Stukuls 1999, p. 541).

Attacking homosexuality has been a particularly common political strategy due to the nature of Latvian politics, which have been dominated by
the right and centre-right since the country regained its independence. As
there has been no left or centre-left presence in Latvian governments since
1991, the adversarial basis of politics is missing. According to Chantal
Mouffe (2005, p. 30), this is bad for democracy:

> A well functioning democracy calls for a clash of democratic political posi-
> tions. This is what the confrontation between left and right needs to be
> about. Such a confrontation should provide collective forms of identification
> strong enough to mobilise political passions. [...] When political frontiers
> become blurred, disaffection with political parties sets in and one witnesses
> the growth of other types of collective identities, around nationalist, reli-
> gious or ethnic forms of identification.

Given that the governing parties in Latvia are all similar from a policy
perspective, they need to find other ways to differentiate themselves from
their ideological fellow travellers. As a result, the confrontation between
different political positions is replaced by confrontation between 'essentialist forms of identification or non-negotiable moral values' (Mouffe 2005,
p. 30). In other words, in Latvia, the battle between right and left has been
replaced by the battle between right and wrong. The absence of adversarial
confrontation helps us understand why issues of morality, such as LGBT
rights or the promotion of nationalist policies, have become *political* issues
and why the requirement to transpose EU anti-discrimination legislation
failed to result in greater tolerance of non-heteronormative sexualities.[5]

In Serbia it was the political ascendancy of pro-Western reformers in
the late 1990s, threatening the power of the nationalist Socialist Party of
Serbia, that prompted Slobodan Milosević and his allies to divide political actors into 'patriots' and 'enemies of the state', determined by their
rejection or support of LGBT rights, respectively. The instrumental use of
homophobia was facilitated by the ethnicisation of Serbian society during
and following the violent collapse of Yugoslavia in the early 1990s, which
had recast gender and sexual norms in highly traditional terms and raised
heterosexual reproduction to the level of state policy in a bid to ensure
ethnic homogeneity (Bracewell 1996; Veličković 2012). The resultant
heteronormative discourses gave rise to rhetorical and physical attacks on

'sexual non-conformity and non-heterosexual practices', which were further legitimized by the Orthodox Church's strong support for the cultural nationalism of the Milosević regime (Kahlina 2013, p. 8).

Against this backdrop, LGBT rights became a touchstone in the subsequent struggle over the future direction of Serbia—along the nationalist or 'European' path—on the cusp of the new millennium. For nationalists, any Serbian liberal intellectual or NGO (Non-Governmental Organization) fighting for LGBT rights was perceived as '"feminized" and marked both as anti-Serbian and in the service of particular interests' (Greenberg 2006, p. 334). Even the judge assigned to investigate the murder in 1999 of Dejan Nebrigić, president of the LGBT rights association *Arkadija*, characterized the movement not as a civil society organization, but as 'a gateway for all kinds of sects conducting a special war against our country' (Prendergast 2000).

While Serbia was officially granted candidate status in 2012, there remains considerable opposition to integration into the European Union from various political quarters, and the requirement to transpose EU anti-discrimination directives as well as the expectation that Pride Parades be allowed to take place are seen as an attack on traditional national values. In her analysis of political responses to the introduction of the anti-discrimination law, Stakić (2011, p. 32) identified how opponents legitimized their position by constructing homosexuality as abnormal and degenerate, whereby the law was seen as being 'imposed on the Serbian Government by the powerful Western states, and was aimed at destroying the Serbian nation'. Moreover, reflecting the very close ties between nationality and religion in Serbia, the law was considered illegitimate as it had not been approved by the Orthodox Church. The role of the Church as the ultimate arbiter of Serbian national values was evident in its repeated interventions in parliamentary debates over the anti-discrimination legislation—particularly the articles relating to sexual orientation and gender identity (Stakić 2011, p. 33). And while the Church officially condemned the violence against the participants in the 2010 Pride Parade in Belgrade, individual representatives, such as Amfilohije Radović, Archbishop of Cetinje, all but legitimized the attacks:

> Yesterday we watched the stench poisoning the capital of Serbia, scarier than uranium. That was the biggest stench of Sodom that the modern civilization raised to the pedestal of the deity. You see, the violence of wrongheaded

infidels caused more violence. Now they are wondering whose fault it was, and they are calling our children hooligans. (in Stakić 2011, p. 39)

In seeking to discredit those who favour closer ties with the EU, therefore, nationalist politicians in Serbia have used homosexuality as a means to divide the political field into 'friends' and 'enemies', the latter encompassing not just those pushing specifically for LGBT rights, but—given the association of homosexuality with foreignness—also any politicians supporting Western-style reforms (see Pavasović Trošt and Slootmaeckers 2015). The policies of reform-minded activists are either delegitimized by their association with LGBT movements and their Western allies, or the activists are discouraged from participating in social and political activity by the threat of violence, itself legitimized by the need of patriots to protect the nation from homosexuality, as the words of Archbishop Radović demonstrate. The construction of a truth-regime whereby only heterosexuals are patriots limits the political agency of LGBT activists and their allies. Homophobic rhetoric and action, legitimized by the need to 'defend national values' in the face of Western decadence, thus proves to be an effective way of dividing and discrediting political opponents and of legitimizing authoritarian and anti-reform policies.

In Russia, it was the mass demonstrations in protest against the falsification of the results during the 2011 presidential elections that prompted Putin to seek to reaffirm his political legitimacy by protecting 'traditional Russian values' in the face of alien ideas from the West, such as tolerance of homosexual propaganda (President of Russia 2014). While the Russian Federation is neither a member state nor a candidate country of the European Union, the latter's support for LGBT rights also has an impact on attitudes towards homosexuality in Russia in that nationalist politicians can use the EU's more liberal position towards LGBT rights to draw a boundary between the 'decadent West' and 'traditional East' for their own social and political purposes (President of Russia 2013).

Following a number of regional bills banning the spreading of 'propaganda of non-traditional sexual relations', Putin signed the federal law on 30 June 2013. Under the law, individuals and organizations can be fined for disseminating information about 'non-traditional sexual orientations' among minors or promoting 'the social equivalence of traditional and non-traditional relationships'.[6] The inclusion of the phrase 'among minors' ensures that practically every public LGBT event will violate the law. In May 2012, LGBT activist Nikolay Alexeyev was convicted for breaching the regional St. Petersburg law by picketing St. Petersburg

City Hall with a banner, which read 'Homosexuality is not a perversion'. Alexeyev's insistence that there were no minors present at the City Hall can be taken as proof that the law was not motivated by a desire to protect Russian children or the Russian nation more broadly, but was rather the latest in a series of legislative measures used by the state to intimidate political opponents and to generate an atmosphere of legal disquiet.

Appeals to tradition and 'the symbolic resource of the collective past' have thus provided politicians in Russia with a 'powerful lever for political mobilisation' aimed at strengthening national unity in the face of perceived internal and external enemies (Pechersaya 2013, p. 96). According to Wilkinson (2014, p. 368), homophobia in Russia thus 'functions as a Slavophile political shorthand for national identity and traditional values'. Restricting LGBT rights enables Putin to clamp down on actual and potential opponents and shore up support among the conservative majority. In addition, it has allows him to entrench traditional Russian values in the face of the spread of Western liberal ideas, which he blames for corrupting the nation's youth and fuelling opposition to his rule. And, thirdly, tapping into pre-existing antipathy towards sexual minorities, he has been able to use homosexuality as a lightning rod to divert attention from political corruption and Russia's weakening economy.

To ensure that the traditional values/anti-gay discourse resonates with Russian society, Putin frames it as part of a strategy to ensure the survival of the Russian nation. The survival of the physical nation requires a marked increase in the Russian birth rate, which plummeted following the collapse of the Soviet Union. To achieve this goal, according to Putin in a television interview in January 2014, Russia needs to 'cleanse' itself of gay people (Aljazeera 2014). To reinforce its specifically *Russian* identity, the nation needs to define itself against the US and the European Union, rejecting their liberal values. The culture clash between Russia and the West over LGBT rights was evident from the Kremlin-backed human rights report published in January 2014, in which Moscow lashed out at the European Union for its 'aggressive promotion' of the rights of sexual minorities (Ministry of Foreign Affairs of the Russian Federation 2013, p. 7). It was also apparent in Putin's address in December 2013, in which he defended Russia's conservative values as a bulwark against 'so-called tolerance', which was 'genderless and infertile' (President of Russia 2013).

Putin's defence of traditional national values chimes with the Russian belief in its national exceptionalism, which can be traced from medieval Moscow's claim to be the 'Third Rome', through the Slavophiles' insistence on Russia's 'special path' and all the way to Lenin's communist messianism (Duncan 2000). Since the collapse of the USSR, the Russian political elite has been searching for Russia's special mission, and establishing it as the defender of traditional national values against Western decadence and tolerance of homosexuality can be seen as a way for Russia to fulfil its historical destiny. Putin's construction of homosexuality as both non-traditional and thereby non-Russian, in tandem with his rigorous defence of traditional values as the foundation of the Russian nation's greatness, have therefore successfully legitimized the marginalization of the country's LGBT citizens. The international outcry these policies triggered was vociferous, but only further strengthened the association of sexual minorities with the West. Putin could simply provide this Western tolerance of homosexuality at the expense of Russian national values as further proof that he was right all along.

CONCLUSION

While it would be wrong to assume that all nationalists are homophobic, it would appear to be the case that ethnic nations, with their greater emphasis on a shared bloodline and common descent, are more likely to have a patriarchal understanding of gender roles and stricter rules on sexuality. As the ethnic continuity of the nation as well as its internal homogeneity and clear demarcation from the Other are ensured by means of endogenous biological reproduction through the patriarchal family and underpinned by heteronormative and patriarchal conceptions of masculinity and femininity, it is also more likely that ethnic nationalists will perceive sexual minorities as threatening this national narrative by undermining the family, failing to adhere to national stereotypes of masculinity and femininity, confusing the public/private roles of men and women, challenging the nation's internal homogeneity and deviating from its shared norms, especially those derived from religious teaching. Again, while it would be wrong to assume that contemporary nations in Central and Eastern Europe are *a priori* more ethnic than anywhere else, the legacies of communism, the effects of the transition from communism and the nature of politics in certain post-communist states have resulted in ethnic nationalism becoming a key component of social and political life in the region since 1989. Taken together, the ethnicisation of politics and the greater antipathy of ethnic nationalists towards sexual minorities have resulted in a situation where attitudes towards homosexuality in many (but not all) post-communist states are more negative than in most (but not all) West European societies, enabling nationalist politicians to exploit pre-existing homophobia for personal political gain. To return to Freyburg and Richter's (2010) and Schimmelfennig and Sedelmeier's (2005) conclusions that EU norms are less likely to be adopted if they conflict with national identity, we can see that the ability of the EU to promote greater tolerance of sexual diversity by means of 'social learning' is hampered by the fact that in many Central and East European member and accession countries, non-heteronormative sexualities clash with discourses of national identity, which have greater resonance among the population, while politicians in third-countries can also manipulate the EU's tolerance of LGBT individuals as a means of drawing a boundary between the 'decadent West' and 'traditional East' for their own political purposes.

NOTES

1. Indeed, historians of sexuality argue that it was the spread of modern medicine and Freudian psychoanalysis that produced the social categories of homosexual and heterosexual (Schluter 2002, p. 29). Prior to the late nineteenth century, people behaved homosexually or heterosexually—or both— but were never classified as such.
2. This understanding of the relationship between the ethnic nation and the patriarchal family is an example of a non-subjective discourse.
3. Historically, ethnic minorities in some CEE states, such as Bulgaria, have even been forced to adopt the surname conventions of the dominant ethnic group.
4. In addition to homosexuals, other countertypes have historically included Jews, Gypsies, vagrants, habitual criminals and the insane (Mosse 1996, p. 12).
5. For a more detailed discussion of these debates in Latvia, see Mole (2011).
6. The full text is available on the *Rossiyskaya Gazeta Dokumenty* website: http://www.rg.ru/2013/06/30/deti-site-dok.html [Accessed 14 July 2015].

REFERENCES

Aljazeera. (2014). Putin: Russia must 'cleanse' itself of gays, but they shouldn't fear Sochi. *Aljazeera America*, [Online] 19 January. Retrieved April 21, 2015, from http://america.aljazeera.com/articles/2014/1/19/putin-russia-must cleanseitselfofgays.html.

Ayoub, P. M. (2014). With arms wide shut: Threat perception, norm reception, and mobilized resistance to LGBT rights. *Journal of Human Rights, 13*(3), 337–362.

118   R.C.M. MOLE

BBC. (2005). Latvia gay pride given go-ahead. *BBC News*, [Online] 22 July. Retrieved June 23, 2008, from http://news.bbc.co.uk/1/hi/world/europe/4708617.stm.

Brenman, M. & Byrne, C. (2007). Fury at Polish president gay threat warning. *Irish Independent*, [Online] 21 February. Retrieved June 25, 2008, from http://www.independent.ie/national-news/fury-at-polish-president-gay-threat-warning-56059.html.

Breuilly, J. (1993). *Nationalism and the state*. Manchester: Manchester University Press.

Brubaker, R. (1999). *Nationalism reframed: Nationhood and the national question in the new Europe*. Cambridge: Cambridge University Press.

Bracewell, W. (1996). Women, motherhood and contemporary Serbian nationalism. *Women's Studies International Forum 19*, 25–33.

Charles, N., & Hintjens, H. (1998). *Gender, ethnicity and political ideologies*. London: Routledge.

Connor, W. (1992). The nation and its myth. *International Journal of Comparative Sociology, 33*, 48–57

Doty, R.L. (1996). Immigration and national identity: Constructing the nation. *Review of International Studies, 22*, 235–255.

Duncan, P. J. S. (2000). *Russian messianism: Third Rome, revolution, communism and after*. London: Routledge.

Foucault, M. (1978). *The history of sexuality* (vol. 1,). New York: Vintage.

Freyburg, T., & Richter, S. (2010). National identity matters: The limited impact of EU political conditionality in the Western Balkans. *Journal of European Public Policy, 17*(2), 263–281.

Gal, S. (1994). Gender in the post-socialist transition: The abortion debate in Hungary. *East European Politics and Societies, 8*(2), 256–286.

Gellner, E. (1996). *Nations and nationalism*. Cambridge: Cambridge University Press.

Gil-White, F. J. (2001). Are ethnic groups biological "species" to the human brain? Essentialism in our cognition of some social categories. *Current Anthropology, 42*(4), 515–553.

Greenberg, J. (2006). Nationalism, masculinity and multicultural citizenship in Serbia. *Nationalities Papers, 34*(3), 321–341.

Greenwood, P. A. (2007). Crucible of hate. *The Guardian*, [Online] 1 June. Retrieved March 3, 2010, from http://www.guardian.co.uk/world/2007/jun/01/gayrights.poland.

Hall, D. (2015). Antagonism in the making: Religion and homosexuality in post-communists Poland. In S. Sremac & R. R. Ganzevoort (Eds.), *Religious and sexual nationalisms in Central and Eastern Europe. Gods, gays and governments* (pp. 74–92). Leiden, The Netherlands: Brill.

Healey, D. (2001). *Homosexual desire in revolutionary Russia: The regulation of sexual and gender dissent*. London: University of Chicago Press.

Hilpern, K. (2009). Flying the flag: Why pride is still relevant. *The Independent*, [Online] 18 June. Retrieved June 20, 2009, from http://www.independent. co.uk/life-style/love-sex/flyingthe-flag-why-pride-is-still-relevant-1707556. html.

Hobsbawm, E. J. (1995). *Nations and nationalism since 1780*. Cambridge: Cambridge University Press.

Inglehart, R., & Baker, W. E. (2000). Modernization, cultural change, and the persistence of traditional values. *American Sociological Review, 65*, 19–51.

Kahlina, K. (2013). Contested terrain of sexual citizenship: EU accession and the changing position of sexual minorities in the post-Yugoslav context. *The Europeanisation of Citizenship in the Successor States of the Former Yugoslavia Working Paper Series*. Edinburgh: School of Law, University of Edinburgh.

Kohn, H. (1967). *The idea of nationalism: A study of its origins and backgrounds*. New York: Palgrave Macmillan.

Linz, J. J., & Stepan, A. (1996). *Problems of democratic transition and consolidation: Southern Europe, South America, and post-communist Europe*. Baltimore: Johns Hopkins University Press.

Ministry of Foreign Affairs of the Russian Federation. (2013). *Report on the human rights situation in the European Union*. [Online] Retrieved July 14, 2015, from http://archive.mid.ru//BDOMP/Brp_4.nsf/arh/AE1F6F4836 31588444257C60004A6491?OpenDocument.

Mole, R. C. M. (2011). Nationality and sexuality: Homophobic discourse and the 'national threat' in contemporary Latvia. *Nations and Nationalism, 17*(3), 540–560.

Mole, R. C. M. (2013). *The baltic States from the Soviet Union to the European Union. Identity, discourse and power in the post-communist transition of Estonia, Latvia and Lithuania*. Abingdon, England: Routledge.

Mosse, G. L. (1985). *Nationalism and sexuality: Respectability and abnormal sexuality in modern Europe*. New York: Howard Fertig.

Mosse, G. L. (1996). *The image of man: The creation of modern masculinity*. Oxford: Oxford University Press.

Mouffe, C. (2005). *On the political*. Abingdon, England: Routledge.

Mozaïka. (2007). Annex 1, database of quotes. In: Mozaïka. *Homophobic speech in Latvia: Monitoring the politicians*. [Online] Retrieved October 1, 2009, from www.ilga-europe.org/home/what_we_do/ilga_europe_as_a_funder/completed_projects/homophobic_hate_speech_in_latvia_monitoring_the_decision_makers.

Nagel, J. (1998). Masculinity and nationalism: Gender and sexuality in the making of nations. *Ethnic and Racial Studies, 21*(2), 242–269.

Nagel, J. (2000). Ethnicity and sexuality. *Annual Review of Sociology, 26*, 107–133.

Nagel, J. (2003). *Race, ethnicity and sexuality. Intimate intersections, forbidden frontiers*. Oxford: Oxford University Press.

Novikova, I. (2002). Gender, ethnicity and identity politics in Latvia. In R. Ivekovic & J. Mostov (Eds.), *From gender to nation* (pp. 171–187). Ravenna, Italy: Longo Editore.

Parker, A., Russo, M., Sommer, D., & Yaeger, P. (Eds.) (1992). *Nationalisms and sexualities*. London: Routledge.

Pateman, C. (1988). *The sexual contract*. Cambridge: Polity Press.

Pavasović Trošt, T., & Slootmaeckers, K. (2015). Religion, homosexuality and nationalism in the Western Balkans: The role of religious institutions in defining the nation. In S. Sremac & R. R. Ganzevoort (Eds.), *Religious and sexual nationalisms in Central and Eastern Europe. Gods, gays and governments* (pp. 154–180). Leiden, The Netherlands: Brill.

Pechersaya, N. V. (2013). Perspektivy rossiiskoi semejnoi politiki: prinuzhdenie k traditsii [Prospects for Russian family policy: The drive towards tradition]. *Zhurnal Sotsiologii i Sotsialnoi Antropologii, 69*(4), 94–105.

Peterson, V. S. (1999). Political identities/nationalism as heterosexism. *International Feminist Journal of Politics., 1*(1), 34–65.

Plugge-Foust, C., & Strickland, G. (2000). Homophobia, irrationality, and Christian ideology: Does a relationship exist? *Journal of Sex Education and Therapy, 25*, 240–244.

Prendergast, F. (2000). Dead man used to attack Yugoslav gays. *Daily Xtra*, [Online] 26 January. Retrieved August 27, 2015, from http://www.dailyextra. com/toronto/dead-man-used-attack-yugoslav-gays-56882.

President of Russia. (2013). Poslanie Prezidenta Federal'nomy Sobraniyu. [Presidential Address to the Federal Assembly.] *Website of the President of Russia.* [Online] Retrieved July 7, 2015, from http://kremlin.ru/events/ president/news/19825.

President of Russia. (2014). Interv'yu rossiyskim i inostranym SMI. [Interview with Russian and Foreign Media.] *Website of the President of Russia.* [Online] Retrieved July 7, 2015, from http://kremlin.ru/events/president/news/ 20080.

Pryke, S. (1998). Nationalism and sexuality, what are the issues? *Nations and Nationalism, 4*(4), 529–546.

Rivkin-Fish, M. (2006). From "demographic crisis" to "dying nation"—The politics of language and reproduction in Russia. In H. Goscilo & A. Lanoux (Eds.), *Gender and national identity in twentieth-century Russian culture* (pp. 151–173). DeKalb: Northern Illinois University Press.

Rohrschneider, R., & Whitefield, S. (2012). *The strain of representation. How parties represent diverse voters in Western and Eastern Europe.* Oxford: Oxford University Press.

Rowatt, W.C., LaBouff, J., Johnson, M., Froese, P., & Tsang, J-A. (2009). Associations among religiousness, social attitudes, and prejudice in a national random sample of American adults. *Psychology of Religion and Spirituality, 1*, 14-24.

Schimmelfennig, F., & Sedelmeier, U. (2005). *The Europeanization of Central and Eastern Europe*. Cornell: Cornell University Press.

Schluter, D. P. (2002). *Gay life in the former USSR: Fraternity without community*. London: Routledge.

Schöpflin, G. (1993). *Politics in Eastern Europe*. Oxford, England: Blackwell.

Schöpflin, G. (2000). *Nations, identity, power*. London: Hurst.

Slootmaeckers, K., & Touquet, H. (2016). The Co-evolution of EU's Eastern enlargement and LGBT politics: An ever gayer union? In K. Slootmaeckers, H. Touquet, & P. Vermeersch (Eds.), *The EU enlargement and gay politics*. London: Palgrave Macmillan.

Smith, A. D. (1996). *The ethnic origin of nations*. Oxford, England: Blackwell.

Spencer, P., & Wollman, H. (2002). *Nationalism. A critical introduction*. London: Sage.

Stakić, I. (2011). *Homophobia and hate speech in Serbian public discourse: How national myths and stereotypes influence prejudices against the LGBT minority*. MA thesis. University of Gothenburg.

Stukuls, D. (1999). Body of the nation: Mothering, prostitution and women's place in post-communist Latvia. *Slavic Review, 58*, 537–558.

Štulhofer, A., & Sandfort, T. (Eds.) (2005). *Sexuality and gender in post-communist Eastern Europe and Russia*. New York: Haworth Press.

Suny, R. (1993). *The revenge of the past: Nationalism, revolution and the collapse of the Soviet Union*. Stanford: Stanford University Press.

Suny, R. (2001). Constructing primordialism: Old histories for new nations. *Journal of Modern History, 73*, 862–896.

Tajfel, H., & Turner, J. C. (1986). The social identity theory of intergroup behaviour. In S. Worchel & W. G. Austin (Eds.), *Psychology of intergroup relations* (pp. 7–24). Chicago, IL: Nelson Hall.

Turner, J. C. (1987). *Rediscovering the social group: A self-categorisation theory*. Oxford, England: Basil Blackwell.

Veličković, V. (2012). Homofobni nacionalizam i kriza maskulinosti u Srbiji. *Sarajevske Sveske*, pp. 39–40.

Weeks, J. (1992). Foreword. In A. Schmitt & J. Sofer (Eds.), *Sexuality and eroticism among males in moslem societies* (pp. ix–xii). New York: Haworth Press.

Wilkinson, C. (2014). Putting "traditional values" into practice: The rise and contestation of anti-homopropaganda laws in Russia. *Journal of Human Rights, 13*(3), 363–379.

Whitley, B. (2009). Religiosity and attitudes towards lesbians and gay men: a meta-analysis. *International Journal for the Psychology of Religion, 19*, 21–38.

Yuval-Davis, N. (1997). *Gender and nation*. London: Sage.

Yuval-Davis, N., & Anthias, F. (1989). *Woman-nation-state*. London: Palgrave Macmillan.

CHAPTER 6

From Pride to Politics: Niche-Party Politics and LGBT Rights in Poland

Conor O'Dwyer and Peter Vermeersch

INTRODUCTION

In recent years, several post-communist countries in Central and Eastern Europe, among them Poland, have experienced rising levels of political homophobia (Graff 2010; Puhl 2006). Politicians have portrayed LGBT citizens as the ultimate 'other' and have threatened the rights and safety of their communities in order to win electoral support of the majority population. Such instrumental use of homophobia seems to work best in societies where homosexuality remains deep in the realm of the taboo. Russia's laws against 'homosexual propaganda', adopted in 2013, are perhaps the most extreme manifestation of this phenomenon, but across Central and Eastern Europe, the past decade offers plentiful evidence of growing politicization of homosexuality: the indicators range from public opinion data to politicians' rhetoric, to the bureaucratic hurdles encountered by LGBT activists in organizing Pride parades (Ayoub 2013, 2014; Buzogány 2008; Graff 2010; Kuhar and Takacs 2006; O'Dwyer and Schwartz 2010).

Yet in 2011, in Poland of all places, two gay-rights activists were elected to parliament—one of them a transgender person—and in the years since

C. O'Dwyer (✉)
Department of Political Science, University of Florida, Gainesville, FL, USA

P. Vermeersch
Leuven International and European Studies (LINES),
KU Leuven – University of Leuven, Leuven, Belgium

© The Editor(s) (if applicable) and The Author(s) 2016
K. Slootmaeckers et al. (eds.), *The EU Enlargement and Gay Politics*, DOI 10.1057/978-1-137-48093-4_6

then the country has seen a flurry of legislative proposals by the major parliamentary parties regarding one of the Polish gay-rights movement's chief goals, registered partnerships for same-sex couples (Gazeta Wyborcza 2014).[1] We write 'of all places' because, until quite recently, Poland had a well-deserved international reputation for its opposition to gay rights, and it is clear that in large parts of the country, LGBT-related issues remain a societal taboo that can be exploited for political gain.

Previous scholarship has analyzed the early stages of Poland's gay-rights movement, from its origins in the 1990s through the surge of political homophobia in the 2000s (O'Dwyer 2010, 2012). This analysis has given particular attention to the role of the EU in fostering both the movement and, unintentionally, the backlash against it. In this chapter, we seek to contextualize the current debate over registered partnerships for same-sex couples within this broader arc of the Polish movement's development. This trajectory was initially shaped by transnational pressures associated with Poland's integration into the EU—and the ways in which these pressures reframed homosexuality as a political issue (O'Dwyer 2012). At this stage in the broader trajectory, we can discern an increasingly organized and visible movement, one that is capable of framing its cause in a way that resonates with a growing portion of society. These successes notwithstanding, just several years ago few would have predicted that registered partnerships would rise to prominence in national politics, generating legislative proposals from the major political parties that have come within a few votes of passing.[2]

In this chapter, we wish to examine how LGBT rights moved from being a site of social mobilization to one of political mobilization, and how that political mobilization has helped reshape the political party dynamic around registered partnerships. In particular, we analyze the entry of a new political party in 2011, Your Movement (*Twój Ruch* [TR]).[3] TR's entry into the party system was in large part the consequence of Poland's culture wars around EU membership—wars in which homosexuality was one of the primary battlegrounds. At the same time, as we show, TR's arrival fundamentally altered the political opportunity structure faced by the movement. It destabilized the set of elite arrangements in the party system, forcing the center right to engage with an issue that it had previously ignored.[4] Thus, although social change regarding tolerance of homosexuality remains frustratingly slow (Siedlecka 2015), between 2011 and 2015 Poland's long ostracized gay rights movement experienced rapidly expanding political influence. We offer an explanation of why this has occurred and close with some reflections on Poland's broader lessons for other parts of post-communist Europe.

Two Key Factors: EU Accession and Niche-Party Politics

We seek to understand how the Polish gay-rights movement successfully crossed two critical thresholds of social movement development: (1) the threshold between social protest and politically engaged protest (or *politicized* protest) and (2) the threshold between politically engaged protest and electoral mobilization (i.e. entering the field of party competition). In this section we argue that crossing the former threshold can be understood in terms of the broader politics of EU accession, while the second threshold is best understood in terms of party system dynamics, i.e. domestically. To separate the two phases in this way is not to remove causal connections between them; on the contrary, we see both phases as part of one broad process in which international shocks have unfolding consequences for domestic politics and the organization of gay-rights activism over time. Since we focus on just one case, we are not seeking to generalize beyond to the rest of the region (though we suspect that the dynamics analyzed here are not unique to Poland). In order to analyze these two phases, we apply theory from (1) the extant literature on Europeanization and gay rights and (2) the dynamics of niche parties.

The First Threshold: From Social to Political Protest

The first threshold of Poland's gay-rights debate was dominated by the politics of EU accession. The requirement that applicant states adopt labor market policies reflecting EU norms of non-discrimination and minority rights meant that, as a legal matter at the very least, the issue of homosexuality would require some form of political accommodation (Kochenov 2007). Given the mix of external incentives for policy change, on the one hand, and the lack of resonance between EU and domestic norms on the other, scholars saw in Europeanization a ready framework for analyzing the emergent debate over gay rights in applicant states like Poland (Schimmelfennig and Sedelmeier 2005). Europeanization scholarship did not offer much ground for hope, however, especially when it came to rights gains *after* accession. As a number of earlier pieces argued (O'Dwyer and Schwartz 2010; O'Dwyer 2010), the leverage of conditionality would decrease after countries like Poland gained EU membership, and the weak character of social learning during the accession process augured poorly for activism going forward. By extension, Europeanization literature would have placed poor odds on registered partnerships proposals in new member states such as Poland.

The relationship between gay rights and accession did not play out as straightforwardly as Europeanization scholars would have suggested, however. Yes, the shift from applicant status to membership status (and the consequent weakening of conditionality) did result in an almost instantaneous homophobic backlash (see below). But it also resulted in a re-founding of Poland's gay-rights movement, setting in motion a process of social movement mobilization that has made the Polish movement one of the strongest in contemporary Eastern Europe. In a 2012 piece, O'Dwyer advanced a theoretical framework drawing on social movement theory, as opposed to Europeanization theory, to explain these developments (O'Dwyer 2012). It is not our intention to recapitulate this framework here, but we wish to highlight the following causal mechanisms by which EU accession helped transform the movement, albeit in ways not anticipated by Europeanization scholarship.

The catalyst for these mechanisms is that of backlash, a 'moral panic' on the part of socially conservative political elites in the accession country. These elites use political homophobia to mobilize their constituencies for electoral gain: they link EU membership requirements with the propagation of homosexuality, painting them as threats to national norms regarding the family (see Mole 2016). Often—and Poland is certainly a good example—this kind of political homophobia proves quite effective as a tool for electoral mobilization. Typically overlooked, however, are a backlash's follow-up effects for the targets of homophobia, particularly gay-rights groups. O'Dwyer (2012) enumerates three such effects, arguing that they can be seen as mechanisms strengthening activism. The first is increased visibility to homosexuality as an issue. Because homosexuality under communism was deeply underground in both the discourse and in everyday life, gay rights lacked not only political salience but also basic visibility (Gessen 1994; Graff 2010; Long 1999). Second, the experience of being politically targeted draws gay-rights activists together, minimizing the threat of splits within the movement over goals, tactics, and so on. Third, the linkage between homophobic backlash and EU accession helps activists win elite allies outside the movement. The latter find common cause with a group that otherwise would have escaped their attention, but who are now 'symbols' of EU values.

The last of these mechanisms, winning elite allies, can at a broader level be thought of in terms of the political opportunity structure, which social movement theorists define broadly as 'the institutional structure or informal power relations of a given national political system' (McAdam et al. 1996, p. 3). Elite allies may range from media outlets to financial donors to public figures, but the allies that interest us here are political parties; this is the second threshold of movement development. As McAdam and Tarrow (2010, p. 533) write, social movements and political parties may become linked in a multitude of ways. They mention at least six: (1) movements may introduce new forms of collective action that influence election campaigns; (2) they may join electoral coalitions or, in extreme cases, turn into parties themselves; (3) they may engage in proactive electoral mobilization; (4) they may engage in reactive electoral mobilization; or (5) they may polarize political parties internally; and, finally, (6) shifts in electoral regimes may have a long-term impact on mobilization and demobilization. In Poland, as we will show, the movement's entry into party politics brought unprecedented attention to its campaign for registered partnerships. It certainly stands to reason that when LGBT demands become part of the agenda of a political party they have a higher chance of leading to legislative victories. Yet even if we recognize that in 'turning to the electoral option [movements] can exert considerable influence over domestic politics' (McAdam and Tarrow 2010, p. 533), the question for gay rights in Poland thus remains: how is the linkage between parties and movements formed? Why should political parties choose to respond to a political issue that does not enjoy great public support?

The Second Threshold: From Political Protest to Party Politics

We seek to answer these questions by turning to recent work by Bonnie Meguid (2008) on how niche parties reshape party competition by shifting the policy agenda of bigger, more mainstream, and more established political parties. Meguid's research looks at the phenomenon of parties that define themselves primarily in terms of a single issue. In Western Europe, such 'niche parties' include three types, often treated separately: green, radical-right, and ethno-territorial parties. In Poland, a niche party with an anticlerical orientation, Your Movement (TR), has emerged in the party system. The party has strong links to the gay-rights movement both in terms of leaders and program. Like the Western European niche parties that Meguid describes, TR is outside the mainstream of conventional ideological competition, and its programmatic profile is sharply defined by one overarching position, i.e. anticlericalism.[5] Also, like niche parties in Western Europe, TR's entrance into the party system has been a disruptive event.

For our purposes, Meguid's key insight is that the entry of a niche party into the electoral arena has strong repercussions for the strategic choices of mainstream political parties regarding those issues at the center of the niche party's program. To focus on the relevant theoretical propositions for our analysis of Poland, Meguid argues that mainstream parties respond to the appearance of niche parties in one of three ways: by ignoring them, by actively countering their program, or by accommodating (or co-opting) key aspects of that program. By ignoring the niche party's issue, a mainstream party seeks to lower its political salience. By accommodating or co-opting it, a mainstream party attempts to steal the niche party's potential voters. By countering the issue, a mainstream party, in effect, heightens its salience and increases the niche party's perceived ownership of the issue. In a party system such as Poland's in the 2000s—in which two to three major parties dominate—the combination of the major parties' responses is critical to the electoral success of the niche party.[6] If one of the mainstream parties ignores the issue while the other actively counters it, Meguid's model predicts electoral success for the niche party.

Niche parties thus may lead mainstream parties to endorse certain topics that they would normally never endorse. In doing so they change the political opportunity structure both directly and indirectly. They spur direct change inasmuch as their appearance provides social movements with an ally in the political system, together with all the legitimacy and policy-making leverage that an ally can provide. Equally, they spur indirect change by reshaping the competitive dynamics in the party system, forcing the mainstream parties to reevaluate their strategic choices about which policies they engage and which they ignore. In this way, niche parties may open up alliances for the movement with *other* parties as well. The end result is to activate the variety of mechanisms of party-led social movement mobilization outlined by McAdam and Tarrow (2010) above.

FROM SOCIAL PROTEST TO PARTY POLITICS: THE TRAJECTORY OF THE POLISH GAY-RIGHTS MOVEMENT SINCE 1989

Having laid out our theoretical framework, in the following sections we apply it to give a more detailed view of the trajectory of the Polish gay-rights movement since 1989. We divide the movement's development into three overarching periods: from 1990 to 1997, from 1998 to the accession of Poland to the EU in 2004, and from 2005 to the present. Dividing the movement's development arc in this way helps to capture the interplay between EU factors and domestic dynamics. In the first period, the movement was weakly organized and oriented toward self-help and service provision rather than political goals. In the second period, international pressure—in particular, the requirements of EU accession—politicized the topic of homosexuality. This politicization initially took the form of political homophobia—a backlash against gay rights as threatening social norms regarding the family—but it also catalyzed a re-founding of the movement on more organized and political terms. By the end of these first two periods, the Polish gay-rights movement had, therefore, crossed the first of our two thresholds. During the third period, after accession, it crossed the second threshold, from politicized movement to electorally mobilized movement. At this point, domestic political dynamics become critical and the process of 'Europeanization' seems less important; we highlight in particular the role of niche-party politics as a factor in the advancement of legislative proposals for registered partnerships.

The Social Protest Stage (1990–1997)

As earlier literature has described, until recently, LGBT rights in Poland were mainly a matter of social protest and grassroots campaigning (Gruszczynska 2009a; Holzhacker 2012; Owczarzak 2009; Walczyszyn 2012). Activist groups have existed since the mid-1980s (Zboralski 1991), but they were at that time small and confined to urban areas such as Wrocław (where the 'Etap' group was active), Łódź, Gdańsk, and to some extent, Warsaw. Although groups like *Filo, Warszawski Ruch Homoseksualny* (Warsaw Homosexual Movement) and, shortly after the fall of the socialist regime, *Lambda*, as well as individual activists such as Ryszard Kisiel, all openly opposed government policies, a broader LGBT movement did not emerge as a visible part of the main oppositional networks of the time (Szyk and Urbańczyk 2010). In the 1990s, individual activists and local groups continued to provide self-help and information to LGBT communities, but not until the beginning of the first decade of the 2000s did this lead to attempts at broader movement formation (Chetaille 2011, p. 122). The largest Polish LGBT organization, Campaign Against Homophobia (*Kampania Przeciw Homofobii* [KPH]), was established in 2001, during the period in which EU accession was at the center of attention (see below). During the 1990s, the movement was not engaged in direct political action, and it certainly did not manage to influence political party programs. The legal recognition of same-sex couples was absent from political debates, and no proposals were formulated or introduced. For the better part of the 1990s, groups working on behalf of LGBT people in Poland did not conceive of their agenda in political terms. Advocacy meant organizing support services, combatting prejudice, and educating the public; it did not mean campaigning for political rights (Owczarzak 2009).

Not surprisingly, then, an analysis of the party programs of the parliamentary elections during this time reveals the virtual absence of direct references to LGBT rights in party programs.[7] We do, however, find many references to the importance of 'traditional family values' in the programs of conservative and right-wing political parties. These references were clearly a component of a broader tradition in post-1989 Polish electoral mobilization—that of emphasizing Catholic moral preferences, particularly with respect to debates on euthanasia and abortion. The salience of family values grew in the latter half of the 1990s, in particular in the run-up to the elections of 1997, which many scholars saw as a turn to the right (e.g. Vermeersch 2013). In these elections, the regrouped center-right parties of the Solidarity Electoral Action (*Akcja Wyborcza Solidarność* [AWS]) campaigned under the slogan 'zAWSze Wolność-Własność-Rodzina' ('Always Freedom-Ownership-Family'), and became the largest group in parliament with 38.83 per cent of the vote (Piasecki 2012, p. 112). In sum, one can say that during this period the movement did not go beyond the stage of social protest, and that by 1997 it was faced with a palpable traditionalist force.

The Politicization of the Movement: Backlash Against Gay Rights and the Politicization of Homosexuality (1998–2004)

At the end of the 1990s and during the early 2000s, LGBT issues became more salient politically as Poland went into a process of transposing European anti-discrimination legislation—a process that was slow and would in the end take a full decade to complete. It is, however, in the context of coming closer to the EU membership date that the first proposals for a law on registered partnerships emerged, albeit very tentatively. For example, in its 2001 election campaign, the SLD made vague promises about same-sex partnership legislation—in addition to liberalizing Poland's highly restrictive abortion law—but once in power, it dropped work on both (Gruszczynska 2009b, p. 29). A later proposal for same-sex partnerships in 2002 by Maria Szyszkowska, a professor of philosophy at Warsaw University who was also a senator with the SLD, was passed by the Polish Senate but failed to attract support in the Parliament, even in Szyszkowska's own party. Her sponsorship of the doomed measure was generally credited with ending her political career (Gruszczynska 2009b, p. 24). Over the course of the early 2000s, the campaign for registered partnerships lived on in a kind of suspended animation in the parliament, while in the civil societal sphere, NGOs and advocacy groups became increasingly engaged with it.

Simultaneously, however, political opposition against LGBT rights became increasingly palpable. It was an important topic in the program of the League of Polish Families (*Liga Polskich Rodzin* [LPR]), which stated in its election manifestos that that the party was 'opposed to abortion, euthanasia, human cloning, homosexual relations and every legislation which contradicts Christian ethics' (reprinted in Skłodowska and Dołbakowska 2006, pp. 66–76). The LPR also proposed to introduce the death penalty for 'murderer-pedophiles', an idea that received support from members of the Law and Justice party (*Prawo i Sprawiedliwość* [PiS]). In the Polish political debate the terms homosexuals and pedophiles have often been (deliberately) conflated, and the LPR's language had a clear subtext: gays were a danger to the nation's children. The LPR subsumed all these ideas under the rubric of a broader political project: regaining independence for the Polish nation from the outside world, in particular the EU, and taking power out of the hands of left-wing politicians who were accused of being puppets in the hands of foreign rulers.

While the topic of homosexual relations had not been a key element of the political programs of mainstream political parties for most of the 1990s, in the years before the 2004 accession date the topic rose to prominence as a symbol of differentiation between the mainstream left and right, and by extension, between pro- and Eurosceptic politicians. Key politicians in PiS began to comment on the issue and sometimes promoted policies against LGBT groups in order to tap into nationalist feelings. For example, in 2004 Warsaw's then-mayor, Lech Kaczyński, banned the March of Equality in Warsaw and allowed homophobic counter-demonstrations. Protestors held up signs with slogans like 'God, Honor, Fatherland' and, in a direct reference to Poland's nationalist–populist demagogue of the interwar period, 'Roman Dmowski, Pride of Poland' (O'Dwyer and Schwartz 2010, pp. 7–8). The idea that 'a gay is like a Jew' ('gej, czyli Żyd', quoted in Graff 2008, p. 113) was a powerful and efficient slogan in the hands of radical groups, who used it as a way to connect anti-gay protest with the defense of (a particular interpretation of) Polishness. These tactics pushed gay activists into the middle of a polarized debate over the status of nationalism and anti-Semitism (Graff 2008, p. 122). As Agnieszka Graff (2010, pp. 584–585) has written:

> lack of acceptance for sexual minorities (or "deviants" and "promoters of homosexuality", as conservatives refer to them) was construed as Poland's distinctive national feature in Europe—to be cherished or eradicated, depending on the speaker's standpoint. Although the link was rarely as clear as the neo-Nazis' signs proclaiming "Europa=Sodoma", homosexuality became closely linked to Europe in public discourse.

PiS' anti-gay and nationalist platform may be seen as shoring up its position vis-à-vis the LPR on the right flank and the SLD on the left. The latter was consistently portrayed by PiS as being a threat to the nation because of its involvement in corruption, its ties to former communists, its willingness to conform to the demands of the EU, and its openness to gays and lesbians.[8]

This politicization—and polarization—was in many ways a boon for Poland's gay-rights movement (O'Dwyer 2012; Walczyszyn 2012). In the years right before the EU accession, it brought new visibility to the issue, knitted together a previously disparate network of advocacy groups and service organizations, and attracted domestic allies from outside the movement. As it gained strength, the Polish movement increasingly framed its goals in political terms. Whereas in the 1990s, LGBT advocates organized primarily as self-help groups and as educators against intolerance, after 2000 advocacy efforts began to take on political goals, moving from EU-mandated policies such as antidiscrimination to newer ones, e.g. registered partnerships. The latter became a topic not only of politicization but also of political party competition in the years that followed.

From Politicization to Party Politics (After 2004)

Immediately after the EU accession, Poland elected its most socially conservative and nationalist government since 1989. During the period of this PiS-LPR government (2005–2006), Polish gay-rights activism found international support as EU and affiliated institutions strongly criticized Poland for discrimination (see e.g. reports by Amnesty International and international governmental organizations).[9] The European Parliament passed several resolutions condemning homophobia in Poland (in January and June 2006, and again in April 2007). But while international pressure opened up opportunities for Polish LGBT activists to participate in public discussions and to protest against discrimination, it also sparked opposition from the Polish right. Thus, increased visibility mostly took the form of opposition against LGBT rights. The topic was at that time a prominent tool of political mobilization in the hands of those politicians who sought to challenge the main political parties associated with a pro-EU standpoint.[10]

This post-accession backlash made one thing very clear: EU conditionality could no longer be used to shape the politics of homosexuality. The dynamics of domestic party competition—namely, niche-party politics—were becoming the main factors shaping the issue. In this section, we describe how the dynamics of party competition, and especially the emergence of Your Movement (TR), upended the politics of this issue and put the enactment of registered partnerships into play. Following the model outlined earlier in the chapter, niche-party politics vaulted the campaign for registered partnerships from the sidelines into the midst of mainstream party politics. The critical element in this process was the entry of a new party, Your Movement (TR), into the party system in 2011. Up to this point, gay rights had been an issue of potential salience to three of Poland's mainstream political parties: PiS (*Prawo i Sprawiedliwość* [Law and Justice]), PO (*Platforma Obywatelska* [Civic Platform]), and SLD (*Sojusz Lewicy Demokratycznej* [Democratic Left Alliance]).[11] The PiS had established a strong reputation in opposition to the issue. The PO and SLD meanwhile had both sought to establish themselves as moderate, liberal alternatives to the PiS across a range of issues; however, because of society's generally negative view of homosexuality, they had also tried to avoid being drawn into any clear position on gay rights (O'Dwyer 2010, p. 242). When TR entered the party system in 2011, it focused on gay rights as one of its defining issues. TR's subsequent electoral success came at the expense of the center-left SLD (Wojtasik 2012) and served as a warning to the center-right PO. Both parties had failed to engage post-materialist issues like gay rights, an omission that TR capitalized on. In short, the competitive threat represented by TR to Poland's mainstream alternatives to the PiS explains why, in the period since 2011, both the PO and SLD have shifted from trying to ignore homosexuality as a political issue to engaging with it more directly, and both parties have become more supportive of registered partnerships. In the remainder of this section we trace the main stages of this process.

Your Movement was founded by Janusz Palikot, a self-made millionaire who originally entered politics as a member of the PO and rose to national prominence through his aggressive criticism of the nationalism-tinged social conservatism of the PiS and its partners in government. In

April 2007, he appeared at a public news conference wearing a t-shirt that said 'I am gay' and 'I am with SLD'.[12] Palikot explained that he wished to draw attention to the rights of minorities because the PO, his party at the time, was not striving hard enough to protect them. The t-shirt's messages were anathema to the core philosophy and image of the Kaczyński-led government, which defined itself primarily in terms of Christian-nationalism and anti-communism. No Polish politician had ever so brazenly challenged the twin taboos of the Polish hard right. Perhaps even more shocking than the expression of solidarity with the SLD, the slogan 'I am gay', while not strictly accurate, served as a symbol for a new kind of political identity: anticlerical, anti-nationalist, and iconoclastic.[13] These became the defining elements of Palikot's movement and a political career sustained by provoking controversy to generate publicity, beginning with homosexuality.[14]

Even if Palikot's emphasis on homosexuality as a political topic may have been in part a matter of political calculation and strategy, it affected how the registered partnership debate developed in the years that followed, as a comparison of the debate on registered partnerships before and after 2011 shows. In 2007, the PO, now the governing party, was continuing its quiet avoidance of gay-rights issues: it voted, for example, to keep the remnants of Szyszkowska's registered partnerships proposal from consideration by parliament. Meanwhile, the opposition SLD continued to consider some form of registered partnerships in the period from 2008 to 2009, though these proposals seemed half-hearted and did not progress beyond the discussion stage. During this time, the registered partnerships campaign was gaining steam *outside* of parliament and among NGOs and advocacy groups. A new group working to create legislation for registered partnerships, the Initiative for Registered Partnerships (*Grupa Inicjatywna ds. Związków Partnerskich*), was established in June 2009.[15] This group brought together representatives of the Green Party and three of Poland's largest LGBT groups, KPH, *Lambda Warszawa*, and *InnaStrona*. For two years, this group convened town-hall style meetings throughout Poland to gather feedback on legislation for registered partnerships. In summer 2011, the group wrote draft legislation.

This proposal would doubtless have languished in obscurity had TR not decided to make it a centerpiece of its campaign for the upcoming 2011 election campaign. For Palikot, registered partnerships were a means to broaden his appeal among voters who had previously voted for the PO or SLD but were now disappointed by the failure of these parties to get this legislation accepted. TR could position itself as trustworthier and less likely to be indulgent to conservative political forces. Moreover, when the SLD failed to give gay-rights activist Robert Biedroń and pro-abortion campaigner Wanda Nowicka positions on its election lists—something the party had promised earlier—TR made use of the occasion to position itself as the more vigorous defender of liberal issues (Szczerbiak 2012, p. 22).

By July 2011 the stage was set for a debate on registered partnerships legislation among the main political parties. Palikot had become more than simply a politician of the opposition; he represented a party with a constituency.[16] TR threw its support behind the Initiative for Registered Partnerships' proposal, promising that it would be one of the first legislative items that it would pursue if elected. In response, the PO made its first steps toward engaging the issue. Characteristically, these amounted to a vague promise to consider it at some future time, as PO leader Donald Tusk declared that he believed 'the time was ripe for the Polish [Parliament] to adopt civil partnership laws following the elections' (Kawiński 2012; Walczyszyn 2012, p. 91).

As Fig. 6.1 shows, the elections were a breakthrough for TR. It received a stunning 10.02 per cent of the vote and, in effect, vaulted past the two most established parties in the political system: the Peasant Party and the Democratic Left Alliance. This development added further visibility to gay rights in Polish party politics. Not only had the issue of registered partnerships been part of the election debates, but during the campaign TR had also allied with transgender activist Anna Grodzka as well as with Robert Biedroń, the leader of Poland's largest gay-rights NGO. Even more significantly, both were elected to parliament on the party list. The inclusion and foregrounding of these two prominent activists on the TR ticket conferred unprecedented political legitimacy to openly gay activists, acknowledging them as political actors in a system in which they were previously invisible.

Comparative research suggests that the election of openly gay candidates to national political office tends to presage a tipping point before the enactment of broader LGBT rights (Reynolds 2013). After the elections of 2011, both the PO and the SLD became far more openly supportive of the gay-rights movement's signature project of registered partnerships than at any time previous. Three full-fledged parliamentary proposals (and votes) on the issue followed in the months after the elections, which was more than in all the years previous. In January 2012, TR and the SLD jointly submitted two draft legislative proposals for registered partnerships, and in April of the same year the PO followed with its own version.

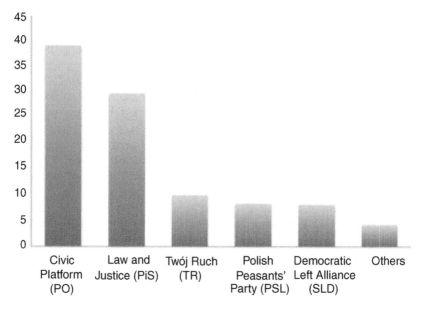

Fig. 6.1 Vote share (in %) by party in the 2011 parliamentary elections. *Source:* Parties and election in Europe database, http://www.parties-and-elections.eu/poland.html

Furthermore, the issue has raised the stakes within parties as well as among them. This became clear in the events surrounding PO politician Jarosław Gowin, who was Minister of Justice in Tusk's cabinet. In April 2013, he was sacked after making homophobic statements during a debate over the PO's proposal on registered partnerships. The PO-led government had issued the proposal in February 2013, but following Gowin's initiative, 46 MPs from the PO party voted against it. As a result, the proposal failed to pass, though only just barely: the final vote was 228–221.[17] Despite the setback, Tusk signaled his continued support for some form of registered partnerships, but whether this was a return to the old strategy of words over deeds remains to be seen. Optimists can take heart at his dismissal of Gowin. They can also note his government's acceptance of the nomination of the transgendered Anna Grodzka for the post of Deputy Speaker of the Polish parliament (Adekoya 2013). For Tusk, her nomination was a way to put down Gowin's revolt within the PO and distance himself from the opposition Law and Justice party. A pessimist, on the other hand, would point out that the PO has remained cautious in its support, with Tusk also stating that going too quickly on the matter of registered partnerships would be counterproductive.[18]

While this latest stage in the Polish gay-rights movement has not yet led to the acceptance of registered partnerships, to simply dismiss the recent debates on the issue would be to miss the momentous shifts in the movement since the 1990s. Even looking to the more recent past, there has been an important shift since the elections of the 2011 in the way such legislative proposals have become a visible topic in party competition. While there were some discussions and even proposals for registered partnerships in Parliament before 2011, none came close to finding broad support. Since 2011, TR's appearance has catalyzed what could be called a legislative stage in the LGBT movement, in which all three liberal parties have sponsored parliamentary proposals that have since been voted on. The issue can no longer be shoved to the margins of politics and safely ignored.

CONCLUSION

We conclude by considering what 'lessons', if any, the Polish gay-rights movement's path from social protest to party politics offers to other countries in the region. First, let us briefly recapitulate the main points of the argument. We argue that, despite significant headwinds from widespread negative social attitudes toward homosexuality, opposition from a politically influential church, and a wave of political homophobia in the mid-2000s, the Polish gay-rights movement has succeeded in overcoming two very significant developmental hurdles: (1) social protest against politicization of the movement and (2) movement politicization to party politics. The latter stage is evident in the rapidly evolving debate over registered partnerships, which has generated a slew of legislative proposals. Few would have foreseen these developments from the vantage point of the late 1990s, when homosexuality was politically invisible and the movement moribund.

In order to explain these developments, we have suggested that two key changes in the broader political opportunity structure were critical. First, the requirements of EU accession, particularly in the area of labor market antidiscrimination policy, made homosexuality one of the central points in a hard-right backlash immediately following EU accession. This period of heightened political homophobia, we argue, also politicized the movement, bringing unprecedented public visibility to its issues, forging deeper ties of solidarity among activists, and winning allies outside of the movement (O'Dwyer 2012). The latter dynamic, concerning extra-movement allies, became particularly important in 2011, when a newly founded political party, TR, forged close links with activists from the leading gay-rights groups. This moment can be seen as a shift within the opportunity structure of domestic politics (McAdam and Tarrow 2010). Rather than leave the analysis at that level of generality, though, we employ a model of niche-party politics (Meguid 2008) to understand more precisely *how* the political opportunity structure affected the movement's goal of registered partnerships legislation. We believe that these factors offer a good account of the Polish case; we would like now to briefly consider their wider usefulness for other post-communist countries, especially with regard to registered partnerships.

The first 'lesson' to be drawn from our analysis is that EU accession can strongly shape the domestic political field in which gay-rights movements organize. More importantly, though, the mechanisms by which these EU pressures operate can run quite counter to the 'external incentives' and 'social learning' mechanisms described in standard Europeanization theory (e.g. Schimmelfennig and Sedelmeier 2005). Second, the terms of debates over registered partnerships proposals—which have occurred (or are occurring) in the Czech Republic, Slovenia, Hungary, Estonia, Latvia, and most recently, Croatia, and Slovakia—are not the same across countries and over time (see also Kuhar and Mecin Čeplak 2016). Gay-rights advocates enter these debates in very different positions depending on the strength of the movements they represent and the political allies that they bring with them. Our argument should, above all, draw attention to the role of political homophobia and backlash in politicizing movements and, potentially, in strengthening them. The third lesson from our case study is that party-system dynamics become critical as movements cross the second threshold of development. Poland's case is especially interesting because those dynamics have followed a specific logic, that of niche-party politics. With the victory of Andrzej Duda in the 2015 presidential elections, and of the PiS in the parliamentary elections of October 2015, the Polish political party landscape has shifted again; the eclipse of the left will likely limit the Polish gay-rights movement's legislative opportunities for the near future. Whether movements in other countries can take advantage of niche-party dynamics is an empirical question that will require further comparative work. However, in a region in which scholars have often argued that a secular-liberal/religious-nationalist cleavage is more salient than the standard left-right socioeconomic one, we might expect more space for niche parties like TR (Benoit and Laver 2006; O'Dwyer 2014; Rovny and Edwards 2012).

A comparative study of this would allow us to sharpen our theory of how elite allies discovered during periods of homophobic backlash may help movements cross the 'second threshold' into electoral mobilization. Poland highlights the niche-party linkage; other cases may highlight other linkages. Examples of countries where this has led to results may offer hope to Polish activists that their goals can be achieved.

NOTES

1. For simplicity, here and throughout the paper, we use the term 'gay rights' to include rights for lesbian, gay, bisexual, and transgender people; we use it interchangeably with the abbreviation LGBT. For purposes of the larger movement and the issue of registered partnerships, specifically, these groups are largely united, and it makes sense to analyze them collectively.

2. This period also saw the introduction, and subsequent failure, of the Gender Accordance Act, which aimed to give better legal protection to transgender citizens. Introduced by Anna Grodzka in May 2012, the bill was first passed by the Sejm in July 2015, but was later vetoed by the president. In early October 2015, the Sejm failed to override the veto.

3. The party was initially named after its founder, Janusz Palikot, and was called Palikot's Movement (*Ruch Palikota*). It changed its name in October 2013. For simplicity, we will refer to it as *Twój Ruch* (TR) throughout.

4. The stability of elite arrangements is one of the key features defining the political opportunity structure according to literature on social movements. For a discussion of the other features, see McAdam (1996, 26–29).

5. Meguid's definition of niche parties depends on three crucial characteristics: rejection of class-based politics, the championing of issues outside the conventional left–right divide, and a focus on a narrower set of issues than those of the mainstream parties (2008, pp. 3–4). TR's anticlericalism meets all three. First, it prioritizes values of self-expression and individual freedom over pocketbook issues (see below). Second, it is difficult to classify in classic left–right terms (Stanley and Czesnik 2014), since it is 'left' on issues like legalization of drugs and 'right' on issues like adopting a 'flat tax'. Last, its strong emphasis on an anticlerical, antinationalist program limits its mass appeal, especially among the Polish electorate.

6. Since 2005, the dominant parties have been two: PiS (*Prawo i Sprawiedliwość*, Law and Justice) and PO (*Platforma Obywatelska*, Civic Platform). Historically, however, the post-communist SLD (*Sojusz Lewicy*

Demokratycznej, Democratic Left Alliance) party has also been a major political player. While its fortunes have ebbed since 2005, it may still be considered a mainstream contender.

7. The party programs were published in the following publications: Paszkiewicz (1996); Skłodowska (2001a); Skłodowska (2001b); Skłodowska (2003); Skłodowska and Dołbakowska (2002); Skłodowska and Dołbakowska (2004); and Skłodowska and Dołbakowska (2006).

8. Former president Aleksander Kwaśniewski (SLD), for example, enjoyed strong support among gays and lesbians (Selinger 2008, p. 26).

9. Amnesty International Poland, 'Polska: Prawa mniejszości seksualnych zagrożone', 24 November 2005; Amnesty International. 'Lesbian, Gay, Bisexual and Transgender Rights in Poland and Latvia'.15 November, 2006, http://web.amnesty.org/library/Index/ENGEUR010192006?op en&of=ENG-375. See also e.g. European Parliament resolution of 26 April 2007 on homophobia in Europe, P6_TA(2007)0167.

10. The conservative Law and Justice (PiS) and League of Polish Families (LPR) parties used it as an argument mainly against the social democrats (SLD), who were known to have no particular problem with issues of sexual orientation, but also against the liberal politicians who were once with the Freedom Union (UW) or with the pro-Round-Table section of the former Solidarity movement. And it has also been used as a tool for mobilizing against the governing Civic Platform (PO)—a party that was, at the time, reluctant to address the topic.

11. For the fourth major party, the Polish Peasant Party, gay rights were not a salient issue of party competition.

12. In Polish, 'Jestem gejem' and 'Jestem z SLD'—SLD here being the postcommunist Party of the Democratic Left.

13. Curiously, Janusz Palikot's entry into Polish politics was inconspicuous and showed little sign of the political style to come later. In 2005, he used his wealth to win a seat in parliament in the Lubelski region as part of the then still-new Civic Platform party (PO). He looked like the typical PO politician—middle of the road politically and certainly not someone identified with 'values issues'. In fact, to curry support for his candidacy in his home district, he bought over the regional Christian-nationalist weekly *Ozon* (Kocur and Katarzyna 2013, p. 48). For his first two years as an MP, Palikot's main work was on a commission to build transparency and accountability in the state administration.

14. Although his stance on LGBT rights has been of key importance, other elements have certainly also contributed to Palikot's political fame. See e.g. his response to the crash, on April 10, 2010, of the Polish airliner carrying President Lech Kaczyński (PiS) and 95 Polish dignitaries and state officials en route to Smolensk. The crash was a bombshell in Polish politics and, not surprisingly, also a turning point for Palikot. Among the Polish right,

accusations swirled of possible Russian involvement, while the left suggested possible criminal negligence by the government in planning the flight. Palikot pushed his critique of PiS to new levels. Charging that Kaczyński himself was responsible for the crash—for insisting that the pilot land the plane in bad weather—he established the Movement for the Support of Palikot, which was intended to represent Poles seeking an investigation of the circumstances leading to the fateful plane flight. He announced in a televised interview that 'the Janusz Palikot whom you all know died with Lech Kaczyński on the 10th of April' (Quoted in Kocur and Katarzyna 2013, p. 50).

15. See http://www.zwiazkipartnerskie.info/.

16. Any description of the history of his party must of course acknowledge how closely it is linked to its founder, who originally named his party after himself (it was the Palikot Movement first and later it became TR). However, an equally striking feature of the party's founding and subsequent development is the degree to which each stage of this development occurred in engagement with, or perhaps more accurately, in reaction to the champion of socially conservative, national-Catholic Poland, i.e. the Law and Justice party (PiS). This clash between PiS and TR's world views—patriotic Christian values vs. anticlerical liberalism—is how Palikot defined the party, even if, with characteristic braggadocio, he initially named it after himself (For more on Palikot, see the study by Polish analysts Anna Kocur and Katarzyna Majczak, 'Who Are You, Mr. Palikot?' (2013)).

17. See http://www.wbj.pl/article-61741-gowin-seizes-spotlight-as-conservatives-snub-pm.html.

18. See http://www.rp.pl/artykul/738665,1020055-Tusk–Zwiazki-partnerskie–Przesada-moze-przyniesc-odwrotne-skutki.html.

REFERENCES

Adekoya, R. (2013). A transsexual deputy speaker could open people's eyes in Poland. *The Guardian*, [Online] 8 February. Retrieved August 28, 2008, from http://www.theguardian.com/commentisfree/2013/feb/08/transsexual-deputy-speaker-polish.

Ayoub, P. M. (2013). Cooperative transnationalism in contemporary Europe: Europeanization and political opportunities for LGBT mobilization in the European Union. *European Political Science Review, 5*(2), 279–310.

Ayoub, P. M. (2014). With arms wide shut: Threat perception, norm reception, and mobilized resistance to LGBT rights. *Journal of Human Rights, 13*(3), 337–362.

Benoit, K., & Laver, M. (2006). *Party policy in modern democracies*. London: Routledge.

Buzogány, A. (2008). Joining Europe, not sodom: LGBT rights and the limits of Europeanization in Hungary and Romania. In: AAASS (American Association for the Advancement of Slavic Studies), The National Convention of the American Association for the Advancement of Slavic Studies. Philadelphia, PA, 20–23 November.

Chetaille, A. (2011). Poland: Sovereignty and sexuality in post-socialist Times. In M. Tremblay, D. Paternotte, & C. Johnson (Eds.), *The lesbian and gay movement and the state: Comparative insights into a transformed relationship*. Surrey, England: Ashgate Publishing Limited.

Gazeta Wyborcza. (2014). Organizacje chcą wznowienia prac nad ustawą o związkach partnerskich. *Gazeta Wyborcza*, March 14.

Gessen, M. (1994). *The rights of lesbians and gay men in the Russian federation: A report of the international gay and lesbian human rights commission*. San Francisco, CA: International Gay and Lesbian Human Rights Commission.

Graff, A. (2008). *Rykoszetem. Rzecz o płci, seksualności i narodzie*. Warszawa, Poland: WAB.

Graff, A. (2010). Looking at pictures of gay men: Political uses of homophobia in contemporary Poland. *Public Culture, 22*(3), 583–603.

Gruszczynska, A. (2009a). *Queer enough? Contested terrains of identity deployment in the context of gay and lesbian public activism in Poland*. Ph.D, Aston University.

Gruszczynska, A. (2009b). Sowing the seeds of solidarity in public space: Case study of the Poznan March of equality. *Sexualities, 12*(3), 312–333.

Holzhacker, R. (2012). National and transnational strategies of LGBT civil society organizations in different political environments: Modes of interaction in Western and Eastern Europe for equality. *Comparative European Politics, 10*(1), 23–47.

Kawiński, M. (2012). PO powalczy o miłość gejów i lesbijek. Wprost, [Online] 17 February. Retrieved April 4, 2016, from http://www.wprost.pl/ar/306171/306171/.

Kochenov, D. (2007). Democracy and human rights—not for gay people?: EU Eastern enlargement and its impact on the protections of the rights of sexual minorities. *Texas Wesleyan Law Review, 13*(2), 459–495.

Kocur, A., & Katarzyna, M. (2013). Kim Pan Jest Panie Palikot, Czyli Krótka Biografia Wydawcy, Przedsiębiorcy, i Polityka. In R. Marzęcki & Ł. Stach (Eds.), *Dlaczego Palikot?* (pp. 41–54). Warszawa, Poland: Dom Wydawniczy 'Elipsa'.

Kuhar, R., & Čeplak, M. M. (2016). Same-sex partnership debates in Slovenia: Between declarative support and lack of political will. In K. Slootmaeckers, H. Touquet, & P. Vermeersch (Eds.), *The EU enlargement and gay politics*. London: Palgrave Macmillan.

Kuhar, R., & Takacs, J. (Eds.) (2006). *Beyond the pink curtain: Everyday life of LGBT people in Eastern Europe*. Ljubljana, Slovenia: Peace Institute.

Long, S. (1999). Gay and lesbian movements in Eastern Europe: Romania, Hungary, and the Czech Republic. In B. D. Adam, J. W. Duyvendak, & A. Krouwell (Eds.), *The global emergence of gay and lesbian politics: National imprints of a worldwide movement* (pp. 242–265). Philadelphia, PA: Temple University Press.

McAdam, D. (1996). Conceptual origins, current problems, future directions. In D. McAdam, J. McCarthy, & M. Zald (Eds.), *Comparative perspectives on social movements: Political opportunities, mobilizing structures, and cultural framings* (pp. 23–40). New York: Cambridge University Press.

McAdam, D., McCarthy, J., & Zald, M. (1996). Introduction: Opportunities, mobilizing structure and framing processes—toward a synthetic, comparative perspective on social movements. In D. McAdam, J. McCarthy, & M. Zald (Eds.), *Comparative perspectives on social movements: Political opportunities, mobilizing structures, and cultural framings* (pp. 1–22). New York: Cambridge University Press.

McAdam, D., & Tarrow, S. (2010). Ballots and barricades: On the reciprocal relationship between elections and social movements. *Perspectives on Politics, 8*(2), 529–542.

Meguid, B. (2008). *Party competition between unequals: Strategies and electoral fortunes in Western Europe.* New York: Cambridge University Press.

Mole, R. C. M. (2016). Nationalism and homophobia in Central and Eastern Europe. In K. Slootmaeckers, H. Touquet, & P. Vermeersch (Eds.), *The EU enlargement and gay politics.* London: Palgrave Macmillan.

O'Dwyer, C. (2010). From conditionality to persuasion? Europeanization and the rights of sexual minorities in postaccession Poland. *Journal of European Integration, 32*(3), 229–247.

O'Dwyer, C. (2012). Does the EU help or hinder gay-rights movements in postcommunist Europe? The case of Poland. *East European Politics, 28*(4), 332–352.

O'Dwyer, C. (2014). What accounts for differences in party system stability? Comparing the dimensions of party competition in Eastern Europe. *Europe-Asia Studies, 66*(4), 511–535.

O'Dwyer, C., & Schwartz, K. S. (2010). Minority rights after EU enlargement: A comparison of antigay politics in Poland and Latvia. *Comparative European Politics, 8*(2), 220–243.

Owczarzak, J. (2009). Defining democracy and the terms of engagement with the postsocialist state: Insights from HIV/AIDS. *East European Politics and Societies, 23*(3), 421–445.

Paszkiewicz, K. A. (1996). *Polskie partie polityczne: charakterystyki, dokumenty.* Wrocław, Poland: Hector.

Piasecki, A. K. (2012). *Wybory w Polsce, 1989–2011.* Kraków, Poland: ARCANA.

Puhl, J.. (2006). Poland's parade of democracy: Gays in Eastern Europe fight mounting homophobia. *Der Spiegel*, [Online] 16 June. Retrieved Agustus 28, 2015, from http://www.spiegel.de/international/spiegel/0,1518,419770,00.html.

Reynolds, A. (2013). Representation and rights: The impact of LGBT legislators in comparative perspective. *American Political Science Review, 107*(2), 259–274.

Rovny, J., & Edwards, E. (2012). Struggle over dimensionality: Party competition in Western and Eastern Europe. *East European Politics and Societies, 26*(1), 56–74.

Schimmelfennig, F., & Sedelmeier, U. (Eds.) (2005). *The Europeanization of Central and Eastern Europe.* Ithaca, NY: Cornell University Press.

Selinger, M. (2008). Intolerance toward gays and lesbians in Poland. *Human Rights Review, 9,* 15–27.

Siedlecka, E., 2015. Na papierze w Polsce nie ma dyskryminacji. Bo przepisy ustawy równościowej są niejasne. *Gazeta Wyborcza,* 24 January.

Skłodowska, I. (Ed.) (2001a). *Wybory 1991. Programy partii i ugrupowań politycznych.* Warszawa, Poland: Instytut Studiów Politycznych Polskiej Akademii Nauk.

Skłodowska, I. (Ed.) (2001b). *Wybory 1993. Partie i ich programy.* Warszawa, Poland: Instytut Studiów Politycznych Polskiej Akademii Nauk.

Skłodowska, I. (Ed.) (2003). *Wybory prezydenckie. Programy kandydatów.* Warszawa, Poland: Instytut Studiów Politycznych Polskiej Akademii Nauk.

Skłodowska, I., & Dołbakowska, M. (Eds.) (2002). *Wybory 2001. Partie i ich programy.* Warszawa, Poland: Instytut Studiów Politycznych Polskiej Akademii Nauk.

Skłodowska, I., & Dołbakowska, M. (Eds.) (2004). *Wybory 1997. Partie i ich programy.* Warszawa, Poland: Instytut Studiów Politycznych Polskiej Akademii Nauk.

Skłodowska, I., & Dołbakowska, M. (Eds.) (2006). *Wybory 2005. Partie i ich programy.* Warszawa, Poland: Instytut Studiów Politycznych Polskiej Akademii Nauk.

Stanley, B., & Czesnik, M. (2014). Poland's palikot movement: Voice of the disenchanted, missing ideological link or more of the same? *Party Politics,* [online before print] doi:10.1177/1354068814560911.

Szczerbiak, A. (2012). Poland (mainly) chooses stability and continuity: The October 2011 Polish parliamentary election. *SEI Working Paper No. 129,* Retrieved from https://www.sussex.ac.uk/webteam/gateway/file.php?name=sei-working-paper-no-129.pdf&site=266.

Szyk, A., & Urbańczyk, A. (2010). Tęczowa Solidarność. In *Trójmiasto. Przewodnik Krytyki Politycznej.* Warszawa: Wydawnictwo Krytyki Politycznej, pp. 220–234.

Vermeersch, P. (2013). Nationalism and political competition in Central Europe: The case of Poland. *Nationalities Papers, 41*(1), 128–145.

Walczyszyn, C. M. (2012). *From anti-gay politics to frustration: The formative relationship between the Polish right and gay rights activists.* Undergraduate Thesis, Department of International Relations, Tufts University.

Wojtasik, W. (2012). Sukces Ruchu Palikota w Świetle Czynników Możliwego Sukcesu Politycznego. *Preferencje Polityczne, 3,* 159–174.

Zboralski, W. (1991). Wspomnienie weterana. *Inaczej, 9,* 2–5.

CHAPTER 7

Same-Sex Partnership Debate in Slovenia: Between Declarative Support and Lack of Political Will

Roman Kuhar and Metka Mencin Čeplak

INTRODUCTION

'Nothing much', replied one Slovenian gay activist when asked by a Western journalist what had changed for the LGBT community in Slovenia after 1989. The fall of the Berlin wall and the political changes in the European socialist countries at that time may have been a crucial turning point for some of the Eastern European LGBT communities, and the first opportunity for the LGBT movement that would eventually emerge in some of the post-socialist states, but that was not the case in Slovenia. 'Nothing much' referred to the fact that, in 1991, when Slovenia gained its independence, the gay movement had been already active for seven years, and the most important political demands for equality had already been voiced and acted upon. The change in the political system did not alter the essence

R. Kuhar (✉)
Faculty of Arts, Department of Sociology, University of Ljubljana, Slovenia

M. Mencin Čeplak
Faculty of social sciences, University of Ljubljana, Slovenia

© The Editor(s) (if applicable) and The Author(s) 2016   147
K. Slootmaeckers et al. (eds.), *The EU Enlargement and Gay Politics*, DOI 10.1057/978-1-137-48093-4_7

of these demands, but it did create a new, post-socialist context, and for a moment, raised high hopes that demands for equality would soon be met. Why this did not happen is the focus of this chapter, which provides an overview of the trajectory of the Slovenian gay and lesbian movement. It focuses on the three decades of struggles aimed at deconstructing the heteronormative to emphasize the ideological and political dimensions of the same-sex partnership debates in Slovenia, we use the concepts of heteronormativity and sexual prejudices and avoid using the term homophobia[1] foundations of partnership and family legislation in Slovenia, and shows that while Europeanization and international norms might have been important factors in these debates, the delays in and resistance to the adoption of marriage equality legislation are best explained by the internal relations between and within the parties that made up the ruling coalitions in Slovenia over the past 20 years. Furthermore, the role of the conservative movements and political parties—often in close relationship with the Roman Catholic Church—cannot be ignored.

The debate surrounding same-sex partnerships in Slovenia has revealed a wide set of contradictory beliefs, attitudes, opinions and 'truths' about sexuality (and gender) and sexual (and gender) norms, from overt moral condemnation of those who break from these norms, to the deconstruction of dominant heteronormative ideologies and practices. It has also illuminated the fundamental discontent, controversy, contradictions and ambiguities in the gay and lesbian movement itself and in the dynamics between dominant and oppositional ideologies and politics in which gender and sexual norms are advocated as a distinctive element of political orientation, principles and programs. Attitudes towards same-sex partnership (and towards homosexuality in general) are considered indicators of 'democracy', 'open-mindedness' and 'Europeanness' or, conversely, as indicators of a sense of responsibility to protect a nation's existing social order, the traditional family unit, and even biological reproduction. These ideological (political) struggles attest to the relevance of Foucault's thesis that sexuality is a privileged object of bio-power, one of the most instrumentalized phenomena in power relations in the Western world, as it exists at the intersection of body and population (Foucault 1978, p. 145).

The structure of this article follows the development of policy debate on same-sex partnerships and families in Slovenia over the past 30 years. We distinguish four periods.

In the first period, from the establishment of the movement in 1984 through the mid-1990s, homosexuality became a political issue. The so-called new social movements in Slovenia that emerged in the 1980s opened the door for alternative politics by addressing and politicizing issues including ecology, peace and women's rights, as well as homosexuality. The second period from the late 1990s until 2004, when Slovenia joined the EU, was characterized by the placement of the politicized issue of homosexuality into a broader, international context. The requirements of EU accession fostered debate on LGBT issues and helped provide a framework of understanding within which activists legitimized their political demands for equality. Although the issue had already been brought into the political agenda, the EU accession process served as an argument against the political opposition. But the effects of this period of 'Europeanization' were short-lived, and failed to foster a fundamental change in sexual prejudices or the way in which society, the Church and the political system have dealt with sexuality and gender norms, as (implicit) nationalism continues to be an underlying force in perpetuating a heteronormative Slovenian society.

The third period, from 2005 to 2012, saw the adoption of very limited (in terms of rights) same-sex registered partnership legislation by the right-wing government, partly as an effect of the EU accession process. The outcome, however, was rather disappointing, as the right-wing government used the EU accession argument to legitimize very reactionary policies that intensified the legal and symbolic distinction between registered same-sex couples and married heterosexual couples. Furthermore, at the end of this period the movement was faced with an increasingly organized backlash by anti-gay groups and civil organizations, whose common denominator was the fight against the so-called gender theory. Here we will examine the role of the Roman Catholic Church (RCC) in this debate and the changes in their political tactics, which moved from direct intervention in policy debate on same-sex partnerships, towards more 'covert' interventions through right-wing political parties and civil groups functioning as the Church's satellite organizations.

Finally, the last period is characterized by what O'Dwyer and Vermeersch (2016) describe as crossing the second threshold, when political protests move towards party politics. In 2014, a new political party, United Left, entered the parliament, filling a void in Slovenian politics: a 'true' left-wing party. Similar to political parties such as the Greek *Syriza* or Spanish *Podemos*, United Left addresses issues that are 'too uncomfortable' or 'unsafe' for the mainstream parties. It adopted marriage equality as one of its key issues, forcing other parliamentary parties to reopen the discussion and, in early 2015, to adopt amendments to the Family Code that introduced marriage equality.

THREE DECADES OF STRUGGLE FOR SAME-SEX PARTNERSHIP LEGISLATION

The first marriage equality initiative in Slovenia dates back to 1989. To understand its context, we must first examine the phenomenon of the 'new social movements' in the 1980s and the broader context of the dissolution of Yugoslavia. We will then focus on similar initiatives, ending with the public referendum on the Family Code in 2012 and the latest legislative proposal from December 2014, which sought to de-gender the legal definition of marriage, putting same-sex and opposite-sex couples on equal legal footing.

The First Period: New Social Movements and Public Articulation of Gay and Lesbian Political Demands

Towards the end of the 1970s and into the 1980s, as conflict between centralistic and autonomist forces in Yugoslavia intensified, a specific citizens' space emerged in Slovenia, where cultural and political movements tried to redefine politics as a conduit for citizens initiatives. This period was characterized by growing criticism of the discrepancies between the declared principles of human rights and civil freedoms and the actual state of affairs in the socialist regime. Furthermore, human rights violations regarding gender, sexual, and ethnic minorities and subcultures were increasingly met with serious resistance and vocal protest from the public.

Beginning already at the end of the 1970s, but intensifying from the mid-1980s onwards, youth subcultures in Slovenia—particularly peace, ecology, feminist, gay and lesbian, spiritual, and punk movements (known as 'new social movements')—were active in opening up this citizens' space. They demanded autonomous social spheres, 'human rights and civil freedoms, legal security and the rule of law, social control over the actions of state organs (particularly repressive organs), the boundary of state activity and an independent public' (Mastnak 1992, p. 56).

New social movements had rather extensive media support, especially by the weekly magazines *Mladina* [Youth] and *Radio Študent* [Radio Student]. Theoretical reflections of younger intellectuals in Slovenia (but also from Zagreb and Belgrade) on the relationship between the state, society, and the political system and the alternative praxis of the new social movements were also given strong support by the League of Socialist Youth of Slovenia (LSYS), which had its own representatives in the federal and republic state apparatuses. LSYS was considered the youth branch of the League of Communists, but it managed to shake off the League's patronizing role, and evolved into a political organization that took its political role seriously.

Despite a certain level of discomfort on both sides of the alliance between the LSYS and the new social movements, their cooperation was fairly productive in terms of opening up the political space. LSYS was more or less successful and persistent in implementing the demands and suggestions of the new social movements in the official institutions of the socialist system.

This wide network of movements and civil initiatives created a means for the public questioning of heteronormative ideology. Although Slovenia, Croatia and Montenegro decriminalized homosexuality in 1977,[1] the first gay organization, Magnus, was established only in 1984, and Škuc LL, a lesbian organization, in 1987. It was then that discrimination on the basis of sexual orientation became a relevant political issue. In 1986, for example, LSYS demanded decriminalization of homosexuality throughout the entire territory of Yugoslavia, although its efforts, unfortunately, were not successful.

After 1987, a new type of civil society emerged, aimed at 'national emancipation' (Pavlovič 2006, p. 133), and began to compete with the earlier (emancipatory and leftist) concepts of civil society in Slovenia. Its most visible adherents were the intellectuals gathered around the journal *Nova revija*. Many of them later became key actors in the Democratic Opposition of Slovenia (DEMOS) coalition, which gained power during the first democratic elections in 1990. Despite huge ideological and political differences among these civil movements (i.e. national emancipation vs. new social movements), they settled into a sort of 'peaceful coexistence', largely due to their collective oppositional position.

Against the backdrop of exacerbated conflict between the political leadership of the Socialist Federal Republic of Yugoslavia (SFRY) and the Socialist Republic of Slovenia (Repe 2000; Luthar et al. 2013), and because of the approaching multi-party elections in Slovenia in 1990, the social influence of the 'national intelligence' strengthened (Mastnak 1992), as it appealed to those who saw communism, the federal centralism of Yugoslavia, and Serbian hegemonic tendencies as a threat to the status of the Slovenian nation.

However, towards the end of the 1980s, another 'threat' emerged: that of a low reproductive rate among Slovenian women. This was the 'birth of ethnopolitics', which brought about essentialist and primordial concepts of 'nation'. In other words, the notion of 'biological reproduction of the nation' (Yuval-Davis 1997) started to gain relevance under the growing influence of nationalist discourse. Such rhetoric gradually narrowed the path for civic initiatives among the new social movements that had upheld the rights of ethnic, gender and sexual minorities. The larger story of Slovenian independence corroborated the idea that sexuality and nation are intertwined constructs: according to Foucault (1978), Mosse (1985), and Yuval-Davis (1997), nationalism is closely connected to patriarchy and to gender and sexual dichotomies and hierarchies.

Nevertheless, the initiatives of the gay and lesbian movement still occupied an important place in the electoral programs of LSYS. At the 13th LSYS congress in November 1989, when the league was transformed into a political party and announced participation in the first democratic elections in 1990, it adopted the initiatives of the gay and lesbian movement, including the demand to amend legislation to allow marriage between persons of the same sex. These initiatives became part of the agenda of this political party, and have remained with that of its successor, the Liberal Democracy of Slovenia (LDS). They represent the beginning of the struggle for equality within the institutions of the political system and mark the beginning of legislative initiatives, but also the delays, compromises and willful ignorance that would ensue. Nevertheless, this issue has never really disappeared from the Slovenian political atmosphere.

After Slovenia gained independence in 1991, however, the process of re-traditionalization and rehabilitation of the RCC began. Pushed to the margins of society during the socialist regime, the Church gradually regained its position as the 'collective intellectual', providing answers to important social and political questions (Kerševan 1996). It began (in concordance with conservative political parties) promoting traditional family structures and portraying abortion as evil. Within this context, rhetoric about gays and lesbians as non-productive, immoral and pathological degenerates emerged. Gays and lesbians were interpreted—similarly to attitudes towards 'careerist' women, immigrants and the state, which is unsupportive of (large) families—as a threat to the biological and cultural reproduction of Slovenians (Mencin Čeplak 2013b).

In the new political climate after the 1990 elections, left-wing political parties demanded explicit constitutional guarantees of equality regardless of sexual orientation. Members of the National Assembly in opposition pointed to the 'contestability' of the phrase 'sexual orientation', claiming that 'the term allows or even supports pathology' and that there should be 'a more professional term'.[2] The Commission of the Assembly of the Republic of Slovenia for constitutional issues proposed a compromise: although the constitution does not mention 'sexual orientation', the official commentary in Article 14, in fact, prohibits discrimination on the basis of sexual orientation.[3] Three years later, however, the new criminal code seamlessly incorporated an explicit reference to 'sexual orientation' in its antidiscrimination provisions, proclaiming discrimination on the basis of sexual orientation to be a criminal offense.

The first concrete initiative for eliminating discrimination in the context of marriage and family legislation occurred in 1993, when a gay couple filed a complaint with the Constitutional Court challenging the constitutionality of the articles in the Marriage and Family Relations Act (adopted in 1976 and still valid today) defining marriage as a union between a man and a woman. Specifically, the act excludes the possibility of marriage between persons of the same sex and does not legally recognize same-sex unmarried couples (but it does recognize heterosexual unmarried couples[4]).

In accordance with the law, the Constitutional Court asked for the opinion of the Ministry of Labour, Family and Social Affairs. Both institutions deemed the complaint to be unfounded, claiming that the social significance of marriage was the formation of a family. The state, they contended, should protect families only as defined in the Universal Declaration of Human Rights, which stipulates that a family is a 'natural and fundamental group unit of society'.[5]

Also in 1993, an informal group was established in order to prepare concrete proposals for amendment legislation in the area of marriage and family relations. The group proposed a simple 'technical' solution: degendering of the marriage definition. Specifically, in the three articles of the Marriage and Family Relations Act addressing a union between a man and a woman, the phrase 'man and woman' would be replaced by 'two people' or 'two persons'. This would open the concept of marriage to include both heterosexual and homosexual couples.

The proposal easily gained the institutional support of the Office for Women's Policy, who in October 1994, in accordance with formal procedure, sent the proposal to the Ministry of Labour, Family and Social Affairs.[6] The Ministry dismissed the proposal, claiming that because of the numerous initiatives in the areas of family and marriage legislation, a detailed analysis would be needed. The Ministry (1994), however, expressed the opinion that 'it would be necessary to address this issue in the context of a special law on registered partnership and not in the context of the Marriage and Family Relations Act'.[7] This would be the official stance of the Ministry for the next 15 years (until 2009, when the new Family Code was presented). Their reasoning was first explained in 1998 with their first proposal for a special law on registered partnerships. The proposal acknowledged that the Marriage and Family Relations Act discriminated against same-sex partnerships, as it did not provide protection equal to that for partnerships of men and women. While some experts within the Ministry group that dealt with the proposal suggested that there should be no legal distinction between heterosexual and homosexual partnerships, the legal experts in the group insisted that 'there is no doubt that the Marriage and Family Relations Act addresses the creation of a family in a natural way'. The assessment that 'a union of same-sex partners does not assume the legal consequences that are typical for marriage',[8] was presented as an additional argument justifying the differences between the treatment of same-sex and heterosexual partnerships.

Such argumentation is based on the capacity for biological reproduction in a relationship between a man and a woman, and refers to the alleged internal logic of the Marriage and Family Relations Act. However, this interpretation is misleading or—at least—incomplete, in that the act does not mandate the creation of a family 'in a natural way': it does not exclude heterosexual couples who cannot have children (because of age or other reasons), as they are allowed to marry. Thus the act regulates relations between partners regardless of whether they are able to have children, and it also takes social parenthood into account (it governs adoption and relationships in adoptive families). As such, the rights and duties of the partners are not derived from (biological) parenthood or from the 'natural reproductive capability' of their relationship, but rather from the 'ethics of care', meaning the caring relationship between a child and a (biological/ non-biological) parent.

This shows that the 'crucial difference between heterosexual and same-sex couples', which some legal experts took as grounds for legal differentiation between the two unions, was not because heterosexual couples met the requirements of the act while homosexual couples did not. The crucial difference, rather, was that heterosexual unions met heteronormative hegemonic norms and expectations, and those of same-sex couples did not. Thus, what appeared to be a solid legal argument was in fact an ideological stance.

The Second Period: EU Accession and the Soft Law Phenomenon

Because of the inability to resolve the conflicting opinions, the 1998 proposal to regulate only the registration of partnerships and property matters was never subjected to parliamentary procedure. The first bill to enter parliamentary procedure (i.e. three readings in the parliament) was drafted between 2001 and 2004. It was also during this time that the 'argumentation method' changed dramatically. While the Ministry still insisted on differentiation between same-sex and heterosexual unions due to their 'nature', the opponents of the law shifted their arguments away from the legal jargon described above, and afterwards focused on the 'interests of children and the nation'.

This period was marked politically by an intense EU accession process. As part of the political vocabulary, the phrase 'Examples from EU' became pure gold when invoked in order to achieve political goals. At the same time, the incorporation of the EU legal framework into Slovenian legislation was under way, which meant that the framing of policy proposals in accordance with the EU standards had become a *conditio sine qua non* of the political process. All of these factors shaped the debate on legal regulation of same-sex partnerships as well.

This process is often referred to as 'Europeanization' (Radaelli 2000; Olsen 2002; Howell 2004), as the 'European standard' becomes the reason/argument for the adoption of specific legislation. Howell (2004) suggests that Europeanization should be understood as an interactive process, which consists of three parts: streaming policies from the European to the national level (downloading), 'dispensing' policies (uploading) and 'transferring' policies (cross-loading). Such a broad understanding of Europeanization is especially important in the case of policies for which there are no binding directives at the EU level, such as the regulation of families and partnerships.[9] However, even 'soft law norms can have profound and transforming effects on European states' policies' (Kollman 2009, p. 51), which was certainly the case in Slovenia.

In a Slovenian post-socialist context, Europeanization served a dual purpose. On the one hand, it ensured the incorporation of the European standards into national legislation. On a symbolic and identitarian level, it represented a further step towards the consolidation of the Slovenian national identity as European—or, rather, 'non-Balkan': the nationalist rhetoric referred to Europe (as a phantasmatic superior civilization) in order to marginalize everything that was understood as non-European or Balkan. On the other hand, when it came to human rights of gays and lesbians, these same voices claimed that we should avoid following European examples at all costs—rather, we should protect 'our nation' and 'our children'. In other words: the dual function of Europeanization manifested itself in the political discourse as a simultaneous struggle between ensuring and denying human rights.[10] However, activists in Slovenia have used the accession process to legitimize the political demands that they first voiced 15 years ago. They see this as a window of opportunity to have these demands met and to take advantage of the 'transnational normative pressure' exerted by what Paternotte and Kollman (2013) call the LGBT 'velvet triangle': EU and national policy elites, legal activists and LGBT social movement organizations.

Against this political backdrop, gay and lesbian non-governmental organizations asked the Ministry to establish a new expert group to prepare same-sex partnership legislation that would address not only material issues of same-sex relationships, but social security as well. These organizations justified their demands by placing them within the context of Slovenia's accession to the EU, claiming that elimination of discrimination was an 'accession condition for the EU'.[11] The drafting of this initiative illustrates how the lack of binding directives regarding family and partnership relations in the EU caused these groups to shift their focus to discrimination on the basis of sexual orientation. In the absence of any concrete EU regulations specifically addressing same-sex families and partnerships, framing the issue as 'discrimination' rather than 'partnership and family' seemed to be most tangible in the context of Europeanization.

At the end of 2001, the Ministry of Labour, Family and Social Affairs formed an expert group to prepare a new version of the same-sex partnership act. The state secretary at the Ministry reached an agreement with the expert group that the law would address same-sex partnerships in the same way as heterosexual partnerships, but that it would not regulate the issues of adoption and same-sex families. The agreement was justified as a rational decision based on the expectation that addressing same-sex adoption would jeopardize passage of the legislation, and thus a step-by-step approach was proposed. Despite a certain degree of discontent among gay and lesbian organizations, the decision was seen as politically pragmatic, and was officially endorsed by the groups.

This political pragmatism, however, led to two types of exclusion. The first relates to the justification of discrimination against same-sex couples in the interpretation of the act, which refers to the 'natural' differences between homosexual and heterosexual couples. 'The bill takes into account the fact that same-sex unions are naturally different from heterosexual unions. For that reason the law does not symbolically nor formally equate a same-sex union with a matrimony union as a life union of a husband and a wife'.[12]

A second exclusion introduced by the proposal is linked to the creation of 'second-class citizens' among the gay and lesbian minority: gays and lesbians with children (i.e. same-sex families). Same-sex families were thus offered as a 'sacrificial lamb' in order to earn the respect and legal protection of the human rights of 'others'—i.e. same-sex couples. As such, lawmakers recognized the existence of same-sex families and the need to address their position, while at the same time sending them a message to 'wait a bit longer', as society was not yet ready for them. Furthermore, same-sex families represented a threat to the validity of the claim of 'natural' differences between heterosexual and homosexual couples with respect to reproduction, as same-sex families are undeniable evidence that same-sex couples can and do create their own families.

The same-sex partnership bill was sent to parliament at the end of 2003, but the Slovenian People's Party, a proponent of conservatism and nationalism that was part of the governing coalition at the time, blocked it during the first reading. The party argued that legal recognition of same-sex partnerships was not a human right, and that same-sex partnerships did not represent values for which our society should strive. They claimed that such a law would encourage new same-sex partnerships, which would have a negative effect on Slovenian demographics. Same-sex partnerships should be tolerated, but not promoted, they declared, as anything else would have been considered political suicide.[13] In this way, overt nationalistic rhetoric entered into institutionalized politics through wide open doors.

In the course of political events, the Slovenian People's Party subsequently withdrew from the coalition (for reasons not related to the same-sex partnership bill), and the bill was approved at the first reading in June 2004. The second reading was planned for the autumn of the same year, after the parliamentary elections, but the left-wing government was defeated. Thus, in the parliamentary and public debate, the political pragmatism of the Ministry had failed. Despite the fact that the proposal did not address adoption, same-sex families and adoption were a recurring theme of political debate on the bill. Moreover, the non-recognition of adoption for same-sex couples did not make the bill 'more acceptable' for those who opposed it. The problem thus was not the extent of rights for gays and lesbians, but something much more basic: homosexuality as such. Public and parliamentary debate still framed homosexuality in the context of 'peripheral' sexualities, medical and psychiatric problems— a deviation from the norm of heterosexual monogamy. Thus, sexuality remains the fundamental basis of biopolitics (Foucault 1978), and heteronormativity remains a key element of the dominant ideology. It is this ideology that proclaims heterosexuality as the self-evident and 'natural' norm, while homosexuality—following the logic of deviation from the norm—is 'unnatural' and therefore in need of correction. Although the culture of political correctness that permeated this debate often concealed sexual prejudices, it nevertheless could not completely erase them.

The Third Period: After the EU Accession and the New Family Code

The new conservative center-right coalition withdrew the 2004 bill from further proceedings. Instead, it adopted the Registered Same-Sex Partnership Act in the summer of 2005, and Slovenia became a unique example of an EU member country adopting such legislation under a conservative rather than liberal government. However, the adoption of the act was not a sign of progressiveness on the part of the Slovenian conservative government. Rather, it was a matter of political calculation, as the coalition parties had previously actively opposed the adoption of any such legislation. By the time the conservative right-wing government came to power in the autumn of 2004, however, the public was well aware of the issues surrounding legal recognition of same-sex partnerships, and the bill prepared by the previous left-wing government had been widely discussed in the media. As the previously introduced bill passed the first reading in June 2004 and the new government withdrew it from parliamentary procedure, they were obliged to prepare a replacement bill. Thus, the conservative government, under pressure from gay and lesbian non-governmental organizations, proposed its own 'watered-down' version of the law (the Registered Same-Sex Partnership Act), which made a clear legal and symbolic distinction between marital unions and registered same-sex partnerships. The law had numerous inconsistencies and shortcomings, which the gay and lesbian organizations and some other 'defenders of equality' pointed to, but the lawmaker refused to take their suggestions into consideration. For example, the law regulates the duty of one partner to care for the other partner in case of sickness, but does not confer the right to sickness leave as it does for heterosexual couples. The act also regulates inheritance rights, but again not in the same way as for heterosexual couples.[14] It does not regulate any social, health, pension or similar issues, and it does not confer the status of next of kin—the basis for all social rights—to partners. According to Žnidaršič Skubic (2006, p. 224) the act 'places part of the burden that would otherwise fall on the state, on the (same-sex) partners. In other words: the lawmaker primarily achieved equalization with heterosexual partners on the level of mutual obligations, but not on the level of rights'.

Similar to the same-sex partnership legislation previously proposed by the left-wing government, the right-wing's Registered Same-Sex Partnership Act is based on the 'distinctiveness' of same-sex partnerships. According to lawmakers, the limited number of rights granted to same-sex unions is a result of their uniqueness (i.e. their 'non-reproductive nature'). However, this is simply not true: same-sex couples are denied numerous social rights that are granted to heterosexual couples without children. This distinctiveness, inscribed into the law, was justified by heteronormative ideology, rendering the act overtly discriminatory.

The law is also problematic on a symbolic level. It refers to the process of solemnizing a partnership as a 'registration', but the verb 'to register' has very specific connotations in Slovenian language, as it is used, for example, in reference to the registration of businesses, associations and cars. However, lawmakers refused to change the name of the law from 'registration' to 'solemnization' of a partnership.

For the right-wing conservative government, the adoption of such legislation was a political and social victory: on one hand, the conservative government managed to throw some 'legal crumbs' to the gay and lesbian community, which could no longer decry the lack of legal recognition of same-sex partnerships, and on the other hand, the law preserved the symbolic and legal superiority of civil marriage and the heterosexual family, which is best illustrated by the fact that registration of same-sex couples is just a bureaucratic procedure in a municipality's office. While heterosexual couples can be married in a public ceremony on Saturday mornings, registration takes place only during on weekdays in an office. According to anecdotal evidence of one registered lesbian, the procedure takes about 'seven minutes, including parking the car outside the municipality build-ing'.[15] When asked during a TV news interview why the procedure was not festive like that of a marriage ceremony, a government representative explained that the law was drafted with homosexual people from rural areas in mind. Because of the homophobia prevalent in society, it would be literally impossible, he claimed, to conduct a celebratory registration of same-sex partnerships in rural Slovenia. It was for that reason, he con-cluded, that the registration process was treated discreetly.

The government representative correctly identified the issue in Slovenian society—dominant heteronormative ideology and sexual preju-dices against or even hostility towards gays and lesbians. However, the proposed solution serves only to perpetuate the problem. Rather than con-fronting the issue, the government's answer was to symbolically eliminate the 'disturbing element' (i.e. same-sex couples), making it even less visible. Ironically, however, the symbolic erasure of the homosexual community brought even greater visibility to the inequality (as it now became part of legislation). It is also important to note that 'coming out' (of the closet) is an inherently political act, which affects how society sees and understands itself. If it were possible to conduct same-sex partnership ceremonies in the same places where wedding ceremonies were held, same-sex couples would certainly become more 'visible' and symbolically equal to hetero-sexual couples—and that is exactly what lawmakers sought to prevent through their attempts to keep the heteronormative fibers of society intact.

This period of struggle for same-sex partnership legislation—before the EU accession and immediately after—was also characterized by the entrance of the RCC into public debate on this issue in Slovenia (cf. Ayoub 2014). Following the first media reports on the government's intention to legally recognize same-sex partnerships in 2002, the Church joined the public debate on the suitability or unsuitability (immorality) of such a law. Although it is true that the political debate on same-sex partnerships intensified in the new millennium, and as such sparked greater public reac-tion, including that of the RCC, the intensity of the RCC's reactions can be attributed in part to the different styles, personalities and agendas of Ljubljana's successive archbishops. In particular, Archbishops Dr. Franc Rode (1997–2004) and later Anton Stres (2010–2013) introduced a tougher and very conservative line in the Slovenian RCC. The entrance of the Church into Slovenian policy debate must also be understood within a broader context, specifically in terms of the intensification of the Vatican's policies against same-sex partnerships. For example, in 2003—during the debate on same-sex partnership legislation in Slovenia—the Vatican issued a document calling on Catholic politicians across Europe to vote against legal recognition of same-sex unions, claiming in fact that 'all Catholics are obliged to oppose it', as 'approval or legalization of evil is something far different from the toleration of evil'.[16]

In his interview on national TV in 2003, Archbishop Rode notoriously declared that homosexuality was 'an abomination', referring to the Book of Leviticus in the Bible. He added that homosexuality was against the laws of nature and immoral, but it was nevertheless a private issue and according to him should remain as such:

> We do not concern ourselves with the private lives of individuals; nonetheless, the issue at stake here is that of the public good. The state should promote everything that ensures a future for society and for the nation and not put things that are of a purely private concern on the same level as those that benefit the community.[17]

One of the most important points of departure for the Church in agitating against legal recognition of same-sex partnerships and families is its interpretation that the introduction of same-sex marriage would diminish the symbolic importance of the (traditional heterosexual) family. Such an understanding was also a premise for the right-wing government's drafting of the same-sex partnership registration bill in 2005. It is for this reason that the RCC ceased to be very vocal in public against the legal recognition of same-sex couples once the right-wing government proposed and later adopted a watered-down version of the registered same-sex partnership bill.

The discussion on the Registered Same-Sex Partnership Act took place after Slovenia had joined the EU, so the pressure of Europeanization had abated. This does not imply that certain discussions were not framed within the context of EU recommendations and assimilation of policy from other European countries, but the prevailing theme during the debate was that the EU had no binding directives that would require the adoption of such legislation. The proposed law was therefore interpreted as the 'good will' of lawmakers (cf. Kollman 2009).

In the years that followed, parties from the ruling coalition that had adopted the law prided themselves on their tolerance, having succeeded in legalizing same-sex partnerships in a matter of just a few months—in contrast to the center-left parties that had failed to do so after more than

12 years of being in power, despite their declarative support for the LGBT community.

In 2009, under the leadership of a left-wing government, the Ministry of Labour, Family and Social Affairs announced a complete revision of the Family Code, which was adopted in the Socialist Federal Republic of Yugoslavia and, with several amendments, had been valid for nearly 40 years. The two changes that resonated most with the public were the new inclusive definition of family and the opening up of marriage to same-sex couples.

The Family Code proposed a broader, more inclusive definition of family, moving away from an exclusively biological model of the nuclear family and towards a more inclusive ethics of care as the basis of family relations. Previously defined as a 'union of parents and children', family was now defined as a union between one or more adults and one or more children. In this way, a plurality of family models was recognized, while the link between an adult and a child could be either biological or social.

The government's announcement also showed its determination to address same-sex partnerships not in a separate law, as it had previously done, but to adopt one basic law that would address both types of partnerships and all types of families and put them on equal legal—and symbolic—footing, including the right of same-sex partners to second-parent and joint adoption.

The latter, similar to policies elsewhere in Europe, shifted the public debate away from the issue of legal recognition of same-sex partnerships towards issues dealing with the well-being of children. Even the parliament's most conservative opponents of the new code voiced no protest against legal arrangements for same-sex partnerships, as the conservatives had already adopted (limited amounts of) such arrangements in 2005, and public opinion had also shifted towards acceptance. The new bone of contention, rather, would be the issue of same-sex families and adoption of children by same-sex couples. The new Family Code was part of a broader European trend, a policy convergence not only in terms of 'outcomes' and 'specific instruments used to recognize same-sex couples' (Paternotte and Kollman 2013, p. 2), but convergence also in terms of framing the opposition and the struggle against so-called gender theory (cf. Paternotte 2014).

As the government sought to make the adoption of the Family Code as transparent as possible, they invited civil society actors, including the RCC, to actively participate in the parliamentary debate. The opponents of the Family Code began their campaign against the law already during its first presentation, in which the moral disqualification of lesbians and gays (and of the supporters of the proposal) was a common refrain. Lesbians and gays were branded as 'neurotic', 'confused', 'contaminated' and incapable of long-term relationships, and some critics of equality even went so far as to attribute a tendency towards sexual abuse to gays. In order to maintain the appearance of objective rationality, some also made use of (mistaken and ill-intentioned) interpretations of sociological and psychological studies, which were not even relevant to the regulations contained within the Family Code. Among the 'arguments', one could find obvious lies—for example, the claim that the European Convention on the Adoption of Children prohibited adoption by same-sex couples.

After three years of public debate, the Family Code was finally adopted by parliament in 2012. However, this was a 'compromised version', wherein same-sex partners were given the right to civil partnership (not marriage) with legal consequences equal to those ascribed to matrimonial unions, but with one exception: same-sex couples were granted only second-parent rights and not the right to joint adoption.

However, while the Family Code was adopted by parliament, it was rejected by public referendum in March 2012, as the conservative group Civil Initiative for the Family and the Rights of Children (CIFRC) managed to collect the 40,000 signatures needed for a public referendum to go forward. During the campaign against the adoption of the new Family Code, the CIFRC and other opponents—while citing scientific research—claimed that a child needed both a father and mother to ensure healthy growth. Furthermore, they cited that gays and lesbians were prone to alcoholism, drugs and sexually transmitted diseases, and as such, were unfit for parenting—again, an argument backed up with results from scientific research. However, it would be later shown that the 'results' of these studies were misinterpreted and misrepresented by the CIFRC to support their political ideology.

The wider framework of the CIFRC's activities was the preservation of Slovenian national and cultural norms, which can be best illustrated in a speech by the leader of the CIFRC to the parliament during the first public presentation of the Family Code. He said: 'I never thought that I would speak in the Parliament for the first time with such an honorable task: to defend the family and the foundation of our culture'. His speech was a well-orchestrated spectacle of sexual prejudice and hatred against a group of society, hidden under the guise of caring for children and the future of the Slovenian nation. The CIFRC campaign was thus based on nationalistic rhetoric, viewing LGBT people as a threat to the 'Slovenian family'. Furthermore, the 'other' comprised all who did not meet the standards of 'Catholic church morality', particularly gays and lesbians, same-sex families, single women and prostitutes.

It appeared at first that the RCC—which also opposed the new Family Code—was not connected to the CIFRC, although their messages were similar. But it was later discovered that the CIFRC website was hosted on the official server of the Slovenian RCC. Furthermore, the organization that owned the CIFRC website had been officially established by a visible representative of the RCC. It thus became clear that there was a close connection between the RCC and CIFRC and that their actions were jointly orchestrated. The CIFRC leader, for example, gave speeches during Sunday masses and on religious holidays, and the group collected signatures against the Family Code outside churches. The close connection between the Church and the civil group is reminiscent of the Proposition 8 campaign in California, USA. It seems that the Slovenian RCC had copied at least some of the tactics of the conservative American religious powers' efforts against gay marriage, including the creation of civil groups that then operate as satellite organizations of the Church. Similar trends were identified in France, Croatia, Slovakia and other countries during the protests against 'gender ideology' (cf. Paternotte 2014, Hodžič and Bijelić 2014).

During the debate on registered same-sex partnerships between 2001 and 2005, the Church often framed its arguments in terms of God's will, God's plan and biblical interpretations of homosexuality as immoral and unnatural. Five years later, during the Family Code debate, such framing was completely absent. A crucial turning point in the Church's discourse on same-sex partnerships and family had arrived: God and the Bible were replaced by 'science'. In order to appeal to the general public, the Church refrained from 'biblical discourse', and instead employed 'secularized discourse' such as the results from scientific research—albeit presented in a highly populist manner and often deliberately distorted—to show that same-sex families were dangerous and an unhealthy environment for children (cf. Kuhar 2015).

A key figure representing the Church in the parliament was a young teaching assistant of moral theology and applied ethics at the Faculty of Theology. Interestingly, he rarely appeared in public wearing clerical clothing. His public persona was that of a young, highly educated person who was an expert in bioethics and who employed rational discourse. At the same time, the bishops and the archbishop rarely appeared in public commenting on the Family Code. The image of the institution of the Church was relegated to the background, precisely because its public image, largely due to economic scandals in Slovenia[18], was no longer a positive one. God and the Bible were moved out of the picture—not only on the level of discourse, but also on the level of public representations—and were replaced by science.

Civil counter-movements by proponents of the Family Code were also well organized. Gay and lesbian non-governmental organizations, in a broad coalition with other progressive non-governmental organizations and youth political groups, established the Campaign for All Families (CFF) to counterbalance the rhetoric being used by the CIFRC and the RCC. Unlike the CIFRC, the official objective of the CFF was to avoid any kind of populism. Just prior the referendum, the CFF transformed itself into the political group Movement for the Family Law, which moved away from scientific discourse and focused on political tactics to address the public. Nevertheless, the new Family Code referendum was rejected by the public. Voter turnout was typically low (30 percent). Forty-five percent of voters supported the law and 55 percent voted against it. In other words, the Family Code was rejected by a minority—16 percent of the electorate. Based on voter turnout, we posit that the majority of citizens were ambivalent and did not take part in the referendum, and as such, had a decisive influence on the outcome (cf. Mencin Čeplak 2013a).

The public referendum on the Family Code was probably the most talked-about episode of the 30-year struggle for legal recognition of same-sex partnerships and families in Slovenia. Although the LGBT community lost the legal fight for equality, socially its members came out the winners of the three-year long debate. Drawing on O'Dwyer's (2012) insightful observation about the 'secondary consequences' of episodes of mass mobilization against equality, we must note that the Family Code debate worked in favor of the LGBT community. First, it provided increased and long-lasting visibility of same-sex partnerships and families in the media and public discourse. The issue became a common topic of conversation. Second, the brutality of verbal attacks on gays and lesbians during the Family Code debate helped to forge alliances with people outside the movement who became active supporters of marriage equality precisely as a reaction to the increased and vocal intolerance. Finally, this episode helped to consolidate the LGBT movement and community on the inside, as it felt threatened by the enemy outside.

The Fourth Period: Niche Politics

The principle of equality regardless of sexual orientation remains a battlefield in every election campaign. The last campaign, in the summer of 2014, was no exception. The new government of Miro Cerar, who had initially refused to sign a pre-election commitment issued by Slovenian LGBT organizations that called for equal rights for LGBT people, eventually promised to finally address same-sex partnerships and families, granting them equal rights and equal legal protection. However, similar commitments in the past had turned out to be empty promises, and so the LGBT community in Slovenia was reluctant to be too optimistic too soon.

In December 2014, the oppositional party United Left took over the government's attempts to address same-sex partnerships and families. The United Left is reminiscent of the niche party phenomenon as described in the Polish case (see O'Dwyer and Vermeersch 2016). Originating in the Slovenian uprisings of 2012 and 2013 during the mass protests against neoliberal austerity measures (Kirn 2013), the new party filled a void in the Slovenian political landscape from the lack of 'true' left-wing party, as most parties migrated towards the center. United Left took on 'unpleasant' economic and social issues, including marriage equality, and consequently forced the new governing coalition to deal with same-sex marriage.

The United Left reissued the 'technical' proposal from 1993 to de-gender the definition of marriage in the Marriage and Family Relations Act, claiming that this was indeed the only systematic and comprehensive solution for marriage equality. The simple change from 'marriage is a union of a man and a woman' to 'marriage is a union of two persons' would thus grant the same rights and obligations to both heterosexual and homosexual married couples (including the possibility of joint adoption of children), as all these rights (encompassing over 80 different laws in Slovenia) are based on the status of next of kin, or spouse. To much surprise, the government did not object to the proposal. On 3 March 2015, the Parliament passed the bill in a 51-to-28 vote, making Slovenia the first post-communist country in Europe to allow same-sex marriage.

The opponents, however, were not silent. The main actors from CIFRC established a new civil initiative, *Za otroke gre* (It is about children), and by March 10 had collected over 80,000 signatures to call for the referendum. This time the role of the Church was quite explicit: the leaders of the Church, in close collaboration with civil organizations, instructed all priests in Slovenia to invite their flocks to sign a petition against the new definition of marriage. They were even instructed to organize transportation for those who were old, sick or without their own transportation in order to take them to the municipality office to officially file their signature for the referendum.

In October 2015, in a tight 5-to-4 vote, and despite the fact that referendums on human rights are not allowed in Slovenia, the Constitutional Court allowed the referendum to go forward. The Court provided a rather technical explanation, contending that the referendum was not unconstitutional, as the Marriage Act had not yet been evaluated by the court as a human rights matter. While the latter is within the Court's capacity, and it could have evaluated the act through a human rights lens, it refrained from doing so, instead concluding that a referendum on the Marriage Act was, at that time, in line with the Constitution. Referendum took place on 20 December 2015. Marriage equality legislation was again overturned with 63% of voters rejecting the law. However just two days later an independent MP Jani Möderndorfer proposed the bill on civil partnership, which gives same-sex partners all the rights of marriage, except from the right of joint adoption and in vitro fertilization. The government adopted the law on 21 April 2016 in a 54-15 vote. As the Civil initiative *Za otroke gre* publicly opposed this law it is possible that the third attempt to secure (a proxy of) marriage equality in the past seven years in Slovenia will face yet another referendum.

CONCLUSION

In the 1980s, the struggle for equal rights regardless of sexual orientation became (and has remained) part of a broader movement for equality which, from the very beginning, crossed the boundaries of identity politics. This is what distinguishes Slovenia from other former Yugoslav republics, and from the former Czechoslovakia, Poland and Hungary, where LGBT movements were excluded from democratic civil society movements (cf. Mastnak 1992). However, the rise of (conservative) nationalism at the end of the 1980s and early 1990s has delayed the realization of this political goal indefinitely.

Why did it take over 25 years from the first initiatives to the actual adoption of marriage equality legislation, despite the fact that the LGBT movement in Slovenia enjoyed at least declarative support from the left-wing parties? Kollman (2009, p. 51) suggests that while international norms and treaties promote recognition of LGBT human rights, this pressure is 'filtered through domestic mediating factors' such as the party composition of ruling coalitions. Such filtering, in terms of the external and internal dynamics between Slovenian parliamentary political parties, seems to bear a reasonable share of responsibility for the delays and inconsistencies. The history of legal recognition of same-sex partnerships and families in Slovenia has been characterized by a great deal of ambivalence and discontent on both ends of political spectrum. Liberal center-left governments on the one hand have declared their support for equal treatment of gays and lesbians, while on the other they have continued to delay legislation to grant complete legal equality in order to satisfy opponents of the legislation. Such an approach was found to be the best means of disguising their own ambivalence towards same-sex partnerships and families (and homosexuality itself). Conservatives also tried to conceal their prejudices in a discourse of tolerance, at the same time placating their voters who oppose homosexuality. The result of this duplicity was the Registered Same-sex Partnership Act of 2005, which recognizes rights to the extent considered to be in line with 'public opinion' and acceptable to Slovenian society, but does not really consider the problems of those individuals who are addressed by the law. In other words, the political reticence of the left-wing parties enabled the determined conservative faction to quickly adopt a rather useless law on registered partnerships, and then to remove the issue from the political agenda for several years. We should also note that the same-sex partnership issue was not utilized as a catalyst in favor of or against joining the EU, as the political parties at both ends of the spectrum supported the accession process.

The 30-year debate on legal recognition of same-sex partnerships and families in Slovenia has raised important questions about gender and sexual discrimination, about the unequal treatment of people living in non-heteronormative life unions, and about the role of the state in providing legal and social protection for individuals regardless of their partnership arrangements. In wide (temporary) coalitions with various emancipatory movements (Invisible Workers of the World, anarchists, Erased, feminists, etc.), the LGBT movement has contributed to the establishment of broader goals of emancipatory politics in Slovenia.

However, the battle for legalization of same-sex partnerships has generated deep controversy about the 'nature' of the movement, its goals, achievements and political rationales, which have has been explicitly problematized by certain groups within the Slovenian LGBT movement. Do they deconstruct relations of domination, subordination and exploitation, striving for radical equality, or do they simply expand on the concept of normalcy and the criteria of inclusion? Is legalization of same-sex marriage a result of emancipatory politics, or subordination to the heteronormative order? These dilemmas are inextricably linked to the very concept of identity and identity politics, and cannot be resolved by an answer to one or the other. Ambivalent and contradictory beliefs, feelings and rhetoric on sexuality, phantasms about the threat posed by gays and lesbians, that they will lead to the collapse of the nation and human civilization in general, are evidence that the struggle for the legalization of same-sex partnerships and for the social and legal recognition of same-sex families threatens the dominant heteronormative ideology and reveals the very fragility of the heteronormative foundation of the social order. Therefore, resistance and transgression can undermine ruling norms, but as Foucault (1994) observed, new ones always arise.

Notes

1. To emphasize the ideological and political dimensions of the same-sex partnership debates in Slovenia, we use the concepts of heteronormativity and sexual prejudices and avoid using the term homophobia. *Phobia* in its original (clinical) meaning points at something that is fundamentally different from what is commonly understood by homophobia. Namely, the object of phobia is not the original source of the anxiety and fear. Furthermore, people tend to get rid of phobias, as they understand that their phobias or anxieties have no real foundations. On the other hand, prejudices are rationalised and more or less emotionally defended. While we recognize that the usage of terms 'homophobia', 'homophobic hatred' or 'political homophobia' (cf. Bosia and Weiss, 2013; Currier, 2010), might be productive in the context of politics, in academic discourse we prefer to use the concept of sexual prejudices.
2. Other Yugoslav republics legalized homosexuality only in the 1990s.
3. Draft Constitution, the Assembly of the Republic of Slovenia 1990: 27.
4. Article 14 of the Constitution stipulates that 'in Slovenia everyone shall be guaranteed equal human rights and fundamental freedoms irrespective of national origin, race, sex, language, religion, political or other opinion, material standing, birth, education, social status, disability or any other personal circumstance'. Former LSYS (then LSYS—LP (Liberal Party)) and the Green Party put forward an amendment, demanding the inclusion of sexual orientation into Article 14, but the lawmaker was reluctant to list it explicitly. *The Commission for Constitutional affairs of the Parliament of the Republic of Slovenia* then conferred an official interpretation that 'the term "personal circumstances" included in Article 14 of the Constitution

encompasses the "same-sex" orientation of an individual. The prohibition of discrimination on the basis of sexual orientation is thus contained in this article. The Commission for Constitutional affairs did not refer explicitly to any special personal circumstance, as ordinarily they are not explicitly enumerated in the conventions or constitutional texts, rather their judicial and other protections are secured in this more general manner.'

5. Article 12:

(1) A durable living community of a man and a woman who have not concluded marriage, shall have the same legal consequences for them under this Act as if they had concluded marriage, provided there is no reason by which marriage between them would be invalid; in other fields, such a community shall have a legal consequence if the law so determines.

(2) If a decision on rights or responsibilities is dependent on the question of the existence of a living community under the previous paragraph, a decision on this question shall be made in a proceeding for establishing these rights or responsibilities. A decision on this question shall have legal effect only in the matter in which this question was resolved.

6. Opinion of the Government, 1993, and Opinion of the National Assembly's Secretariat for Legislation and legal Affairs, 1993.

7. Initiative for amendments to the Law on Marriage and Family Relations, 1994.

8. Opinion of the Ministry of labor family and social affairs in relation to the initiative for amendments to the Marriage and Family Relations Act (1994). Document no. 588-012/94 TP (4.11.1994).

9. The Institute for civil, comparative and international private law at the Faculty of law in Maribor (1998): The bill on registered same-sex partnership.

10. Article 9 of the EU Charter of Fundamental Rights stipulates, 'the right to marry and the right to found a family shall be guaranteed in accordance with the national laws governing the exercise of these rights.' This article does not prevent the adoption of the same-sex partnerships and families legislation, but is also does not impose such legislation upon member states.

11. One right-wing MP, for example, claimed during the parliamentary debate on same-sex partnership in 2005: 'We cannot uncritically accept all models and patterns from the Netherlands. (...) In the Netherlands, the negative trends of too much liberality and of decisions that were made too quickly are already obvious.' In Slovenian public debates, the Netherlands often function as »heaven in the West« for gays and lesbians. Excerpt from the parliamentary debate on the Bill on Registered Same-sex Partnership, 7th Plenary Session of the Parliament of the Republic of Slovenia, June 17, 2005.

12. The letter to state secretary Alenka Kovšca (May 21, 2001) from Škuc LL and Škuc Magnus. Reprinted in Lesbo (2003), no. 19/20, pp. 48–49.

13. The proposal of the Same-sex partnership Act (71st regular sitting of the government of Slovenia, April 22, 2004).
14. The letter of Slovenia's People Party to deputy groups of LDS, ZLSD, Desus and the Ministry of labor, family and social affairs (January 20, 2004).
15. In its 2009 decision, the Constitutional Court changed this provision. Now, inheritance rights are recognized equally for married heterosexual couples and registered same-sex couples. In another Constitutional Court decision from 2011, these rights are also now recognized for same-sex couples who are not registered but have lived in a 'long-lasting' partnership. The same goes for heterosexual couples who live out of wedlock.
16. Personal correspondence.
17. Congregation for the Doctrine of Faith (3 June 2003), Considerations regarding proposals to give legal recognition to unions between homosexual persons, at http://www.vatican.va/roman_curia/congregations/cfaith/documents/rc_con_cfaith_doc_20030731_homosexual-unions_en.html (accessed 8 November 2013).
18. TV Slovenia, telecast 'Aktualno' (19 August 2003).
19. Maribor Archdiocese had run EUR 800 m in debt. See more: Top Church Dignitaries Step Down in Wake of Financial Scandal, The Slovenia Times, August 3, 2013, http://www.sloveniatimes.com/top-church-dignitaries-step-down-in-wake-of-financial-scandal (January 30, 2015).

REFERENCES

Ayoub, P. M. (2014). With arms wide shut: Threat perception, norm perception, and mobilized resistance to LGBT rights. *Journal of Human Rights, 13*(3), 337–362.

Foucault, M. (1978). *History of sexuality, Vol. I: The will to knowledge*. New York: Pantheon Books.

Foucault, M. (1994). *The order of things: An archeology of the human sciences*. New York: Random House, Inc..

Hodžič, A., & Bijelić, N. (2014). *Neo-conservative threats to sexual and reproductive health & rights in the European Union*. Zagreb, Croatia: CESI.

Howell, K. E. (2004). Developing conceptualizations of Europeanization: Synthesizing methodological approaches. *Queen's Papers on Europeanization*, 3/2004.

Krševan, M. (1996). Cerkev v postsocializmu. *Družboslovne razprave, 12*(21), 43–56.

Kirn, G., 2013. Social uprising in Slovenia against neoliberal austerity measures. *Global Research*, [Online] February 25. Retrieved July 10, 2015, from http://www.globalresearch.ca/social-uprising-in-slovenia-against-neoliberal-austerity-measures/5324218.

Kollman, K. (2009). European institutions, transnational networks and national same-sex unions policy: When soft law hits harder. *Contemporary Politics, 15*(1), 37–53.

Kuhar, R. (2015). Playing with science: Sexual citizenship and the Roman Catholic Church counter-narratives in Slovenia and Croatia. *Women's Studies International Forum, 49*(1), 84–92.

Luthar, O., Grdina, I., Šašel Kos, M., Svoljšak, P., Kos, P., Štih, D., et al. (Eds.) (2013). *The land between: A history of Slovenia.* Frankurt am Main: Peter Lang.

Mastnak, T. (1992). *Vzhodno od raja.* Ljubljana, Slovenia: Državna založba Slovenije.

Mencin Čeplak, M. (2013a). Heteronormativity: School, ideology, and politics. *Pedagogický časopis, 4*(2), 162–187.

Mencin Čeplak, M. (2013b). Heteronormativnost in regulacije rodnosti. *Annales Series historia et sociologia, 23*(2), 403–414.

Mosse, G. L. (1985). *Nationalism and sexuality: Respectability and abnormal sexuality in modern Europe.* New York: H. Fertig.

O'Dwyer, C. (2012). Does the EU help or hinder gay-rights movements in post-communist Europe? The case of Poland. *East European Politics, 28*(4), 332–352.

O'Dwyer, C., & Vermeersch, P. (2016). From pride to politics: Niche-party politics and LGBT rights in Poland. In K. Slootmaeckers, H. Touquet, & P. Vermeersch (Eds.), *The EU enlargement and gay politics.* London: Palgrave Macmillan.

Olsen, J. P. (2002). The Many Faces of Europeanization. *Journal of Common Market Studies, 40*(5), 921–952.

Paternotte, D. (2014). Christian trouble: The Catholic Church and the subversion of gender. *CritCom*, [Online] 8 May. Retrieved January 3, 2015, from http://councilforeuropeanstudies.org/critcom/christian-trouble-the-catholic-church-and-the-subversion-of-gender/.

Paternotte, D., & Kollman, K. (2013). Regulating intimate relationships in the European polity: Same-sex unions and policy convergence. *Social politics, 20*(4), 510–533.

Pavlovič, V. (2006). *Društveni pokreti i promene.* Beograd, Serbia: Službeni glasnik.

Radaelli, C. (2000). Whiter Europeanization? Concept stretching and substantive change. *European Integration Online Papers, 4*(8), 1–12.

Repe, B. (2000). Slovenci v osemdesetih letih (drugi del). *Zgodovinski časopis, 54*(2), 233–262.

Yuval-Davis, N. (1997). *Gender & nation.* London: Sage.

Žnidaršič Skubic, V. (2006). Pravna narava zakonske zveze. In Z. Kobe & I. Pribac (Eds.), *Prava poroka? Dvanajst razmišljanj o zakonski zvezi* (pp. 211–236). Ljubljana, Slovenia: Krtina.

PART III

Close-ups of the Western Balkans

CHAPTER 8

The Struggle for Visibility and Equality: Bosnian LGBT Rights

Safia Swimelar

INTRODUCTION

In 1995, the Dayton Peace Accords (DPA) brought an end to the entrenched three-year war in Bosnia-Herzegovina (hereafter 'Bosnia' or 'BiH') and set the stage for the construction of a new state that was to be based on the rule of law, democracy, and human rights. As the narrative is now familiar, while the DPA supported and created relative peace and better human rights protections, it has not been able to create a civic identity, a well-functioning state or democracy, or the strong implementation of human rights. The Dayton constitution has (along with informal state and societal practices) institutionalized ethno-national identities and representation in a way that is keenly felt today in almost all areas of Bosnian political life (Mujkić 2008). During the late 1990s and early 2000s, Bosnian political elites and the international community were focused not on minority rights, but instead on immediate security concerns, rebuilding the economy and country, creating a functioning state, and capturing and prosecuting war criminals. Especially since 2006, elites have been unable

S. Swimelar (✉)
Department of Political Science and Policy Studies, Elon University, North Carolina, USA

© The Editor(s) (if applicable) and The Author(s) 2016
K. Slootmaeckers et al. (eds.), *The EU Enlargement and Gay Politics*, DOI 10.1057/978-1-137-48093-4_8

175

and/or unwilling to compromise and reform the political and electoral system in line with European Union (EU) expectations and requirements. However, the recent coming into force of the Stabilization and Association Agreement (SAA) with the EU may signal a change. In this unfavorable environment, with so many crises needing to be solved, the rights and status of LGBT (lesbian, gay, bisexual, transgender) citizens in Bosnia are weak, and observers describe LGBT issues as 'irrelevant'.[1] The LGBT community faces discrimination and marginalization in all spheres of life, and is often fearful of coming or being 'out'. There have been high-profile cases of violent attacks on LGBT events and numerous other cases of assaults and hate crimes against LGBT individuals (Vasić et al. 2014). Of the countries of the former Yugoslavia, Bosnia ranks toward the bottom in terms of LGBT rights, but improvement was noted between 2014 and 2015 (ILGA-Europe 2015). Societal homophobia is high and is reinforced by the political homophobia used by elites.

However, awareness and visibility of LGBT issues and citizens is beginning to change, as one might expect of a transitioning country aiming to join the EU. Today, general knowledge about LGBT issues in the country has increased, and more public events are held that highlight the everyday lives of LGBT people. Legal protections are starting to be more seriously enforced. Civil society organizations focused on LGBT rights and gender issues are very active and visible, and are now in direct communication and cooperation with government institutions on reforms. Activists have more opportunities to meet and organize, while the EU and other external actors such as foreign embassies provide tangible and intangible support for LGBT rights, and media coverage of LGBT issues has improved to some extent. In short, this chapter argues that, despite continued marginalization, minimal norm diffusion is occurring, and the LGBT rights norm over the past decade has become *empowered* within Bosnia.[2]

It is hard to underestimate the wide-ranging effects that Bosnia's war (1992–1995) has had on political, social, cultural, and economic life, and this includes attitudes toward gender and sexual minorities (Fischer 2007; Pickering 2007; Mujkić 2008). Of the wars in the former Yugoslavia during the 1990s, the Bosnian war was the most destructive in terms of human life lost, the wounded, and the destruction of the social and economic infrastructure. The protracted war cost over 100,000 lives, displaced millions of people, and eventually divided the country into two largely ethnically homogenous entities: the Serb Republic (RS) and the Federation (Bosniaks and Croats), and a more independent, ethnically mixed district, Brčko. The Bosnian Serbs' policy of ethnic cleansing and the genocide of over 7000 Bosniak (Bosnian Muslim) men and boys in Srebrenica, along with the widespread war crimes against civilians committed by all three groups, have left deep scars that have reinforced ethnic divides and elevated ethnic belonging and identity. The widespread use of violence, particularly against women, the post-war impunity of many perpetrators, and the continued denial of these crimes have allowed violence to persist in other forms and in more subtle ways that have affected treatment toward LGBT people.

Bosnia has been characterized for the majority of the post-war period by a mostly paralyzed and inefficient political system, a divided and weak state with competing sub-state entities, corrupt ethnic political parties, weak opposition civic-based parties, a poor economy with high unemployment, a segregated and mono-ethnic education system, and weak implementation of human rights laws, to name but a few examples (Bieber 2004, 2006; Freedom House 2014). Ethno-national identities are institutionalized constitutionally, electorally, politically, in the education system, and beyond. At the same time, in a 2008 survey of LGBT-identified individuals, a third of the respondents said they did not identify themselves by nationality—meaning that they do not identify with *any* of the ethno-national groups (Đurković 2008, p. 27).

In this chapter I will do the following: (1) trace and analyze changes in LGBT rights in terms of law, policy, civil society development and activism, and overall empowerment of the LGBT rights norm (using the 'spiral model' of human rights norm diffusion as a framework) (Risse et al. 1999, 2013); (2) analyze factors that have led both to increased LGBT visibility and equality, and to continued homophobia, violence, and discrimination. Norm diffusion is understood as the process of a state's adoption of the norms or standards of a given community and identity (Katzenstein 1996, p. 5). In addressing these main issues, I will analyze the role played by discourses of 'Europeanness' and the Europeanization process, Bosnia's unique political context and development, and the challenge of nationalism as factors limiting the diffusion and empowerment of the LGBT rights norm. I argue that over the last few years, LGBT rights have progressed and have become empowered within Bosnia due to a combination of EU conditionality and the increasing strength of LGBT/human rights non-governmental organizations (NGOs), but that Bosnia's ethno-national divisions and war legacy, its complicated relationship with Europe, and lack of state capacity have slowed and created challenges to the institutionalization and development of LGBT rights. The chapter first lays out the concepts of Europeanization and norm diffusion, specifically as they relate to LGBT rights. Next, I provide a brief overview of the situation for LGBT citizens in Bosnia. I then describe, trace, and analyze civil society, legal, and political developments of LGBT rights primarily since 2009, and provide some final discussion and conclusions.

EUROPEANIZATION, NORM DIFFUSION, AND HUMAN RIGHTS/LGBT RIGHTS

The process and discourse of Europeanization is a key aspect to understanding and explaining the development of and resistance to LGBT rights in the Eastern European region more widely, and in Bosnia in particular, as it has received much more direct and indirect European and international oversight than any other country in the region. Europeanization is broadly seen as the processes of construction, diffusion, and institutionalization of formal and informal rules, procedures, shared beliefs, and norms within national/domestic discourse and policies (Featherstone and Radaelli 2003, p. 17). Scholars have analyzed how the EU accession process has influenced domestic policy adoption and norm change in East European states in a number of areas, such as national minority rights, LGBT rights, and environmental policy (Ayoub 2015; Fagan 2008; Kelley 2006; Schimmelfennig and Sedelmeier 2005; Swimelar 2008).

One of the central models of the norm diffusion process, the 'spiral model', focuses specifically on human rights as a policy and examines the role played by state and non-state actors in pushing a target state to commit to human rights norms (Risse et al. 1999, 2013). The model argues that a norm-violating (or target) state passes through five phases in the process of norm change whereby both interests and identities are expected to change: repression, denial, tactical concessions, prescriptive status, and rule-consistent behavior with human rights norms. Thus, a target state in the first phase actively represses rights, and in phase two denies that there is a human rights problem, with little to no public discourse on the issue, while phase three is the turning point, where improvements are made as concessions to transnational pressures (from inter-governmental organizations [IGOs] and NGOs). In phase four, states start to actively institutionalize the rights and become socialized to accept these rights as appropriate given their new identity; and finally, the last phase of rule-consistent behavior should find the target state following the norms out of habituation and out of reasons of belief more than for purely instrumentalist purposes.

The spiral model argues, along the lines of the two main models in the Europeanization literature, that states may adopt new norms due to a rationalist external incentives model and/or due to a more constructivist social learning approach. The external incentives model essentially argues that states will formally comply with new EU norms and standards if the benefits of EU rewards outweigh the domestic adoption costs (Schimmelfennig and Sedelmeier 2005). The most cost-effective way to comply is through partial compliance or formal compliance with EU norms (Grabbe 2006). The social learning model focuses on the key role of norms and identities and on mechanisms of persuasion, argumentation, and learning to explain norm diffusion and specifically the process of Europeanization (Checkel 2001; Börzel and Risse 2003). The spiral model framework argues that the two approaches are complementary, and that states initially may adopt new human rights norms for rationalist reasons, but the model predicts and has shown in many cases that, over time, through argumentation and persuasion, these rights may be institutionalized to a greater degree as a result of shifts in states' identity and social learning.

Over the last several years, there has been a burst of new scholarship seeking to explain and understand various aspects of LGBT rights, politics, and activism in Eastern Europe and, to a lesser extent, in Southeast Europe (Ayoub and Paternotte 2014; Ayoub 2014, 2015; Berger 2004; Fejes and Balogh 2014; Kulpa and Mizielińska 2011; O'Dwyer 2010, 2013; Mikuš 2011). Recent research in this area supports both the external incentives and social learning models (Ayoub 2015; O'Dwyer 2010, 2013). Supporting the external incentives or conditionality model, O'Dwyer (2013) found that a state's proximity to the EU appeared to influence its LGBT rights—states that are members or potential members had stronger LGBT rights than non-members or candidates. However, one study found that in Poland and Latvia, EU conditionality was weak and that national identity challenged successful norm adoption (O'Dwyer and Schwartz 2010). Another study found that the EU was lacking strong social learning mechanisms—once EU accession was achieved in Poland, for example, the country backtracked on LGBT rights (Ayoub 2014; O'Dwyer 2010).

There are significant domestic factors that can affect the norm diffusion process, particularly in terms of the cost–benefit analysis and risk associated with norm compliance (Risse-Kappen 1995; Schimmelfennig and

Sedelmeier 2005). International or regional norms that more closely culturally 'match' or 'normatively fit' with domestic norms are more likely
to be adopted (Checkel 1999; Cortell and Davis 1996; Swimelar 2008).
Nationalism, religion, and local traditions are important domestic contextual factors that can affect and present challenges to the norm diffusion
process, as has been shown in the case of LGBT rights in Eastern Europe
(O'Dwyer 2013).

Especially during the enlargement in the Western Balkans, the EU made
the protection of sexual minorities a condition of accession (Slootmaeckers
and Touquet 2016). The EU has specifically required decriminalization of
homosexuality, anti-discrimination legislation, and no obstructions to free
assembly (such as banning gay pride parades) (COM (2013) 700, Final),
but at the same time, EU bodies advise states that they should have higher
standards, such as hate crimes legislation. In short, despite the diversity of
LGBT rights across the region,[3] Europe has gone the farthest in advocating for and enshrining LGBT rights in both EU and national member
state laws, and using their diplomatic soft power and rhetorical power
to persuade others that LGBT rights are central to European values of
human rights more broadly.

Despite the diversity of policies within the EU on LGBT rights, scholars have shown how the 'idea of Europe is seen as related to tolerance
and respect for sexual minorities'; there is a historical and contemporary
'special relationship between LGBT rights and a certain idea of Europe,
in which Europe as a concept extends beyond strict institutional categories' (Ayoub and Paternotte 2014, p. 2). Similar to how transnational
non-state actors invoke international human rights standards to advance
their cause, LGBT activists have used the idea and symbol of Europe or
'European values' to advance their rights (Ayoub and Paternotte 2014;
Butterfield 2013; Greenberg 2006; Kulpa and Mizielińska 2011; Mikuš
2011; Wilkinson 2014).

THE SITUATION FOR LGBT CITIZENS IN BOSNIA: A BRIEF OVERVIEW

Prior to the wars of the 1990s, there was a nascent lesbian and gay community and movement in the former Yugoslavia, but this appears to have
been in the republics of Slovenia, Croatia, and Serbia, and not in Bosnia
(Đurković 2008). Instead, Bosnian LGBT activism and visibility has come
only after the war, particularly in the mid-2000s, and primarily in the capital

of Sarajevo, though organizations have recently been created in other large cities such as Banja Luka, Tuzla, and Mostar. Survey data and personal narratives from LGBT citizens in Bosnia reveal a precarious environment and evidence of human rights abuses in numerous realms of society, from within the family to schools, workplaces, and public places. Despite some legal and sociocultural progress in the late 2000s, ILGA-Europe confirmed that, 'experiences of homophobia and transphobia remain very common in Bosnia and Herzegovina with limited or no action taken by authorities to address such discrimination, harassment or violence' (ILGA-Europe 2013). According to a survey of LGBT individuals, the largest challenges reported are (in order of priority) lack of public acceptance; a primitive, homophobic and conservative environment; a non-democratic state lacking laws and human rights protection; an uninformed and uneducated Bosnian public; and uninformed and unorganized LGBT citizens (Đurković 2008).

These findings are corroborated by interviews with numerous activists in 2014 and by NGO reports on the state of the LGBT community. Many activists perceive that the war served to reinforce or elevate homophobia. LGBT citizens speak of having to be very vigilant about the safety of their public surroundings and of becoming accustomed to verbal comments, teasing, or threats from strangers. Regarding the extent to which LGBT individuals are accepted for their sexual orientation, 50 % of respondents report a lack of acceptance sometimes, often, or very often, and only 22 % say they are accepted (Đurković 2008). In this same survey, over half the respondents reported facing indirect discrimination and harassment, while just under 10 % reported having been physically attacked. There is also evidence that the vast majority of LGBT individuals who have faced abuse did not report it to anyone (Đurković 2008). Levels of homophobia among the public are high, with the vast majority having negative views of homosexuality, believing it to be detrimental to Bosnian society, and thinking of it as an illness. At the same time, the Sarajevo Open Center (SOC) believes that there is some degree of tolerance, as 90 % of the respondents in one survey said they would *not* use physical or verbal violence against LGBT people and about 75 % said they would help an LGBT victim of violence (Popov-Momčinović 2013).

LEGAL AND POLITICAL DEVELOPMENTS ON LGBT RIGHTS

There have been some minimal legal and political changes in the rights of LGBT people, illustrating that these human rights norms are starting to become more empowered and protected domestically. However, despite years of pressure and requests, there has not been an investigation or report by *any* government or parliamentary body on the situation of the LGBT community as a vulnerable minority. For example, over a dozen NGOs have appealed to the BiH Human Rights Ombudsman to research and write a report on the status of LGBT citizens, and the United States Agency for International Development (USAID) has offered to provide financial and legal resources as needed (US Embassy 2014). However, similar to the Ministry for Human Rights and Refugees, given that this body comprises political appointees from major parties that do not support LGBT rights, they have not prepared this report (US Embassy 2014). Additionally, until 2015, no government or parliamentary body or representative had directly addressed LGBT issues or rights, or acknowledged the pervasive discrimination sexual and gender minorities face.[4]

One can roughly divide the changes or the advancement of LGBT legal rights and policy changes into a period before 2009, when there was none to minimal progress, and a period since 2009, and particularly in the last few years, where there have been some advancements in multiple arenas. At the legal level, homosexuality was decriminalized in the Federation entity of Bosnia in 1996 and in the RS in 1998, which was a requirement for Council of Europe membership and compliance with other new legislation. On the institutional and legal front, there are Gender Centers at the state level (since 2000) and within both entities that are tasked with advocating, promoting, monitoring, and serving as expert government bodies on gender equality, whose mandate includes equality on the basis of gender identity, gender expression, and sexual orientation. The main law that these bodies are tasked with monitoring, and the first law in Bosnia to address sexual orientation, is the Gender Equality Law of 2003 that prohibits discrimination on the grounds of sexual orientation and gender.[5]

Similar to most human rights laws in Bosnia, the greatest deficiency is in implementing and enforcing the law. But equally challenging—and more unique to sexual minorities—is that victims of discrimination are reluctant to make use of the law through the judicial process, because many of them are not 'out' to family or friends (much less the public and media), and this process could put them in the public spotlight and result in even more harassment, discrimination, or ostracization. A representative of the Gender Center in the Federation of BiH said that members of the LGBT community are involved in their training and events, but that they have not appealed to the center or to the courts on behalf of the law.[6]

Another area that IGOs and LGBT advocates have focused on is the need for hate crimes (and hate speech) laws that would increase punishment for crimes when sexual orientation or gender identity was a motivating factor. Hate crimes legislation has been adopted at the BiH state level, in RS, and in the district of Brčko, but has been stalled in the Federation.[7] The RS entity and Brčko District have also adopted hate speech legislation that includes sexual orientation and gender identity. The SOC reported more than 60 cases of hate speech and hate crimes, for example, in 2014.

Due to pressure and obligations connected to the European Union accession process (specifically, the visa liberalization process), the BiH government adopted comprehensive anti-discrimination legislation in 2009. European Union progress reports prior to 2008 briefly mentioned that discrimination on the basis of sexual orientation was common (and that comprehensive legislation was needed), but in 2008, they went farther in addressing the *LGBT community* specifically and calling out the government (SEC (2008) 2693, final).

Religious critics strongly criticized a draft of this anti-discrimination law when it was first announced. According to the SOC, it was only due to subsequent pressure by the international community that the law was eventually adopted despite the local critics.[8] The law concerns discrimination in access to goods and services, education, and employment. Despite passage of the law, numerous interlocutors have identified many problems with the law. First, it states that individuals are protected from discrimination on the basis of 'sexual expression or sexual orientation' (in addition to other, more traditional protected categories)[9]; this language has been criticized as confusing and incomplete. Informants have reported that judges and prosecutors are not clear and have not been trained on how to interpret or use this law. The SOC has also criticized the law and its implementation for the failure to review how other legislation could lead to discrimination, and for the lack of a comprehensive strategy or national action plan to deal with societal attitudes and stereotypes that lead to direct and indirect discrimination (Barreiro and Vasić 2013). The most recent legal and political developments that may signify a turning point in the diffusion of LGBT rights are outlined and analyzed in a section below.

CIVIL SOCIETY DEVELOPMENT, ACTIVISM, AND STRATEGIES

Prior to 2008 and 2009, there was little civil society organization or activism focusing on LGBT rights. Organization Q, Bosnia's first registered LGBT organization, was established in 2004 and was active in the following years in many areas: collecting information and data about the LGBT community, tracing the violations and abuses of the LGBT community by the Bosnian state, educating about human rights laws, and organizing public events to spread awareness of LGBT citizens and rights. As further described below, while the NGO and civil society community has been plentiful in the post-war period, much of the activity has been driven by foreign and international interests and organizations, with little participation or connection to local citizens. With respect to LGBT rights specifically, given the pressures of peace-building, education reform, and human rights more generally, LGBT issues received no attention. However, a community did exist and was starting to make itself and its precarious situation known.

One of the major events and flash points for the LGBT community was the violent attack upon activists and participants at the Queer Sarajevo Festival (QSF) in September 2008 by Wahhabi Muslims and football hooligans. This incident, the widespread discourse surrounding it in the media, and the fact that it was not condemned by political elites provides a window into the norm diffusion process at this time—specifically, that Bosnia was in the denial phase of LGBT rights. The event was framed through several identity discourses—Europeanness, Islam, and nationalism—thus illustrating the constructivist view that identity plays a key role in setting out what human rights policies may be acceptable or unacceptable. Moreover, this event illustrates that increased LGBT visibility and activism often creates a backlash and greater anti-gay resistance, and thus the incident should be seen as evidence that civil society actors and LGBT issues are gaining strength and visibility, causing apprehension in conservative segments of society who fear change.

Organization Q organized the four-day art event at the Academy of Fine Arts in central Sarajevo to bring public visibility to LGBT people and issues. On the first night of the QSF festival, a group of Wahabbis and other protestors stood across the river from the festival site and hurled insults at the participants. Some shouted 'Allahu Akbar' (God is great) and yelled, 'May dear Allah give your children to Dutch queers to make porno films' (AKI 2008). The demonstrators physically attacked participants, injuring eight of them; the police did not prevent the attackers from advancing toward the building.[10] The violence and fear continued, as many participants, including the organizers, were followed, harassed and even attacked. One of the leading conservative Bosniak newspapers, *Dnevni Avaz*, published the names and birthdates of all participants who were injured and taken to the hospital.

Tensions were evident weeks before the event, and media discourse revealed that the festival was symbolic in terms of its relationship to the complex and negotiated identity of contemporary Bosnia and the challenges to LGBT rights norm diffusion. The conservative and more religious media outlets (print and online) consistently verbally attacked the founder of Q, Svetlana Đurković, and her co-leaders (and any journalists appearing to support or cover the event as well), and homophobic graffiti could be found around town.[11] In contrast, the liberal media, best represented by the weekly *Dani* (which had the most coverage of QSF, with 60 articles), generally provided support to the event and saw it as a litmus test for the notion of Sarajevo as a modern, multicultural metropolis (Kajinic 2008).[12] While Bosnia's state identity is complicated and mixed, one can argue that there is a definite strand within the public and the elites that sees Bosnia as a European country that should align its policies—including human rights and LGBT rights—with Europe. However, there is another strand at the levels of both political (and religious) elites and the masses that is skeptical of Europe and seeks to construct a different, more indigenous identity. Part of this mixed identity can be seen in an urban–rural split on political and social attitudes. Understanding the construction of Bosnia's state identity is more complicated than other Balkan states such as Croatia and Serbia, whose supportive and opposing post-war stances toward Europe, respectively, have been instrumental in explaining their interests and policy choices (Subotić 2011). The uniqueness of Bosnia's lack of a strong centralized state and the power of its sub-state- or entity-level identities also means that constructing (and deciphering) a 'state' identity that would inform interests and policy, such as LGBT rights, is a challenge.

Another important feature of the QSF attacks is that they were interpreted through an ethnic or nationalist lens, illustrating the difficulty of promoting a more civic, multicultural identity that would make room for different sexual and gender identities.[13] Some religious opponents argued that Đurković and another main organizer, who have Serb names, should go 'back to Serbia' (they are both from Bosnia);[14] they were also called 'Chetniks'[15] and received online death threats.[16] The re-traditionalization that occurred during the nationalist 1990s also emphasized patriarchy and masculinity in defending 'our' nation from the enemies' nations (Schäuble 2009). As Causević (2010, p. 34) argues, in relation to Bosniak identity, 'anything other than the heterosexual Muslim norm is considered an offense to the victimized image of the Bosniak nation'. In terms of a public response, political and religious elites expressed homophobic views and some sympathy for the anti-gay demonstrators. Their comments support the argument that nationalism and traditional religious attitudes have posed challenges to LGBT norm diffusion. In terms of the spiral model of human rights norm diffusion, the QSF event, and specifically the lack of elite support for freedom of assembly for the LGBT community, and even more so their support of the (violent) protestors, illustrates that Bosnia in 2008 can be characterized as having been still in the 'denial' phase, wherein LGBT rights at the level of both principle and practice were not accepted.

The environment for LGBT citizens and activists following the QSF attacks was very difficult and, according to many, led to a setback in public gatherings and activism. After 2009, and significantly in the last few years, segments of civil society have grown and become stronger, and have begun focusing specifically on LGBT rights, in addition to increasing their cooperation with and acceptance by government authorities and institutions, on the one hand, and their direct social support of LGBT citizens on the other. They have now become an initiator of LGBT visibility and rights given their multiple strategies at different levels, taking advantage of the political opportunity structure of EU accession, and building partnerships and networks with other NGOs, foreign embassies, and international organizations. As the European Union, the Council of Europe, foreign embassies, and other organizations have made LGBT rights part of their agenda, this has meant that funds and support are available to local NGOs such as the SOC, who has been the most active in their broad efforts toward LGBT rights in terms of law, policy, education, and outreach. The SOC has developed partnerships with other civil society organizations that work on gender and human rights, including Fondacija Cure, the Heinrich Boll Foundation, and the Sarajevo Media Center, often working in tandem to promote the recommendations and implement projects of the Organization for Security and Cooperation in Europe (OSCE), the Council of Europe, and the European Union.

The burgeoning civil society sector on LGBT issues has meant that more powerful members of the international community now have knowledgeable and empowered partners to work with to achieve their common goals. According to a longtime human rights officer at the US embassy, in 2008, there was no partner to talk to about LGBT issues until the SOC came along, and now US and other embassies work closely with and financially support them. 'They [SOC] started talking to government—communication is still far from perfect, but [the government] is now acknowledging that they exist'.[17] A Bosnian diplomat at the Dutch embassy pointed out that the SOC has had good results working on policymaking, lobbying, and even broader structural issues to promote societal change, such as police training, their media work, and other educational efforts.[18] For example, one of the most often cited success stories of civil society's ability to partner with government to effect positive change for LGBT protection is the recent police training organized by the SOC. LGBT individuals have reported that they do not feel safe or confident in reporting incidents to the police, and most police officers are not aware of LGBT issues, terminology, and appropriate professional response to citizens' needs. The SOC received permission from the Ministry of Interior to start an informal training program on hate crimes and LGBT issues with Sarajevo police officers, which then transitioned into part of their permanent ongoing education program; in 2014, 1000 officers had received the training (Vasić et al. 2014). With the cooperation of the OSCE, the program will operate in all other cantons within the Federation, and perhaps in the RS. In addition, four main police stations in Sarajevo have appointed specific contact persons to work with LGBT citizens.[19] While some officers may admit that they are homophobic or don't support LGBT equality, they generally do understand that it is their duty to protect all citizens, and they have come to accept it as part of their job.[20] Beyond police education, the SOC has now begun training other civil servants, including judges, prosecutors, and teachers from elementary school and beyond.[21]

While the SOC focuses primarily on political and legal strategies for promoting LGBT visibility and rights within Bosnia, other organizations with different approaches illustrate the growth and diversification of the NGO sector and LGBT community and the contribution to norm empowerment since the early 2000s. For example, Okvir (formed in 2011) is a small grassroots non-hierarchical organization of young queer activists. While they see the benefit of legal and policy changes and lobbying the government, they believe it is just as, if not more, important at this stage of LGBT activism in Bosnia to focus on supporting and building a solid community of secure and empowered individuals and to direct their energies toward direct action and a broad vision of social justice and psycho-social care. Okvir has participated in and created street performances, public art projects, protests, psychological support groups, peer-to-peer counseling, training, and workshops for LGBT activists, multimedia online projects/events, and more. For example, founder and leader Azra Causević commented, 'I like working with people and the empowerment within community; it's not that I don't feel comfortable educating police [as SOC is doing], but I don't want to use my resources if some kid needs me in their house because of suicide'.[22]

Over the past approximately seven years, LGBT rights issues have gained new visibility through specific LGBT activist organizations or by becoming part of the agenda of human rights NGOs. In particular, NGOs have framed LGBT rights explicitly through the lens of human rights and equality, aiming to separate the issue from the more controversial questions of morality and religion, and have taken advantage of the political opportunity structure of the EU accession process. Beyond the capital, several other LGBT organizations were formed in late 2014 and early 2015—B.U.K.A (*Banjalučko Udruženje Kvir Aktivista* [Banja Luka Association of Queer Activists]) in Banja Luka, LibertaMo in Mostar, and TANKA (*Tuzlanska Alijansa Nezavisnih Kvir Aktivistkinja* [Tuzla Alliance for Independent Queer Activists]) in Tuzla—all of which held diverse events in their respective cities in May 2015 for International Day Against Homophobia (IDAHO day) (Ćuzulan 2015). These linkages both across Bosnia and those that exist across the region and with transnational organizations such as ILGA-Europe illustrate what could be called a 'transnational advocacy network' formed around the common principle of LGBT equality and non-discrimination (Keck and Sikkink 1998). Some political elites now see civil society actors such as the SOC as 'partners' and not adversaries, which supports the scholarship on changes in human rights norms that plays a key role in the changing and more cooperative relationship between societal actors and state actors—when state actors are pushed by the civil society sector to make good on promises they have made (Risse et al. 1999, 2013).

RECENT DEVELOPMENTS, 2014–2015: A PROGRESSIVE TURNING POINT?

Between late 2014 and early 2015, Bosnia's score on ILGA-Europe's Rainbow Index, which takes into account a country's LGBT legal and political advancements across a wide range of areas, increased from 20 to 29 % (ILGA-Europe 2015).[23] Several significant events on the legal, political, and activist levels that occurred in 2014–2015 may *suggest* that LGBT rights norms are becoming more empowered among the public and government elites. While it is too soon to say what the long-term outcomes will be, and the challenges described in this chapter still hold, observers on the ground seem a bit more positive.

However, at the same time, the SOC reports that during this period, violence and threats toward LGBT people and human rights defenders have increased (Pandurević et al. 2015; SOC 2015). Moreover, another high-profile attack occurred on 1 February 2014, when 14 hooded men stormed the *Merlinka* film festival during a panel discussion on transexuality and assaulted three people (Jukić 2014; Human Rights Watch 2014; Vasić et al. 2014). Although police protection had been secured weeks in advance, and the police had been informed on the day of the event about a Facebook page threatening the festival directly, the authorities were not present when the attack occurred (Vasić et al. 2014). In contrast, a positive development, illustrating the importance of strong relationships with state agents such as the police, was the success of the February 2015 *Merlinka* film festival. 'They [the police] learned a lesson from last year and resulting from our work with them, they did everything to protect us', said Bošnjak of the SOC.[24]

There have been a few other positive developments. After many years, in late 2014, the Constitutional Court of BiH ruled that the freedom of assembly of LGBT activists at the QSF had been violated and that fines were to be paid to the organizers. While participants at the festival both then and now still lament that none of the perpetrators of the violence were ever punished, this court judgment at least could be considered a symbolic victory on principle. The expansion of the police training by the SOC and in cooperation with the OSCE as outlined above is another example of a progressive event within the last year. On 17 May 2015, IDAHO day, there were even more events and celebrations than usual by several different LGBT- and human rights-related organizations, all occurring without any confrontations or security problems. The US Embassy did its usual lighting of the embassy building in rainbow colors to make a public statement, even though it knew that local officials might not appreciate it.[25]

The most significant development in May 2015 were two seminars or events which brought state actors (government and parliament) together with the SOC and other members of civil society to discuss LGBT rights and the needs of the community. The first was a training event organized by the SOC on LGBT rights in the context of Bosnia's EU integration, in order to educate government representatives such as institutions working on human rights and gender equality (Tinjak 2015). SOC organizers reported that they were surprised at the level of government interest in the topic and the willingness expressed to become more knowledgeable on LGBT issues and to enact reform.

Second, and even more importantly, was a thematic session on LGBT rights held in the Parliament for government institutions and representatives. The event was organized by the SOC on the occasion of IDAHO Day, and was hailed as a 'historic event' by many observers and by the media (Tinjak 2015). According to the SOC, 'we didn't hope for much when we sent them a memo asking for a thematic session, but we said let's do it and see what happens, and actually it did happen'.[26] The range of attendance was broad and impressive: representatives from the parliamentary Joint Commission on Human Rights (within Bosnia's state Parliamentary Assembly), the Human Rights Commission (at the state level), Gender Equality Office (state and entity levels), the Human Rights Ombudsman (from all levels), the Ministry for Human Rights and Refugees and Ministry of Justice (state and entity levels), the Council of Europe, and the OSCE. In addition, many representatives from civil society participated. 'Even though there is not a lot that state government [compared to entity levels] can do in terms of working on LGBT issues within the scope of human rights, this is the most important event [for LGBT rights] in Bosnian history', said Vasić of the SOC.[27]

At the thematic session SOC leadership presented their annual report on the current and challenging situation for the LGBT community, and laid out recommendations and expectations for the new legislative agenda. The new head of the parliamentary commission and a member of the Serbian Democratic Party (SDS), Boric Borislav, gave a speech in which he stated that LGBT citizens in Bosnia remained totally invisible due to fear of violence and discrimination, and that they should have human rights like every other citizen (E-Novine 2015). This was the first time a government official had made a public statement of support for the LGBT community and LGBT rights. As a result, the Human Rights Ombudsman agreed (after many years of pressure) to research and compile an official special report on the human rights situation of LGBT citizens, and there was agreement among the group that the anti-discrimination law should be amended to clarify sexual orientation and other legal terms. According to Bošnjak,[28]

I genuinely believe it is a turning point. We are continuing cooperation with the commission. We have the amendments, we have the solutions and they are supportive. The first step is this newly established relationship with the institutions. [We hope this is] going to bring at least legislative change, but also change on policy level.

Additionally, even though activists at the SOC know that changes to the family law to recognize same-sex unions (or marriage) are not possible in the current political and social climate in Bosnia, they have inserted the issue into public discourse and laid the groundwork.[29] With the support and cooperation of the European Union and Sarajevo's Media Center, the SOC held a workshop to present a draft law on same-sex partnerships to interested government officials—and modeled this on Croatia's successful law of 2014. In short, civil society actors are taking advantage of new opportunities and a potentially more receptive government that is witnessing some progress not only in its own neighborhood (such as Croatia), but globally as well.

Discussion and Conclusions

To what extent have LGBT rights norms become accepted or empowered within Bosnia? In other words, to what extent have prescriptions such as equality and dignity embodied in this human rights norm become a focus of political attention and debate through changes in legislation, discourse, and behavior? Can we identify a norm diffusion process? As illustrated by the narrative and analysis presented in this chapter, over the past two decades, and particularly within the last five years, LGBT equality and rights have become a focus of political attention and debate, both through discourse and through specific behavioral, policy, and legal changes. Thus, I argue that this norm has become empowered domestically and that diffusion is now occurring, although it has much farther to go before substantive changes are felt on the ground by the LGBT community. However, both the LGBT rights norm itself and several domestic factors pose challenges to the application and generalizability of this model and LGBT rights progress more generally. The rhetoric and controversy surrounding the QSF and the data from multiple interlocutors reveal that nationalism, cultural traditions, local political contexts, and weak EU conditionality all present continuing constraints and roadblocks to the socialization process and the further development of LGBT rights.

In applying the spiral model of human rights norm change, Bosnia before 2008 would likely have been in phase two of 'denial', with the state ignoring and violating LGBT rights, and failing to demonstrate through any discourse or policy that LGBT rights are important and necessary. During this period, civil society actors barely exist and are not yet strong enough to successfully advocate for change, and the relationship between state and civil society actors is tenuous and negative. While the EU accession process was ongoing during this period, it was weaker, in part because the SAA was not signed until 2008. I would argue that the post-2009 period is characterized by a 'tactical concessions' phase, wherein Bosnia has made some cosmetic changes, such as formally complying with certain laws, to appease both a more active civil society and pressure from the European Union and other external actors.[30] For example, during the same period, the EU specifically used the visa liberalization process (granting visa-free travel for Balkan citizens) to persuade Bosnia and other Balkan countries to make changes to policies such as anti-discrimination legislation (Muja 2013). But the acknowledgement that LGBT rights are a normal part of a European democracy—which Bosnia must now accept—seems to have become a societal trend only within the past few years. As scholars explaining norm change are aware, it is difficult to separate out the influence of domestic non-state actors (such as the SOC) and inter-governmental actors (such as the EU) in pushing the LGBT rights norm forward. However, it seems most plausible that the EU has been instrumental in bringing the issue of LGBT rights to the fore, while local NGOs have been key players, as the spiral model predicts, in reinforcing the norm through lobbying and pressuring the government to 'walk the walk' and make good on their promises.

The core developments illustrating this phase of 'tactical concessions' are the 2009 anti-discrimination law, the greater visibility of LGBT issues and individuals (both in terms of NGO activities and the media), police education and cooperation between the SOC and the Ministry of Interior, and the recent meetings and commitments on the part of government representatives, civil society, and European regional diplomats. All the informants consulted in this research agreed that the atmosphere, public discourse, and government actions concerning LGBT rights have improved over the past several years, even though there is a long way to go before LGBT individuals feel secure and equal. The context for any pro-LGBT policy or pronouncement, whether large or small, has come from expectations and pressure from the EU. Activists and observers are united in the opinion that without EU conditionality, these changes would not have been adopted at all.

As the Europeanization literature has argued, the mechanisms of norm diffusion at work here appear to be primarily sanctions and rewards, and secondarily persuasion and argumentative rationality. This study more strongly supports the external incentives model of norm diffusion in terms of the conditionality role of the European Union, but as the spiral model would predict, I also argue that we are seeing some aspects of a social learning process wherein some government leaders (and the NGO community) are recognizing that LGBT rights are central to a democratic and European state. All the NGOs working on LGBT rights have taken advantage of the recent political opportunity structure of the EU accession process, and have strongly framed their claims and persuaded the state through the use of a discourse on human rights and basic European standards.

There are also more specific domestic explanations for some of the recent positive developments and possible turning points. Regarding the first parliamentary session on LGBT rights in May 2015 and subsequent commitments by lawmakers, representatives of the new government, and particularly the members of this commission (such as its new leader), were *individually* more interested in human rights protection than their predecessors and genuinely wanted to 'do their job'.[31] One could argue that this may illustrate a social learning mechanism of norm diffusion, since elites over time may be persuaded by both local civil society and European human rights discourse to accept LGBT rights.

Challenges to greater norm diffusion abound. The intrinsic nature of the LGBT rights norm presents conceptual challenges to its diffusion and domestic acceptance, and to the wider application of the spiral model. Thomas Risse argues that the impact that transnational non-state actors have on state policies will vary according to, *inter alia*, the strength and degree of international institutionalization of a norm (Risse 1995, p. 6). There is no global consensus on the value and makeup of LGBT rights, and at a European regional level, while there is a basic minimum expectation regarding the inclusion of sexual orientation in non-discrimination law, the strength of the norm varies greatly among EU members. The position of LGBT rights in the *acquis* is both soft and negligible. Second, the domestic NGOs promoting LGBT rights are either specifically made up of members of that minority group, members of the dominant group that supports them, or a mixture of both. Given that these groups are perceived to represent minority and not majority interests, and that these rights are perceived as so anathema to traditional and conservative religious values, they are already starting from a weaker position in terms of mass public and government support.

Next, as this chapter has illustrated, nationalism and the strength and institutionalization of ethno-national identities have presented challenges to norm diffusion and LGBT norm change. The relationship between nationality and sexuality has historically been constructed in ways that have supported patriarchal relations, traditional or 'natural' gender divisions and roles, and heterosexual relations (Nagel 1998; Yuval-Davis 1997). The fear of a population demographic crisis as a result of growing numbers of LGBT people who allegedly will not reproduce is one of the most common arguments in the post-communist regions where birth rates are rapidly falling. A related challenge to LGBT rights in Bosnia is the way that elites have used political homophobia in relation to nationalism. States often use homophobia to claim political legitimacy and gain authority when faced with challenges to their power (Weiss and Bosia 2013, pp. 17, 21). Bosnia is ripe for political homophobia, since the political elites (and the public) have felt for years that they have little to no control over their country. The notion of state sovereignty often means little in the face of so much European and international influence and pressure; resistance to what are seen as 'foreign' norms and identities can thus be used to gain legitimacy and authority when the state possesses little reserves of either. In short, Bosnia's post-war identity emphasizing the three ethno-national identities (i.e. 'constituent peoples'—Serbs, Croats, and Bosniaks) presents clear challenges to the recognition and acceptance of other identities, particularly those based on sexual orientation or gender.[32] As one Bosnian political scientist commented, 'the queer category is really and truly a point of resistance to nationalism. Nationalism wants to appropriate all institutions, (as in Bosnia) so queer theory [and movement] is a good point of protest and resistance to the overwhelming nationalization [of society]'.[33]

In terms of the institutional level of Europeanization, the main dynamic for the majority of the post-war period has been the consistent expectation by the EU that Bosnian political reforms will occur and the subsequent consistent intransigence by those in power to enact reform. What this means for LGBT rights in practical terms is that EU accession and conditionality has not resulted in additional and stronger public rhetorical and policy support, despite the fact that I argue that it has still had some influence. In addition to the central challenge of a lack of interest and political will, there is the 'lack of credible membership incentive'. The research on EU conditionality in Eastern Europe has found a significant correlation between rule adoption and a 'credible membership perspective' (Schimmelfennig and Sedelmeier 2005, p. 210). For many in Bosnia, the promise of EU membership has been so elusive or unlikely for so long that it has not played the strong role that many observers expected. The EU has thus provided little incentive, and the Bosnian elites themselves have shown little political will to respond to any incentives or sanctions.[34] A clear illustration of this that many interlocutors pointed to has been the unwillingness of Bosnian authorities to implement the 2009 European Court of Human Rights decision in the Sejdic-Finci case, even after the EU cut millions of dollars in funding. There are so many priorities in Bosnia, whether the narrow economic interests of elites, security reform, or—the greatest of all—constitutional reform (Bieber 2010), that LGBT issues have become irrelevant. But this may be changing.

In conclusion, the key factors contributing to the relative shift toward greater LGBT rights have been (1) the growing strength, commitment and ability of human rights NGOs such as the SOC, Okvir, and others to move the LGBT issue from invisibility and from the margins to the public sphere; (2) potential slow shifts in attitudes (social learning) by the political elites and political parties (illustrated by the new Parliamentary Committee for Human Rights session with civil society); and (3) weak but existent EU conditionality and pressure (external incentives).

Recent research on LGBT politics in Eastern Europe reveals a dynamic whereby increased visibility of the LGBT community and increased activism and events can lead to backlash and resistance by societal actors who fear change to traditional gender norms (Ayoub 2014). This has occurred in Bosnia, and should not necessarily be taken as evidence that sociocultural attitudes are becoming *more* homophobic, but as a sign that civil society actors and LGBT issues are gaining strength and visibility, thus causing apprehension in conservative segments of society.

Bosnia is an interesting and relevant case for understanding how competing domestic norms can affect the diffusion of LGBT norms, even though it may be more unique given its war experience and the direct role of the international community in its political development. But the findings here may be useful for a wider understanding of the region, where states are dealing with identity, institutional, and post-war challenges. Nevertheless, in 2015, several pro-LGBT commitments by political elites, peaceful gatherings and events by the LGBT community, and increased civil society–government communication and cooperation have signaled a *possible* turning point for greater LGBT progress in the future.

Notes

1. Given the widespread use of the LGBT acronym globally and within Bosnia, it will be used here, even though transgender issues will not be discussed due to space and focus. Also, according to the Sarajevo Open Center, 'Trans* people are completely marginalized within the BiH society, which is also reflected by the institutional policies. There are no established medical support and procedures for the gender reassignment process in BiH. The official social security system does not cover any costs related to gender reassignment surgeries that are taking place abroad' (Vasić et al. 2014). The anti-discrimination and hate crimes laws do include 'gender identity' as a protected category, but visibility and awareness of trans citizens remains limited.
2. According to Checkel (1999), norm empowerment occurs when 'the prescriptions embodied in a norm become, through changes in discourse or behavior, a focus of political attention or debate'. LGBT rights norms here means basic equality and individual rights applied to LGBT individuals (such as protection from discrimination and violence). But it also includes general awareness and visibility of LGBT people and any issues related to this community. This idea is also called the 'domestic salience' of norms. Greater norm empowerment is not necessarily the same as progress on LGBT rights, but empowerment should be seen as one advancement in this area. See also the work of Cortell and Davis (1996, 2000).
3. For example, Italy and Poland, according to ILGA-Europe, are ranked at the same level as Bosnia, while the UK and Belgium are at the highest levels in the region. See ILGA-Europe (2015).
4. The inclusion of the language of sexual orientation in the 2003 Gender Equality Law discussed below is one exception.
5. The main statement on discrimination does not use the term 'gender', even though the term is used throughout the law. The law focuses on gender discrimination and does not use the terms 'gender identity' or 'gender expression'. While 'sexual orientation' appears at the beginning of the law, the subsequent articles refer only to sex or gender, creating some confusion as to how this law would best apply to LGBT citizens (See the law at: http://www.ilo.org/dyn/natlex/docs/SERIAL/64146/69205/F195754431/BIH64146.pdf.) The comprehensive anti-discrimination law of 2009 has more potential for protecting LGBT citizens.

6. Moreover, the Gender Equality Law has been criticized for its lack of a definition of sexual orientation (and the lack of explicit reference to it after Article 2), for not including 'gender identity' specifically, and for its general vagueness that makes it difficult for prosecutors and judges to interpret (Đurković 2008).

7. The Social Democrats brought up the legislation in 2014, but it did not pass, and now this task has moved to the Ministry of Justice, with observers reporting that it is still under review, but has not been passed yet (Author interview with Vladana Vasić, 5 June 2015, SOC, Sarajevo). One should note the structural complexities of the Federation compared to RS and how it often takes longer for laws to be adopted.

8. Author interview with Vladana Vasić, Sarajevo Open Center, Sarajevo, 29 October 2014.

9. Text of the law at: http://arsbih.gov.ba/wp-content/uploads/2014/02/002-Anti-Discrimination-Law-.pdf.

10. Author interview with Svetlana Đurković, Sarajevo, 25 January 2015.

11. Sarajevo was covered with posters and leaflets promoting 'fascist, racist and xenophobic ideology directed against homosexuals' and media coverage that could be considered hate speech (Helsinki Committee 2008, p. 7).

12. Kajinic explained how both the liberal and conservative media 'explicitly link[ed] the discourse of human rights and "queerness" to "Europeanness" and modernity, but with very different results' (Kajinic 2008, p. 66).

13. Another important topic of the media debate that illustrates the identity conflicts was the timing of the festival. Islamic conservatives and even some political elites claimed that the organizers were intentionally provoking them (and Bosnian society more generally) by holding the festival during Ramadan (the Islamic holy month). In fact, this was not intentional, but an oversight (Author interview with Svetlana Đurković, Sarajevo, 25 January 2015).

14. This semantic ethnic cleansing has been common, where people with Croat or Serb names who are Bosnian are often told to leave the country even though they are not from Croatia or Serbia.

15. 'Chetnik' is the derogatory term used for nationalist Serbs during the Balkan wars.

16. Author interview with Svetlana Đurković, Sarajevo, 25 January 2015.

17. Author interview with US Embassy, Sarajevo, 28 October 2014.

18. Authors interview with Dutch Embassy, Sarajevo, 27 October 2014.

19. Author interview with Vladana Vasić, Sarajevo Open Center, Sarajevo, 29 October 2014.

20. Author interview with Vladana Vasić, Sarajevo Open Center, Sarajevo, 29 October 2014.

21. Author interview with Vladana Vasić, Sarajevo Open Center, Sarajevo, 29 October 2014

22. Author interview with Azra Causević, Okvir, Sarajevo, 29 October 2014.
23. According to ILGA's index, the main improvements from 2014 to 2015 relate to progress on transgender rights (e.g. legal gender recognition, name change allowed, and identity noted on official documents) in addition to having an 'equality body mandate'.
24. Author interview with Emina Bošnjak, Sarajevo Open Center, Sarajevo, 3 June 2015
25. Author interview with US Embassy, Sarajevo, 28 October 2014
26. Author interview with Emina Bošnjak, Sarajevo Open Center, Sarajevo, 3 June 2015.
27. Author interview with Vladana Vasić, Sarajevo Open Center, Sarajevo, 29 October 2014
28. Author interview with Emina Bošnjak, Sarajevo Open Center, Sarajevo, 3 June 2015
29. Progress should not overshadow the fact that among many political elites, there is still resistance to change. Thus, observers are likely skeptical that political elites, even those within human rights institutions, will follow through on their policy commitments. See ILGA-Europe (2013).
30. Note that this claim does not mean that the state is not repressing LGBT individuals, since the police and state agents are clearly still violating LGBT rights. It only means that at the institutional and legal levels and also at the level of discourse, we do not see direct and systematic repression relative to previous years. We do see some cases of assault and violence being investigated and perpetrators being convicted (while other cases are languishing). Thus, progress can coexist with continued discrimination and violence.
31. Author interview with Vladana Vasić, Sarajevo Open Center, Sarajevo, 29 October 2014; Author interview with Emina Bošnjak, Sarajevo Open Center, Sarajevo, 3 June 2015.
32. Author interviews with numerous LGBT activists and University of Sarajevo political scientist, October 2014.
33. Author interview with Asim Mujkić, Sarajevo, 28 October 2014.
34. Risse et al. (1999, p. 24, emphasis added) hypothesize that a 'transition to the third phase of "tactical concessions" primarily depends on the strength and mobilization of the transnational network *in conjunction with the vulnerability of the norm-violating government to international pressures*'. While Bosnia is somewhat vulnerable and needing to convince EU actors of its commitments, it is not in the same position as neighboring Serbia, which is aiming to construct a new identity and be welcomed into Europe after its behavior during the Balkan wars.

REFERENCES

AKI. (2008). Bosnia: Gay festival closes after clashes with hardline Muslims. *Adnkronos International* [Online], 26 September. Retrieved January 18, 2015, from http://www1.adnkronos.com/AKI/English/CultureAndMedia/?id=1.0.2515181716.

Ayoub, P. M. (2014). With arms wide shut: Threat perception, norm reception, and mobilized resistance to LGBT rights. *Journal of Human Rights, 13*(3), 337–362.

Ayoub, P. M. (2015). Contested norms in new-adopter states: International determinants of LGBT rights legislation. *European Journal of International Relations, 21*(2), 293–322.

Ayoub, P. M., & Paternotte, D. (Eds.) (2014). *LGBT activism and the making of Europe: A rainbow Europe?* Basingstoke, England: Palgrave Macmillan.

Barreiro, M., & Vasić, V. (2013). *Monitoring the implementation of the Council of Europe Committee of Ministers recommendation on combating sexual orientation or gender identity discrimination.* Sarajevo: Sarajevo Open Center.

Berger, N. (2004). *Tensions in the struggle for sexual minority rights in Europe.* Manchester: Manchester University Press.

Bieber, F. (2004). Institutionalizing ethnicity in the Western Balkans managing change in deeply divided societies. *ECMI Working Paper #19* [Online]. Retrieved June 30, 2015, from http://unpan1.un.org/intradoc/groups/public/documents/UNTC/UNPAN015487.pdf.

Bieber, F. (2006). *Post-war Bosnia: Ethnicity, inequality, and public sector governance.* New York: Palgrave Macmillan.

Bieber, F. (2010). Constitutional reform in Bosnia and Herzegovina: Preparing for EU accession. *European Policy Centre Policy Brief* [Online]. Retrieved June 5, 2015, from http://www.epc.eu/documents/uploads/1087_constitutional_reform_in_bosnia_and_herzegovina.pdf.

Börzel, T. A., & Risse, T. (2003). Conceptualizing the domestic impact of Europe. In K. Featherstone & C. M. Radaelli (Eds.), *The politics of Europeanization* (pp. 57–80). Oxford: Oxford University Press.

Bosnia and Herzegovina 2008 Progress Report, SEC(2008) 2693, final.

Butterfield, N. (2013). Sexual rights as a tool for mapping Europe: Discourses of human rights and European identity in activists' struggles in Croatia. In N. Fejes & A. P. Balogh (Eds.), *Queer visibility in post-socialist cultures* (pp. 11–34). Bristol, England: Intellect Ltd.

Causević, A. (2010). *Making it queer in post-socialist BiH.* Master's thesis, Central European University, Budapest.

Checkel, J. (1999). Norms, institutions, and national identity in contemporary Europe. *International Studies Quarterly, 43*(1), 83–114.

Checkel, J. (2001). Why comply? Social learning and European identity. *International Organization, 55*(3), 553–588.

Cortell, A., & Davis, J. (1996). How do international institutions matter? The domestic impact of international rules and norms. *International Studies Quarterly, 40*(4), 451–478.

Cortell, A., & Davis, J. (2000). Understanding the domestic impact of international norms: A research agenda. *International Studies Review, 2*, 65–87.

Ćuzulan, J. (2015). IDAHOT 2015: Pregled dešavanju u BiH. *LGBT.ba* [Online], 22 May. Retrieved June 15, 2015, from http://lgbt.ba/idahot-2015-pregleddesavanja-u-bih/.

Đurković, S. (2008). *The invisible Q? Human rights issues and concerns of LGBTQ persons in Bosnia and Herzegovina*. Sarajevo: Organization Q.

Enlargement strategy and main challenges 2013–2014, COM (2013) 700, final.

E-Novine. (2015). Poboljšati položaj LGBT osoba u BiH. *E-Novine*, [Online] 21 May. Retrieved June 13, 2015, from http://www.e-novine.com/region/region-bosna/120748-Poboljati-poloaj-LGBT-osoba-BiH.html.

Fagan, A. (2008). Global–local linkage in the Western Balkans: The politics of environmental capacity building in Bosnia-Herzegovina. *Political Studies, 56*(3), 629–652.

Featherstone, K., & Radaelli, C. (Eds.) (2003). *The politics of Europeanization*. Oxford: Oxford University Press.

Fejes, N., & Balogh, A. (Eds.) (2014). *Queer visibility in post-socialist cultures*. Bristol, CT: Intellect.

Freedom House. (2014). Bosnia and Herzegovina overview. *Freedom House* [Online]. Retrieved June 5, 2015, from https://freedomhouse.org/report/freedom-world/2014/bosnia-and-herzegovina#.VXHd5WTBzGc.

Fischer, M (Ed.). (2007). *Ten Years after Dayton: Peacebuilding and Civil Society in Bosnia Herzegovina*. Berlin: Lit Verlag.

Greenberg, J. (2006). Nationalism, masculinity and multicultural citizenship in Serbia. *Nationalities Papers, 34*(3), 321–341.

Grabbe, H. (2006). *The EU Transformative Power: Europeanization through Conditionality in Central and Eastern Europe*. New York: Palgrave Macmillan.

Helsinki Committee for Human Rights in Bosnia and Herzegovina. (2008) *Report on the status of human rights in Bosnia and Herzegovina: Analysis for the period January 2008–December 2008*.

Human Rights Watch. (2014). Bosnia and Herzegovina: Attack on LGBT Activists. 4 February. Retrieved June 5, 2015, from https://www.hrw.org/news/2014/02/04/bosnia-and-herzegovina-attack-lgbt-activists.

ILGA-Europe (2013). *Annual review of the human rights situation of lesbian, gay, bisexual, trans and intersex people in Europe 2013*. Brussels, Belgium: ILGA-Europe. Retrieved June 10, 2015, from http://www.ilga-europe.org/resources/rainbow-europe/2015.

ILGA-Europe. (2015). *ILGA-Europe rainbow map May 2015*, Brussels, Belgium: ILGA-Europe. Retrieved June 25, 2015, from http://rainbow-europe.org.

Jukić, E. (2014). Sarajevo Queer Fest Violence Condemned, *Balkan Insight*, [Online] 3 February. Retrieved January 27, 2015, from http://www.balkaninsight.com/en/article/sarajevo-violence-over-queer-fest-condemned.

Kajinic, S. (2008). 'Battle for Sarajevo' as 'Metropolis': Closure of the first queer Sarajevo festival according to liberal press. *Anthropology of East Europe Review*, 28(1), 62–82.

Katzenstein, P. (Ed.) (1996). *The culture of national security: Norms and identity in world politics*. New York: Columbia University Press.

Kelley, J. (2006). *Ethnic politics in Europe: The power of norms and incentives*. Durham, NC: Duke University Press.

Keck, M., & Sikkink K. (1998). *Activists Beyond Borders*. Ithaca: Cornell University Press.

Kulpa, R., & Mizielińska, J. (Eds.) (2011). *De-centring western sexualities: Central and Eastern European perspectives*. Surrey, England: Ashgate.

Mikuš, M. (2011). "State Pride": Politics of LGBT rights and democratisation in "European Serbia". *East European Politics & Societies*, 25(4), 834–851.

Muja, A. (Ed.) (2013). *The EU visa liberalisation process in Western Balkans: A comparative assessment*. Pristina: Kosovar Center for Security Studies. Retrieved August 6, 2015, from http://www.qkss.org/repository/docs/The_EU_Visa_Liberalization_Process_in_the_Western_Balkans_Countries-A_Comparative_Assessment_363096.pdf.

Mujkić, A. (2008). *We, the citizens of ethnopolis*. Sarajevo: Center for Human Rights.

Nagel, J. (1998). Masculinity and nationalism: gender and sexuality in the making of nations. *Ethnic and Racial Studies, 21*(2), 242–269.

O'Dwyer, C. (2010). From conditionality to persuasion? Europeanization and the rights of sexual minorities in post-accession Poland. *Journal of European Integration, 32*(3), 229–247.

O'Dwyer, C. (2013). Gay rights and political homophobia in post-communist Europe: Is there an "EU effect"? In M. L. Weiss & M. J. Bosia (Eds.), *Global homophobia: States, movements, and the politics of oppression* (pp. 103–126). Urbana, IL: University of Illinois Press.

O'Dwyer, C., & Schwartz, K. Z. S. (2010). Minority rights after EU enlargement: A comparison of antigay politics in Poland and Latvia. *Comparative European Politics, 8*(2), 220–243.

Pandurević, D., Bošnjak, E., & Kučukalić, N. (2015). *Political parties and the human rights of LGBT people: Monitoring of the general election 2014*. Sarajevo: Sarajevo Open Center.

Pickering, P. (2007). *Peacebuilding in the Balkans: The view from the ground floor*. Cornell: Cornell University Press.

Popov-Momčinović, Z. (2013). Ko smo mi da sudimo drugima. Sarajevo: Heinrich Boll, Foundation CURE, Sarajevo Open Center. Retrieved August 4, 2015, from http://soc.ba/site/wp-content/uploads/2013/11/ko_smo_mi_2013_10_25web1.pdf.

Risse, T., Ropp, S., & Sikkink, K. (1999). *The power of human rights*. Cambridge: Cambridge University Press.

Risse, T., Ropp, S., & Sikkink, K. (2013). *The persistent power of human rights*. Cambridge: Cambridge University Press.

Risse-Kappen, T (Ed.). (1995). Bringing Transnational Relations Back In: Non-State Actors, Domestic Structures and International Institutions. Cambridge: Cambridge University Press.

Schäuble, M. (2009). Contested masculinities: Discourses on the role of Croatian combatants during the "Homeland War" (1991–1995). In C. Eifler & R. Seifert (Eds.), *Gender dynamics and post-conflict reconstruction* (pp. 169–198). Frankfurt am Main, Germany: Peter Lang.

Schimmelfennig, F., & Sedelmeier, U. (Eds.) (2005). *The Europeanization of Central and Eastern Europe*. Ithaca, NY: Cornell University Press.

Slootmaeckers, K., & Touquet, H. (2016). The Co-evolution of EU's Eastern enlargement and LGBT politics: An ever gayer union? In K. Slootmaeckers, H. Touquet, & P. Vermeersch (Eds.), *The EU enlargement and gay politics*. London: Palgrave Macmillan.

SOC (Sarajevo Open Center). (2015). *Written submission by Sarajevo Open Centre on the state of human rights of LGBT people in Bosnia and Herzegovina tot the 2015 progress report*. Sarajevo: Sarajevo Open Center. Retrieved September 28, 2015, from http://soc.ba/site/wp-content/uploads/2015/03/Written-submission_2015-Progress-Report_LGBT-rights_Sarajevo-Open-Centre.pdf.

Subotić, J. (2011). Europe is a state of mind: Identity and Europeanization in the Balkans. *International Studies Quarterly, 55*(2), 309–330.

Swimelar, S. (2008). The making of minority rights norms in the context of EU enlargement: The Czech Republic and the Roma. *The International Journal of Human Rights, 12*(4), 505–527.

Tinjak, A. (2015). Intervju: Vesna Švancer: Svako je Osjetljiv kada njegovo pravo povrijeđeno. *LGBT.ba*, [Online] 28 May. Retrieved February 12, 2015, from http://lgbt.ba/intervju-vesna-svancer-svako-je-osjetljiv-kada-je-njegovo-pravo-povrijedjeno/.

Vasić, V., Gavrić, S., & Bošnjak, E. (2014). *Pink report: Annual report on the state of human rights of LGBT persons in Bosnia Herzegovina in 2014.* Sarajevo: Sarajevo Open Center.

Weiss, M. L., & Bosia, M. J. (Eds.) (2013). *Global homophobia: States, movements, and the politics of oppression*. Urbana, IL: University of Illinois Press.

Wilkinson, C. (2014). LGBT activism in Kyrgyzstan: What role for Europe? In P. M. Ayoub & D. Paternotte (Eds.), *LGBT activism and the making of Europe: A rainbow Europe?* (pp. 50–72). Palgrave Macmillan: Basingstoke, England.

Yuval-Davis, N. (1997). *Gender and nation*. London: Sage.

CHAPTER 9

Whose Pride? LGBT 'Community' and the Organization of Pride Parades in Serbia

Bojan Bilić

INTRODUCTION

Pride parades are increasingly considered a 'litmus test' of the status of LGBT[1] rights in countries acceding to the European Union (EU) (Mikuš 2011; Fagan and Slootmaeckers 2014). Although this indicator function should be problematized rather than taken for granted, it is clear that by participating in such events, segments of the LGBT population intervene into and—at least temporarily—claim public space. Numerous attempts to organize Pride parades in Belgrade over the last 15 years call for sociological attention for at least two interrelated reasons: on the macro level, they represent an explosive intersection between multiple ideological threads pertaining to patriarchy and ethno-nationalism, on the one hand, and the discourses of human rights, democratization and Europeanization, on the other. From a micro perspective, closer to my interests, Pride parades constitute the tip of an iceberg offering us insight into a complex geometry of

B. Bilić (✉)
AISSR, University of Amsterdam, Amsterdam, The Netherlands

© The Editor(s) (if applicable) and The Author(s) 2016
K. Slootmaeckers et al. (eds.), *The EU Enlargement and Gay Politics*, DOI 10.1057/978-1-137-48093-4_9

B. BILIĆ

social practices, forces and interests, not all of which are, individually or in combination, necessarily compatible with the overarching and sometimes illusive objective of advancing the LGBT cause.

This chapter draws upon a variety of empirical data (interviews, documentary sources, Internet forums, social surveys) to examine the extent to which identitarian politics based on non-normative/non-procreative sexualities could operate as an organizing principle of activist engagement in the current social environment characterized by poverty and unemployment. I am interested in the ways in which disparities in wealth, education and professional status, but also skills, connections and geographical locations within the Serbian LGBT population destabilize the grassroots ownership of activist initiatives, and condition the strategic options and perceptions of the LGBT population as well as its willingness to participate in them. As such, my chapter does not engage specifically with the vicissitudes of Europeanizing policies in today's Serbia (Bilić 2016), but focuses on the main tensions within the activist context in which these policies are negotiated and implemented. In other words, I take a closer look at the 'internal' dynamics of the Serbian LGBT activist 'scene'.

Moreover, research on LGBT issues in the post-Yugoslav region is still rather scarce and is focused almost exclusively on lesbians and gay men. Bilić and Stubbs (2015) argue that the Yugoslav and post-Yugoslav space almost never appear in the theoretical literature on political contention in general. The former Yugoslav republics are rarely examined in works on social movements in the context of the post-communist transition of Central and Eastern Europe. This is all the more the case with LGBT activism, which, along with other kinds of social movements, has largely escaped the attention of national/regional social scientists. Because of this, we are, as observers, left believing that LGBT organizations represent a homogeneous group of benevolent actors whose agency is at the mercy of superior forces embodied by patriarchal/conservative governments and the church and/or by different form(ation)s of international power.[2] This scarcity of sociological research flattens the organizational and ideological diversity of the LGBT activist networks and falsely overstates the level of consensus among its member-groups (Stubbs 2007).

The marked absence of empirical work on the dynamics and effects of LGBT organizing (in spite of significant media coverage that it receives around Pride marches) has also rendered LGBT people invisible in their social, generational, political and other forms of heterogeneity. This is not so much related to the methodological dilemmas that accompany attempts to approach such a 'fluid' population[3] that might demonstrate reticence and suspicion towards any sociological 'intrusion'. Rather, such a knowledge gap in the post-Yugoslav space, at least partially, has to do with the 'authoritarian legacies that lead to social scientific and policy research which is mostly elitist and 'top-down' in character and does not really encourage engagement with social movements and alternative groups' (Bilić and Janković 2012, p. 28). Scholarly marginalization of 'non-normative' sexualities as legitimate 'research objects' is a reflection of the wider exclusionary patterns that parallel the processes of ethno-nationalist homogenization that have been, with varying degrees, unfolding in the post-Yugoslav region over the last three decades.

In this regard, I start from the premise that Serbian LGBT (professional) activist groups operate in unpropitious circumstances characterized by a poorly reliable state apparatus, high levels of poverty and unemployment, and strong (re-)clericalization tendencies which, along with the devastating legacy of the Yugoslav wars, provide fertile ground for homophobia and other kinds of prejudice and discrimination (Bilić 2012; Gordy 1999). However, the fact that the situation has been unfavorable cannot be but an argument *for* the urgency of activist initiatives that would, instead of unsuccessfully copying and insisting on foreign/Western models under the EU pressure, try to stimulate solidarity and articulate local grievances through an appreciation of the specificities of their own sociopolitical context.

In this regard, I argue that the vast majority of Serbian LGBT initiatives, especially those associated with the Belgrade Pride, are conceptualized and carried out in a manner that is detached from the broader LGBT population that they are supposed to represent. Highly professionalized activist groups operating within the Serbian political context *precede* (instead of follow) any (spontaneous) instances of protest that would constitute a reaction to local grievances. Thus, in spite of the courage, energy and a huge amount of resources that have been invested in these manifestations, Serbian LGBT initiatives that converge around Pride continue to reflect activist divisions and keep missing an opportunity to articulate LGBT emancipation as a universally oriented political struggle. This raises important questions about the emphasis that has been placed on the role of the Belgrade Pride within the EU enlargement context.

The Context of Serbian LGBT Activism

Serbian LGBT organizations did not appeared at the end of a protest cycle as an offspring of the dissipated collective mobilization for the advancement of LGBT rights, but they instead emerged in the early 1990s on the margins of the anti-war movement which, mostly for pragmatic reasons, rapidly (and not unproblematically) substituted various forms of street protest for highly professionalized institutions devoted to human rights, transitional justice and peace education (Bilić 2012). This is how Lepa Mlađenović (2012, p. 129), a prominent anti-war and feminist lesbian activist from Belgrade, explains what the beginning of the wars of the Yugoslav succession meant for those interested in fighting homophobia:

> In Serbia, when the war started, the peace movement, women's movement and human rights organizations, apart from responding to the urgent needs of the people who survived the war, also became the nuclei of a future civil society. Feminists expected that the human rights organizations would be based on the policy of working against all kinds of discrimination, including sexism and homophobia. And that the principle of indivisibility of human rights would be respected, so that all human rights would be considered equal. However, in the initial years of the anti-war movement this was not the case. The human rights groups that were formed in our cities worked hard to deconstruct nationalism and support refugee rights, but still did not touch the rights of other social groups. We, therefore, came to the point where we could observe that war urged a priority of needs for safety, shelter, food, that the destructive regimes set up a hierarchy of violence, destroying people's lives. Responding to this new terror, the human rights organizations also set up a hierarchy of human rights.

The LGBT 'movement' in Serbia was reinvigorated in the early 2000s (after the removal of Slobodan Milošević), in an atmosphere in which the 'NGO-ized' mode of 'activism' had *always been* there (Bilić 2012). As the anti-war movement could not have positioned the issue of 'gay liberation' particularly high on its agenda, many LGBT activists did not have an opportunity to seek public (either within or outside the LGBT community) 'legitimation' of their engagement.[4] This public legitimacy problem, which has accompanied Serbian LGBT activism from its beginnings, is rooted in a historical particularity: the decriminalization of homosexuality in Serbia (and Yugoslavia) occurred as a result of the routine revision of the penal code and not as the end product of any grassroots engagement or wider societal human rights claims. In socialist Yugoslavia, homosexuality was decriminalized in the republics of Slovenia, Croatia and Montenegro, as well as in Vojvodina, an autonomous province in the Republic of Serbia, in as early as 1977. The penal code referred only to male homosexuality, and made no mention of lesbian sexuality (Dioli 2009). The second wave of decriminalization took place in 1994, in the rest of Serbia, Bosnia and Herzegovina, Kosovo and Macedonia. Jelica Todosijević, a member of the first Serbian LGBT organization, *Arkadija* (founded in 1990), thus sent a report on lesbians in yugoslavia to the International Gay and Lesbian Human Rights Commission, in which she wrote:

> On July 14 (1994), our government adopted the draft of the new criminal law. Before, the old law was banning homosexuality. However, lesbianism was never a part of that ban. The change came as a total surprise to the gay community. NO ONE in the community 'lobbied' for the new law, because it was beyond our power. Our guess is that the change came from someone high up in government. (Todosijević 1995)[5]

In this sense, the issues of the contextual and the temporal become deeply significant.[6] In the USA and much of Western Europe, the first Pride marches were a reaction of a *structurally disadvantaged* population facing an extremely homophobic legal system. To a large extent, the idea to stage Gay Pride came to the rather unfavorable Serbian politico-social environment stripped of its political potency. Much of the controversy (and overt violence) accompanying Pride organization shows that this manifestation was belatedly transferred as a commodified political instrument in the context of (visual) globalization in which the images of Western Prides—inaugurated to commemorate the famous Stonewall riots—are easily available, consequently undermining the idea that such a protest in Serbia 'authentically' stems from local grievances. In the wake of the protest organized after the banning of the 2013 Pride, Boban Stojanović declared:

> Every breach of human rights requires an adequate response. If someone had told me last year that the LGBT community and those supporting it would manage to organize themselves within an hour via SMS, to go into the streets and make a Balkan Stonewall, I would not have believed them, but, you see, it happened.

This quote refers to the 'LGBT community' as if it were a precisely delimited, self-understandable and unproblematic category synonymous with the LGBT population, which is, given sexual variability, itself a problematic notion. Stojanović's words on SMS-ing draw our attention to the fact that the asynchronous and anachronous, but inspiring and resilient, reference to Stonewall should perhaps mostly be read in the context of the current advances in IT communications and the emergence of various forms of computer-mediated social networks over the last couple of decades.[7] Although they are referred to here in the sense of their capacity to facilitate mobilization, social media tools appreciably reduce incentives for direct political engagement because they render LGBT (sexual) encounters much easier in comparison to what was possible just a decade ago. As the LGBT community has become a 'virtual community', the Internet appears as a sort of 'digital closet' (e.g., Gorkemli 2012) that does not substantially challenge stereotypes about non-heterosexual sexualities in traditionally patriarchal environments.

'UNPACKING' THE CURRENT PRIDE PARADIGM

In the remainder of the chapter, I take a closer, if still preliminary, look at the dimensions that prevent the Belgrade Pride from embracing a more inclusive approach that would better reflect not only the complexity of the Serbian sociopolitical situation, but also the inherent heterogeneity of the LGBT population as well as the intersectional nature of discrimination in an impoverished and still highly patriarchal context. I briefly examine the consequences of profound activist professionalization, the dominance of heightened visibility of male activists in LGBT initiatives, the lack of interclass solidarity and the notion of Pride as an exclusively urban phenomenon.

First, the sense of NGOs as the only mode of operation has had important implications for the development of LGBT activism in the Serbian political milieu.[8] Stemming from the cooperation with the feminist antiwar group Women in Black, the major strand of the 'movement' adopted an anti-political stance deeply skeptical of the state and its institutions, which earned them the label of 'national traitors' that often powerfully delegitimizes their efforts (Bilić 2012). More importantly, however, the omnipresence of NGOs has made it difficult to conceive of civic initiatives outside an NGO frame, often (sometimes wrongly, sometimes rightly) associating activists and activism with huge amounts of foreign money, and introducing division regarding its distribution as well as limiting claims to representational legitimacy that could develop on the basis of articulating widely shared local grievances.[9]

Some LGBT activists themselves generate controversy around the association between their engagement and financial benefits. Consider Predrag Azdejković, a prominent activist, organizer of the Belgrade queer movie festival *Merlinka* and editor of the queer magazine *Optimist*, who provoked strong indignation among the wider LGBT population when he stated on the nationally broadcast evening news that he could change his sexual orientation if someone offered him enough money. Reacting to this, a participant in the gay-serbia.com forum, wrote:

> I will not say anything about that idiotic act of Azdejković in which he says that he would change his orientation for money because it is not worth mentioning [...] I can only be disgusted by such a huge amount of stupidity which is by no means harmless and which will now strengthen those who work against us [...] that is one of the more harmful arguments he made [...] and imagine, he is a gay activist! Terrible!

Along with alienating them from their base, the intense process of professionalization has created serious and often insurmountable tensions within the (mainstream) Serbian LGBT activist circles. Although collective action is, to use Melucci's (1995, p. 61) words, always a 'system of tensions', differential access to resources, privileges and speaking positions in an impoverished and highly precarious environment makes compromise difficult and renders the idea of wider-solidarity politics—that which would encompass other discriminated groups—implausible. Competition for financial resources has induced a rapid process of differentiation and a 'division of labor' that gives the impression of a saturated and barely penetrable activist field. As a young gay activist recently told me:

> When I went to the first meeting of LGBT organizations in Belgrade I was full of enthusiasm and I expected that everything would go smoothly because I thought people were gathering around the same objective. However, I soon realized that they were on the verge of even physically fighting with each other.[10]

This was further reinforced by another interviewee of mine who had participated in organizing the Belgrade Pride parades, only to leave the human rights NGO sphere after a few years of engagement to look for a job in the corporate sector. He said:

> I feel just fine in that world [the corporate sector] [...] it was a bit strange in the beginning, I thought that I would feel dirty... but as a matter of

fact I feel much cleaner now than in the NGO sector where the majority is pretending [folira] that they are there because of some political, altruist or who knows what kind of reason [...] the real motives are actually those characteristic of the sector in which I find myself now.[11]

While it would be naïve to think that activism is not an arena of power struggles, it is quite difficult to research the existing tensions among activists. As a matter of fact, some of the most visible (and therefore also overburdened) LGBT activists never replied to my invitations for an interview, while others agreed to be more explicit provided that the interview was not recorded. Some understanding of the deep polarization among LGBT groups/activists can be gained during the relatively rare instances of publicly open discussions or in analyses that follow deeper personal and professional ruptures.[12] It is, however, important to take into account these tensions when we try to understand the current state of LGBT activism in Serbia, and certainly when we analyze the Pride parade.

In the wake of the downfall of the Milošević regime in October 2000, *Labris* (a lesbian activist group founded in 1995 by the lesbian members of *Arkadija*) decided to organize (in cooperation with *Gayten-LGBT*) the first Pride parade. This event was to take place in June 2001 in what was still a highly volatile political climate. Lepa Mlađenović (cited in Kajinic 2003, p. 30), one of the organizers of the first Belgrade Pride, observed:

I have a feeling that a lot of them [lesbian Pride participants] somehow activated some of their old fears there and that they now took hold together with some facts which justify their being afraid. And that this pretty much prevented them in the whole development of their lesbian existence, which was really difficult for me to accept. Because then [...] of course that it would have been better that nothing happened instead of this happening since the whole movement in Belgrade was thrown back. In fact, the women and men activists were thrown in some situation that is much more difficult than it used to be. And the whole thing was supposed to encourage us, to improve things for us. And we are ten times worse than before that day. [...] And on the other hand, this was of course a huge amount of information about the society we live in. So we got completely sobered up then, and not only we!

The event ended with more than 40 injured activists, and as Bilić and Stubbs (2015) argued, the first Pride parade remains a traumatic event in the Serbian/regional LGBT history. This was the moment that Pride parades became associated with brutal violence, and the event inaugurated a series of unsuccessful attempts to organize such a manifestation. As the groundwork was not well executed, the Pride organization lost the potential for a progressive 'momentum' (which it got, for example, in the case of Zagreb) and contributed to the resignation of the LGBT 'community', polarization between gay and lesbian activists and, possibly, to an actual increase in homophobia.

Tensions between gay and lesbian activists also accompanied the organization of the 2013 Belgrade Pride parade, which was yet again banned shortly before it should have taken place. In September, *Labris* issued a statement informing the public about its decision to withdraw from organization of the 2013 Pride. After underscoring the importance of such manifestations, the members of *Labris* reported:

> The reasons for a lack of cooperation have to do with work politics which is, in the case of *Labris*, founded on tolerance and non-violent conflict resolution. However, already during the first meeting of *Labris* and Pride Parade Belgrade [an NGO that organizes Pride], these principles were breached as the *Labris* representative was verbally attacked by a member of *Kvirija* and *Pride Parade Belgrade*.

The experience of being excluded from or marginalized within the Pride 'paradigm' prompted some lesbian activists to organize the Lesbian March that took place in Belgrade on 19 April 2015. This was the first manifestation of its kind in the post-Yugoslav space. One of the organizers, Ana Pandej, remarked:

> Lesbian March is the culmination of the Lesbian Spring which we organized because we think that lesbians are socially invisible on many levels. We are here, we take part in protests, and still we are absent. We are absent from workers' protests, from women's protests, from Pride [...] There are no lesbians anywhere and there is always some other group in the foreground. It is very important that women generally and above all lesbians—and all the others women comrades—claim public space themselves.

In addition to strong patriarchy, which still characterizes the Serbian sociopolitical context, both professionalization pressures and gay–lesbian tensions must be put in the context of strong deindustrialization and high levels of poverty and unemployment. See, for example, what this reader of the daily *Blic* said, reacting to yet another activist announcement that the Pride parade would take place in Belgrade:

> This is a circus. Does not Serbia have anything smarter to do? Where are jobs, factories, more education and better health care? We have the lowest salaries in the region, our children are going abroad and we are here talking about some Pride parade? As if anyone would be better or worse off if that happens. I personally do not have anything against LGBT population, but for God's sake [...] Our country is in tatters, and the issues of LGBT population are the least important ones. Soon we will face a new increase of prices, whereas our salaries and pensions are going down.[13]

This comment implicitly draws upon the widespread trope of 'gay financial superiority', to point to both the supposedly privileged social status of the LGBT population and the hierarchical division of needs and rights in which those pertaining to sexual orientation are of secondary relevance. As an expression of so-called identity politics, the Pride march is usually criticized—within the LGBT community itself—for insularity that fails to take into consideration the class dimension. As gay activist and coordinator of the course on queer studies in Belgrade, Dušan Maljković (2013), says:

> The absence of 'class consciousness' is evident in the lack of any kind of reflection about class question as, for example, in the requests that Pride makes 2012 or in the attitude that Pride organizers have towards the needs of raspberry producers and military reservists, that is to say mostly lumpenproletariat/precariat that gets excluded from the Pride paradigm or is suspiciously perceived as a potential usurper of the Pride itself [...] there is no attempt to bring protests together [...] but instead, there is an insistence on a distance and particularization of protest on the basis of identity politics which fails to see the relationship between the class status and minority sexuality although it is exactly their social subservience that prevents the members of LGBT community to fully enjoy their 'identitarian rights'.

Reacting to criticism about the exclusion of other marginalized groups in the 'Pride paradigm', Boban Stojanović commented (in Radoja 2013):

> Such an idea is always present, but it is not easy. People gathered around non-governmental organizations and minor political parties are struggling for the rights of marginalized groups. They are only in quite unfavorable positions because they are interested in a good image, donors and ratings.

Supporting Pride is not something that brings points. Minority communities do not necessarily show solidarity towards each other because everyone is struggling for his own place under the sun. [...] LGBT community is specific because no one wants to go with it. I have to admit that sometimes I do not understand such insisting. Why would we have to, for example, support workers while there is no one insisting that workers also support gays? That is also a part of the system of marginalization.

Although Stojanović is right in saying that bridging power and identitarian differentials through a more inclusive politics of solidarity 'is not easy', what is problematic about this position—which, one could argue, characterizes mainstream Serbian LGBT engagement—is the polarization between *workers*, on the one hand, and *gays*, on the other. Such reasoning wrongly assumes that these two are discrete and independent groups that should cooperate exactly because there is no overlap between them. This essentializing concept disregards the fact that many gays are actually workers (and vice versa), and as such, it cannot be productive for activist enterprises, because it perpetuates the notion of gay difference, and distances the public from the LGBT movement. This is reminiscent of Žižek's (2010, p. 138) argument concerning the relationship between gay activists and immigrants:

> Our question to the gays should be: what did you do to help the immigrants socially? Why not go there, act like a Communist, organize a struggle with them, work together? The solution of the tension is thus not to be found in the multicultural tolerance and understanding, but in a shared struggle on behalf of a universality which cuts diagonally across both communities, dividing each of them against itself, but uniting the marginalized in both camps.

Class tensions are also a reflection of the different positions that LGBT activist actors assume towards the role of the state in Pride organization. The 2010 Pride parade, organized with the strong involvement of governmental institutions and EU representatives a year after the adoption of the Anti-Discrimination Law, has been labeled by some activists as 'State Pride' (see also Mikuš 2011), and along with the frustration caused by the further cancellations of the 2011 and 2012 marches, has created deep divisions within the LGBT activist community around who is responsible for Pride failures and the extent to which the state should be involved or consulted during the process of Pride organization.

In reaction to this, the members of the Pride Parade Belgrade organization—which does not include those employed in the Gay-Straight Alliance that organized the 2010 parade—in both 2011 and 2012 bypassed the official ban on the parade by undertaking what came to be known as 'mini Prides'. Echoing the tactics and iconography of earlier antinationalist protests, they stopped traffic in the city center for a few minutes, throwing rainbow-colored paint on the roads. The organizers of the Belgrade Pride have recently reported that the Constitutional Court had determined that the banning of the 2011 Pride was unconstitutional, but not discriminatory, and announced that the 2013 Pride would take place in September (Tanjug 2012). When this parade was also banned, the organizers announced yet another, which finally materialized in September 2014, largely as a result of the new government's willingness to attend to the EU's insistence on Pride parades in the context of Serbia's membership aspirations (Bilić and Stubbs 2015).

What is more, alongside the class tensions within the Pride paradigm, there is at least one other contentious aspect of Serbian LGBT engagement: its overwhelming concentration in Belgrade. Pride and LGBT activism seem to be an *exclusively urban experience*, which tends to remain closed to non-Belgrade participants. As such, the operation of LGBT activist groups reflects the profound structural centralization of the Serbian state. As LGBT activist Ksenija Forca (2012) observed:

> There are fewer than 10 non-governmental organizations that are in one way or the other devoted to LGBTIQ activism. Each and every one of them has its own politics and ideology which determine its work. To a very small extent do these organizations work directly with the community, and they are even less familiar with the problems that that community has outside of Belgrade or/and bigger cities. Centralization has not escaped these organizations. With such a focus on Belgrade and big cities, it is so often forgotten that the topic of gay and lesbian existence has not been even minimally raised and 'detabooised' as in Belgrade.

In the wake of the 2010 Pride (the so-called State Pride), General Police Director Milorad Veljović remarked that 'it was very interesting that 60 % of the [249] arrested hooligans did not have their residence in Belgrade, but were coming from the Serbian provinces' (B92 2010). Similarly, in a video clip that was released, one can hear a police officer addressing a hooligan, saying, 'You came here to demolish my Belgrade' (B92 2010). Bilić and Stubbs (2015) have argued that, in accordance with the a rather formalistically oriented allegiance to European values of tolerance, anti-discrimination, and freedom of assembly and expression, this statement draws up and mobilizes deeply entrenched symbolic asymmetries between an urban and rural habitus in the ex-Yugoslav space.[14]

Finally, bearing in mind all of the contentious Pride dimensions that I have touched upon above, it is not surprising that a study of the attitudes of the LGBT population found that after 15 years of intense activism, violence and fear, of it a profound feeling of elementary in security, still mark LGBT people's existence in Serbia (Stojčić 2014). More than one-third (36 %) of the respondents felt that Pride brings more damage than benefits, whereas 42 % agreed that the 'pride parade contributes to the increase of fear and hatred towards LGBT people' (Stojčić 2014, p. 147). The study also revealed an ambivalent attitude towards LGBT organizations. On the one hand, they are seen as playing an important role in empowering, educating and informing LGBT people, and for a considerable number, they represent a kind of safe space and acceptance. On the other hand, they are often seen as disunited, non-transparent, not inclusive of LGBT people and lacking media presence (except, of course, during the period when Pride is organized). In this regard, taking a look back at the outcomes of the 2014 Pride, one commentator noted:

> Without going deep into the problematic of the Belgrade Pride March itself, of the organizer's shady politics, pointless politic demands, their absence during the whole year, seasonal opportunism and the organizer's complete detachment from the LGBT community and the everyday reality of LGBT people in Serbia, we can conclude that Belgrade Pride March 2014 didn't bring ANY positive social change at all. It's obvious it was all fake. Further more [*sic*], Serbia's example of Belgrade Pride Parade was used in the OSCE/ODIHR conference on freedom of assembly as an example of good practice, disregarding the overall status of the LGBT people and freedom of assembly in Serbia, which [are] both deteriorating. Fake in a sense that it was just organized to show that Serbia, as a country, is capable of obeying demands of patrons such [as] the European Union or any other international body, the deity our country is so eager to become a part of. Wishful thinking, dear folks. (Marinkovic 2015)

CONCLUSION

Although they may start with ambitious goals, 'identity-based' struggles tend to reflect, refract and reproduce wider patterns of social inequality. In the context of Serbian LGBT activism, this has important implications for the potential to conceptualize Pride parades as an expression of locally articulated grievances and the capacity of LGBT activists to form coalitions with other oppressed or discriminated groups. Highly professionalized activist engagement that does not fully appreciate class and gender differences repeatedly damages the constitution of an LGBT 'community' and may—contrary to its original goals—promote homophobic intolerance.

The separation of the struggle for 'gay emancipation' from wider political issues, which has plagued the Pride organization in Belgrade from its beginnings, is of course not an exclusively Serbian phenomenon, and is rather a reflection of the fact that at an international level

> lesbian and gay human rights struggles have become disconnected from politics and, moreover, that we have become depoliticized consumers through the fetishization of rights [...] It becomes far too tempting for 'citizen gay' to consume human rights and then withdraw from any kind of progressive politics, especially when those who have bestowed the rights are also pursuing policies that are eviscerating the human rights of others on issues from migration to counterterrorism. (Stychin 2004, pp. 967–968)

With this in mind, the set of elements that I have examined in this chapter underscores the necessity for the Serbian LGBT activist 'community' to broaden the current Pride paradigm and to come up with a clearer political platform that would go beyond the mere insistence on the respect of (individual) human rights. The decade-long absence of such a political program, which would be sensitive to the volatility of the local sociopolitical situation, perpetuates the idea—deeply rooted within the general public—that (homo)sexuality is an exclusively private matter that people should confine to their own 'four walls'. One would be hard-pressed to believe that major advances in the sphere of LGBT rights and social acceptance of non-heterosexual sexualities are at all possible without a greater level of communication and cooperation between the LGBT population and activist groups as well as sustained political initiatives with other discriminated groups.

NOTES

1. According to Binnie and Klesse (2012, p. 445) 'the term LGBTQ signifies a coalitional practice between different collectivities of actors (Lesbian-Gay-Bisexual-Transgender-Queer). The term is controversial because it insinuates a quasi-natural confluence of interests around certain gender and/or sexual subjectivities'. Although aware of the fact that bisexuals (B)

and transsexuals (T) are almost absent from the discussions of Serbian activists politics, I will use this acronym for pragmatic reasons.

2. A meager amount of scholarly interest has been paired with the lack of the (mainstream) activist 'community's' willingness to question its strategic options and examine the potential for Pride parades to substantially advance the LGBT cause under the current sociopolitical climate. As a result of this inflexibility, which sometimes wants to present itself as a matter of perseverance and ideological consistency, parade organizers have also contributed to the perpetuation of a spiral that associates their manifestation with acts of brutal violence.

3. Many have failed to recognize that at least one component of the so-called 'brain-drain' that has seen hundreds of thousands of people leave Serbia over the last 20 years also has to do with the impossibility for many of them to live out their (homo)sexuality in their own country.

4. Opposition to the Yugoslav wars was also associated with homosexuality in the Croatian context. The most illustrative example in this regard is the article that appeared in the Osijek newspaper *Slavonski magazin*, entitled *Serbs, Reds, Leftists and Faggots Lead a War Against the War*. See Pavlović (1999).

5. Originally written in English.

6. Two Polish scholars, Mizielińska and Kulpa (2011), differentiate between a Western 'time of sequence' and an Eastern European 'time of coincidence'. The former concept points to future-oriented linear progress in which later activist strategies take into consideration and build upon the successes and failures of earlier efforts. 'Time of coincidence', on the other hand, stresses the 'coincidental' nature of Eastern European activist engagement.

   According to Mizielińska and Kulpa (2011), Eastern European activists adopt Western labels and create hybrid strategic options that are often detached from local political grievances and positive legislation. Passed under the pressure from the EU to demonstrate respect for human rights in ascending countries, these legal solutions generate controversy, as they precede rather than reflect wider public acceptance of non-normative sexualities (Bilić and Stubbs 2015).

7. The Stonewall riots can be understood only by taking into consideration that American homosexuals in the 1950s and 1960s had to face an extremely homophobic legal system—they were severely threatened by the state. Homosexual acts, even between consenting adults acting in private homes, were a criminal offense in every US state at the time of the Stonewall riots. What is more, Stonewall must be positioned in the context of the civil rights movement and various other anti-war and environmentalist campaigns that all stimulated and fed each other and derived energy through interaction and cooperation.

8. On NGO-ization see, e.g., Stubbs (2012).
9. Discussion on <www.gay-serbia.com/forum> on 7 October 2012, accessed August 2013.
10. Interview with the author, February 2013.
11. Interview with the author, April 2013.
12. Such as the one that took place at the Belgrade cultural center REX.
13. User comment on Lazarević et al. (2014).
14. Overly Belgrade-oriented initiatives are not, however, an exclusive characteristic of LGBT activism, as they were also present within the anti-war engagement that unfolded before and during the wars of the Yugoslav succession. As Bojan Aleksov, an anti-war activist and conscientious objector, remarks, 'There was also the isolationism and self-righteousness of the Belgrade anti-war activists which contributed to the reticence of the deserters to make contact. Most of the Belgrade activists came from the privileged Yugoslav intelligentsia and establishment, whereas rebelling soldiers came from underprivileged rural areas' (Aleksov 2012, p. 123).

REFERENCES

Aleksov, B. (2012). Resisting the Yugoslav wars: Towards an autoethnography. In B. Bilić & V. Janković (Eds.), *Resisting the evil: [Post-]Yugoslav anti-war contention* (pp. 105–126). Baden-Baden, Germany: Nomos.

Bilić, B. (2012). *We were gasping for air: (Post-)Yugoslav anti-war activism and its legacy.* Baden-Baden, Germany: Nomos.

Bilić, B. (Ed.) (2016). *LGBT activism and Europeanization in the Post-Yugoslav space: On the rainbow way to Europe.* London: Palgrave Macmillan.

Bilić, B., & Janković, V. (2012). Recovering (Post-)Yugoslav anti-war contention: A Zagreb walk through stories, analyses and activisms. In B. Bilić & V. Janković (Eds.), *Resisting the evil: [Post-]Yugoslav anti-war contention* (pp. 25–36). Baden-Baden, Germany: Nomos.

Bilić, B., & Stubbs, P. (2015). Unsettling 'the urban' in Post-Yugoslav activisms: *Right to the city* and pride parades in Serbia and Croatia. In K. Jacobsson (Ed.), *Urban movements and grassroots activism in Central and Eastern Europe* (pp. 98–113). London: Ashgate.

Binnie, J., & Klesse, C. (2012). Solidarities and tensions: Feminism and transnational LGBTQ politics in Poland. *European Journal of Women's Studies, 19*(4), 444–459.

B92. (2010). Ko diriguje hiljadama huligana? *B92* [Online] 11 October. Retrieved May 8, 2013, from http://www.b92.net/info/vesti/index.php?yyyy=2010&mm=10&dd=11&nav_id=464440.

Dioli, I. (2009). Back to a nostalgic future: The Queeroslav utopia. *Sextures, 1*(1), 1–21.

Fagan, A., & Slootmaeckers, K. (2014). Too proud to have pride? The EU's (in) ability to promote LGBT equality in Serbia. In European Consortium for Political Research (ECPR), *ECPR Joint Sessions*. Salamanca, Spain, 10–15 April 2014.

Forca, K. (2012). Parada ponosa i Srbija. *Centar za Kvir Studije (CKS)* [Online] 27 October. Retrieved September 10, 2013, from http://www.cks.org.rs/2012/10/parada-ponosa-i-srbija/.

Gordy, E. (1999). *The culture of power in Serbia: Nationalism and the destruction of alternatives.* Philadelphia: The Pennsylvania State University Press.

Gorkemli, S. (2012). "Coming out of the internet": Lesbian and gay activism and the internet as a "digital closet" in Turkey. *Journal of Middle East Women's Studies, 8*(3), 63–88.

Kajinic, S. (2003). *Experiences of lesbians at the Belgrade Pride 2001 and Zagreb Pride 2002.* Master's thesis. Budapest, Central European University.

Lazarević, Z., Petrović, M., Milićević I., et al. (2014). PRAJD 2014 Huligani zapalili autobus i napali zgradu B92! Parada održana uz crkvena zvona i helikoptere. *Blic Online* [Online] 28 September. Retrieved August 31, 2015, from http://www.blic.rs/Vesti/Drustvo/498287/PRAJD-2014-Huligani-zapalili-autobus-i-napali-zgradu-B92-Parada-odrzana-uz-crkvena-zvona-i-helikoptere.

Maljković, D. (2013). *Prajd, da, ali kakav i čiji?* Retrieved October 10, 2013, from http://rexpro.b92.net/ikd/files/Parada%20i%20politika%20-%20komentar%20-%20Dusan%20Maljkovic.pdf.

Marinkovic, L. (2015). At least 2 people beaten up for being gay in Belgrade in the last 2 weeks. *BuzzFeed*, [Online] 17 April. Retrieved August 31, 2015, from http://www.buzzfeed.com/lazaralazara/at-least-2-people-beaten-up-for-being-gay-in-belgr-6qjt?utm_term=.pl0R1aA5N#.eaLJA9yr5.

Melucci, A. (1995). The process of collective identity. In H. Johnston & B. Klandermans (Eds.), *Social movements and culture* (pp. 41–63). Minneapolis: University of Minnesota Press.

Mikuš, M. (2011). "State pride" politics of LGBT rights and democratisation in "European Serbia". *East European Politics & Societies, 25*(4), 834–851.

Mizielińska, J., & Kulpa, R. (2011). "Contemporary peripheries": Queer studies, circulation of knowledge and East/West divide. In R. Kulpa & J. Mizielinska (Eds.), *De-centring western sexualities: Central and East European Perspectives* (pp. 11–26). London: Ashgate.

Mlađenović, L. (2012). Notes of a feminist lesbian in anti-war initiatives. In B. Bilić & V. Janković (Eds.), *Resisting the evil: [Post-]Yugoslav anti-war contention* (pp. 127–136). Baden-Baden, Germany: Nomos.

Pavlović, T. (1999). Women in Croatia: Feminists, nationalists, and homosexuals. In S. Ramet (Ed.), *Gender politics in the Western Balkans: Women and society in Yugoslavia and the Yugoslav successor states* (pp. 131–152). University Park: Pennsylvania State University Press.

Radoja, Ž. (2013). Parada ponosa je desničarima "seksi tema". Interview with Boban Stojanović. *Kontra Press*, [Online] 11 October. Retrieved October 15, 2013, from http://www.kontrapress.com/clanak.php?rub=Razgovori&url=Parada-ponosa-je-desnicarima-seksi-tema.

Stojčić, M. (2014). Summary and final examination. In A. Stojaković (Ed.), *Parada ponosa i LGBT populacija* (pp. 142–155). Belgrade, Serbia: Fund for an Open Society.

Stubbs, P. (2007). Civil society or Ubleha: Reflections on flexible concepts, meta-NGOs and new social energy in the Post-Yugoslav space. In H. Rill, T. Šmidling, & A. Bitoljanu (Eds.), *20 pieces of encouragement for awakening and change: Peacebuilding in the region of the former Yugoslavia* (pp. 215–228). Belgrade, Serbia: Centre for Non-Violent Action.

Stubbs, P. (2012). Networks, organisations, movements: Narratives and shapes of three waves of activism in Croatia. *Polemos: časopis za interdisciplinarna istraživanja rata i mira, 15*(2), 11–32.

Stychin, C. F. (2004). Same-sex sexualities and the globalization of human rights discourse. *McGill Law Journal, 49*(4), 951–968.

Tanjug. (2012). Završen prajd u četiri zida. *Politika* [Online] 6 October. Retrieved September 3, 2015, from http://www.politika.rs/rubrike/Drustvo/Prajd-u-Medija-centru-uz-jake-mere-bezbednosti.lt.html.

Todosijević, J. (1995). Report on lesbians in Yugoslavia. [Email] 13 March. Retrieved September 15, 2013, from http://www.qrd.org/qrd/orgs/IGLHRC/1995/report.on.lesbians.in.yugoslavia-03.13.95.

Žižek, S. (2010). *Living in End Times*. London: Verso.

CHAPTER 10

The Curious Case of Macedonia: A Personal Insight of a Former Head of the EU Delegation in Macedonia

Erwan Fouéré

MACEDONIA'S ROAD TO THE EU

When the Former Yugoslav Republic of Macedonia (henceforth Macedonia) submitted its application to join the European Union in March 2004, it was seen as a courageous move for a country that had experienced an armed (and bloody) inter-ethnic conflict only a few years before. It also showed the determination of Macedonian political elite—at that time, a government coalition led by the SDSM, the Social Democratic Union of Macedonia—to move forward towards the objective of European Union (EU) accession without delay. For them, EU membership would guarantee political stability and security, as well as the best prospects for economic and social development for Macedonia and its citizens.

For the EU, although in no hurry to engage in new accession negotiations so soon, the 2004 Enlargement nevertheless recognized the Macedonian application as a logical follow-up to EU commitment to the

E. Fouéré (✉)
Centre for European Policy Studies, Brussels, Belgium

© The Editor(s) (if applicable) and The Author(s) 2016
K. Slootmaeckers et al. (eds.), *The EU Enlargement and Gay Politics*, DOI 10.1057/978-1-137-48093-4_10

Western Balkans. It was at the EU-Western Balkan Summit in Thessaloniki (June 2003), now known as the Thessaloniki Agenda, that the EU confirmed the membership perspective for the countries of the region. The language contained in the Agenda was very clear: 'The future of the Balkans is within the European Union'.

Following its application to join the EU, the Macedonian government maintained a steady pace of reforms in line with its objective of EU accession. It also pushed through the constitutional reforms required by the Ohrid Framework Agreement,[1] including granting language and representational rights for the ethnic Albanian community (comprising 25 % of the population according to the 2002 census) and other minorities (Serbs, Roma, Bosniaks, Turks and Vlachs).

The consistency with which the Macedonian government pursued all of these reforms received considerable praise from the international community, which hailed Macedonia as a success story in terms of multi-ethnic cooperation in the Balkan region. Rewarding these efforts, the EU formally accepted Macedonia's membership application, granting Macedonia candidate status in December 2005. This positive atmosphere continued into the early stages of the following year, with the expectation that accession negotiations could even start within the year, conditioned on the adoption of further reforms.

2006: A New Government with a Social Conservative Agenda

The optimism did not last very long. The July 2006 Elections saw the current Prime Minister, Nikola Gruevski, take office in a government led by the Internal Revolutionary Organisation–Democratic Party for Macedonian National Unity (VMRO–DPMNE). Since then, Macedonia has lurched from one crisis to another, with periodic flare-ups of inter-ethnic violence and growing polarisation in society.

Although he was elected on a platform of much-needed economic reforms as well as a declared fight against corruption, the ethno-nationalist and populist agenda pursued by the Prime Minister and his ruling party became more and more pronounced. Partly fuelled by Greece's refusal to recognize Macedonia's constitutional name—thereby blocking both accession to the North Atlantic Treaty Organization (NATO) and the start of EU accession negotiations[2]—but also based on its own party ideology, the Prime Minister embarked on a controversial policy of giving citizens a false sense of identity while fomenting dangerous undercurrents that upset the delicate inter-ethnic co-existence.

The most glaring example of this was the official launch in 2010 of the largest monument and statue-building project ever seen in the region: the Skopje 2014 project. Five years on, the capital city centre is replete with statues glorifying Alexander The Great, together with a triumphal arch, lions, fountains, etc., which have the appearances of a Las Vegas theme park. For a country with an unemployment rate of just under 30 %, including one of the highest youth unemployment rates in the region, plus over 30 % living below the poverty line (World Bank 2013), the cost of this vast building project is viewed by many as an extravagance the country can ill afford.

An integral part of this ethno-nationalist and populist agenda of the ruling party is the socially conservative policies it has been promoting from the start. An example of this conservative ethno-national agenda can be found in the party's election manifesto for 2008–2012, where one of the ten key objectives includes: 'Healthier nation that respects traditional Christian values, in clothing the values of the family and children' (VMRO-DPMNE 2008, p. 21, translated by author).

In the years since his first election,[3] the Prime Minister has been using every means available to promote this socially conservative agenda. It included an aggressive campaign promoting child birth, another campaign against abortion, introducing 'family studies' in schools and in universities, introducing a law that offered monetary compensation to families to increase child birth, but that was restricted to the majority ethnic Macedonian families where average childbirth was lower than in the ethnic Albanian community (a law later declared discriminatory and thus unconstitutional by the Constitutional Court), and many other controversial initiatives.

The latest measure pushed through by the Gruevski-led government relates to its efforts to prohibit same-sex marriages. By means of a constitutional amendment defining marriage as a union between a man and a woman, the government has sought to prevent any attempt at allowing the introduction of same-sex marriages. Its first attempt at introducing this constitutional amendment failed in 2013, as both the opposition and even the ruling party's junior coalition partner, the ethnic Albanian Democratic Union for Integration (DUI), considered this to be no priority as well as unnecessary, given existing legislation. The second attempt in

December 2014, however, was successful, albeit in a Parliament boycotted by all the opposition parties after the 2014 elections, which were, according to the Organisation for Security and Cooperation in Europe (OSCE) Election Observation Report, affected by serious irregularities.

To fully grasp the nature of the current regime, it is important to understand the fact that the ruling party exercises full control over all branches of power, whether it is the electoral process, the judiciary or the media. For example, in respect of the latter, Macedonia has the worst media freedom record in the entire Balkan region. In the latest Reporters Without Borders index, Macedonia is ranked 123rd, just above Angola, a drop of almost 90 places from 2009, when it was ranked 34th.[4]

The ruling party does not tolerate any minority or dissenting views, using fear and intimidation to exercise its repressive authority over society. Civil society organizations that seek to promote human rights and greater tolerance in society have also been the target of vitriolic government attacks. Additionally, and further adding to the atmosphere of intolerance, incidences of hate speech, incitement to violence, as well as homophobic statements are common features of popular TV talk shows. These shows, moreover, are periodically graced with the presence of the Prime Minister and even the President, giving the impression they condone such statements and behaviour.

The attitude of the government and the behaviour of its leaders contributed to an increasingly hostile environment where the lesbian, gay, bisexual and transgender (LGBT) community was deliberately targeted. Pro-government media posted photos of people, including journalists, suggesting they were part of the LGBT community and branding them as 'enemies of the state' (cf. Mole 2016). This was accompanied by repeated attacks on the LGBT office, which was established in the capital city in 2012. Even though the attacks were caught on CCTV (the latest attack was in October 2014) with the perpetrators easily identifiable, not one of those responsible has ever been charged, let alone arrested.

ADOPTION OF ANTI-DISCRIMINATION LEGISLATION

Against this background, it should not be surprising that the EU's efforts to have the government adopt the comprehensive anti-discrimination legislation have been so fraught with difficulty. It was in April 2010 that the Parliament adopted a law on prevention and protection from discrimination.[5] The adoption was preceded by a debate that was characterized by the European Commission in the 2010 Progress Report as 'divisive', while 'remarks from civil society and the international community were not considered' (SEC 2010 1332, final, p. 20). Already in the previous year's Progress Report, the European Commission stated:

> Little progress has been made in the area of anti-discrimination policy. Mechanisms to identify, pursue and criminalize all forms of discrimination by State and non-State bodies against individuals or groups do not exist. A framework law on anti-discrimination remains to be adopted. Discrimination based on sex, ethnic origin, disability and sexual orientation persists […] Neither the Constitution nor the existing legislation identifies sexual orientation as a basis for discrimination. Lesbian, gay, bisexual, and transgender (LGBT) people are not protected against direct or indirect discrimination and are stigmatized, particularly in rural areas. (SEC 2009 1335, final, pp. 19–20)

In the months and years preceding the discussion in the government on the proposed anti-discrimination law, major efforts were undertaken by civil society groups in Macedonia to ensure that the draft law being proposed for adoption would be comprehensive and fully reflect the principles contained in the relevant EU legislation as well as in the Charter for Fundamental Rights incorporated into the Lisbon Treaty (cf. Slootmaeckers and Touquet 2016). These efforts were supported both publicly and privately by the EU, with the EU Delegation itself attending many meetings organised on the issue, as well as hosting events with many civil society organizations active in this area.

These efforts initially bore fruit in that the first draft proposed by the government in December 2009 fully reflected the provisions of the relevant EU legislation. However, the situation changed dramatically in the following weeks, with the government announcing a revised proposal on 29 January 2010 that no longer included 'sexual orientation' as one of the grounds for protection.

It is no coincidence that this change of attitude on the part of the government came just a few days after the European Council granted visa liberalisation to Macedonia. The visa liberalisation process launched by the EU the previous year was based on roadmaps where each country had to comply with key reforms in four broad categories, which included security of documents, border controls and illegal migration, public order and security as well as fundamental freedoms. As part of this fourth category of fundamental freedoms, applicant countries were expected to adopt and implement comprehensive anti-discrimination legislation. Unfortunately, Macedonia became the only exception in not fulfilling that commitment, despite being considered as being a frontrunner in the other reform areas of the visa liberalisation process. This was thus a missed opportunity by the EU to ensure proper conditionality in granting visa liberalisation (Kacarska 2015).

In subsequent meetings with the government in the beginning of 2010, the EU sought to emphasise grave concerns at this turn of events to the Macedonian interlocutors. As EU Special Representative, I was given full authority to draw attention to the importance of adopting a law that fully reflects EU legislation, as it would demonstrate the government's commitment to European values. At successive meetings with the Minister and Deputy Minister for Labour and Social Policy, the Deputy Prime Minister and Minister for European Integration, and the Prime Minister himself, as well as with Members of Parliament (MPs) from the ruling party VMRO-DPMNE, we appealed for a return to the original draft. Additionally, the Ambassador of the Netherlands made similar representations to impress upon the government the importance of respecting European values and the EU acquis. These diplomatic actions were joined by statements and advocacy work of international human rights organizations. One of these was Human Rights Watch, which in a letter dated 3 February 2010 reminded the government of its international commitments to human rights—which include principles of equality and non-discrimination on the basis of sexual orientation.

The government's responses to these international interventions were universally weak and unconvincing. The Minister for Labour and Social Policy suggested that lesbian, gay, bisexual and transgender people could still ask for protection as the draft law also referred to 'other grounds' of discrimination. The Prime Minister meanwhile insisted that he was 'bound by the will of his party'. The debate in the Parliament on the government's revised draft, which continued during the subsequent weeks, reflected the deep prejudices and homophobic sentiments prevalent in the ruling party, with some MPs going so far as to contend that homosexuality was a 'disease' that had to be eradicated. Some of these MPs went even further, trying to distort the debate by suggesting that what the EU was proposing would lead to the country being forced to accept same-sex marriages.

This debate in the Parliament was accompanied by homophobic articles in pro-government media as well as on social media, which only increased the atmosphere of intolerance. One entry on social media by the then

Spokesperson of the Secretariat for European Affairs referred to journalists and homosexuals as 'state enemies'. This incident was reported in an article published on 3 February 2010 in *Vest*, which was one of the few independent media existing at the time.

With the time for adoption of the draft law by the Parliament fast approaching and no indication of any change of heart on the government side, the Commissioner for Enlargement, Mr Štefan Füle, sent a letter to the Prime Minister on 31 March 2010. In the letter, the Commissioner underlined that 'the anti-discrimination acquis is at the heart of what the Union stands for', and appealed directly to the Prime Minister to take into account all the recommendations submitted by the European Commission Services. He continued:

> The most urgent issue is that sexual orientation needs to be established as a ground for discrimination in Article 3 of the law. Its absence in the current draft is striking in view of the wide list of grounds which are included. If the current text is adopted it would send a negative message and could paradoxically, be seen as a form of discrimination.

He furthermore strived to counter the misinformation spread by the ruling party on the issue of same-sex marriage, emphasising in his letter:

> Let me assure you that all the Member States have passed legislation in line with the anti-discrimination acquis as regards sexual orientation. On the other hand, I take this opportunity to underline that the acquis does not affect family law, on which Member States maintain significant differences.

The letter was hand-delivered by myself on the following morning, Thursday 1 April 2010, to the office of the Prime Minister—who had already left for the long weekend.[6] The same morning, I personally handed a copy of the letter to the Deputy Prime Minister for European Integration, asking him to make sure the letter would be relayed to the ruling party in Parliament.

Knowing that the law was scheduled for a vote during the course of the upcoming week, I called the Parliamentary leader of the ruling party on Monday to check whether she had received the letter. She replied in the negative. Calls to the Prime Minister's office did not provide any clarity, while the Deputy Prime Minister claimed he didn't know what the Minister had done with the letter. To erase any doubts, my office translated the Commissioner's letter into Macedonian and Albanian and delivered it to the Parliamentary parties on the Tuesday 6 April 2010, when they returned from the Easter break. In light of the obvious lack of communication between the Prime Minister and his parliamentary party, the Commissioner ordered the following day that the letter should be made public.

Despite all of these efforts, the law was passed by the Parliament on 8 April 2010 without any the Commission's recommendations incorporated. To date, the law has not been changed to reflect the EU acquis.

INDEPENDENT ANTI-DISCRIMINATION COMMISSION

Another controversial feature of the anti-discrimination law relates to the monitoring mechanism, which has not been given sufficient resources to function and whose composition remains sadly deficient. The law provides for the establishment of a seven-member Independent Anti-discrimination Commission tasked to monitor and implement the law on Prevention and Protection from Discrimination (Articles 16–24). However, as stated in the 2010 Progress Report: 'The law does not endow the envisaged monitoring and protection mechanism with sufficient administrative capacity' (SEC 2010 1332, final, p. 20).

The appointment of the members of the Commission was itself fraught with irregularities; procedures lacked transparency and serious concerns were raised regarding the qualifications of those appointed. It was only on 27 December 2010, five days before the deadline established by the law, that the Parliament appointed the seven members of the body, voting on a list proposed by the government coalition, ignoring the objections and recommendations of the opposition parties.

Not one single member of civil society was included, despite many excellent candidates who had put forward their name in response to the call for candidatures.[7] While the list of all the applicants remained internal to the Parliament, despite appeals to make it public, several opposition MPs mentioned at least six prominent independent experts who had applied and could have brought the required expertise, professional standing and diversity to the Commission. Those independent experts themselves confirmed they had applied. They included Professor Najcevska, a prominent human rights expert and Zvonko Savreski, who pioneered the rights of people with disabilities (and is suffering from disabilities himself).

Of additional concern was that two of those selected did not appear to fulfil the necessary criteria defined in the law (one of them being a piano teacher and another working as an assistant to one of the ruling party MPs, also known for his hard line views against the LGBT community). To complete this unsatisfactory picture, two of those appointed were senior employees of the Ministry of Labour and Social Policy. As highlighted by the UN Resident Coordinator at the time, having Government representatives with decision-making power on the board of a National Human Rights Institution is against international standards, as it affects the independent functioning and decisions of the Institution.

To this day, the Independent Commission has yet to have an effective impact in the fight against discrimination. The EC 2014 Progress Report, for example, underlines in relation to the Commission's work: 'The ongoing lack of funding and staff shortages continues to hinder its effectiveness' (COM 2014 700, final, p. 46).

CONCLUDING NOTE

The political environment in Macedonia continues to deteriorate. Since the first weeks of February 2015, the country has been shaken by revelations of massive wiretapping of its citizens, over a period spanning several years. According to information provided by the leader of the opposition SDSM, the surveillance operation covered over 20,000 people, including ministers, judges, business people, journalists and even foreign diplomats.

The Prime Minister has tried to blame the wiretapping operation on foreign intelligence services—which he has refused to identify—whilst at the same time accusing the opposition leader of plotting a coup. The opposition leader was subsequently charged with espionage and had his passport removed.

The government's claim of involvement of foreign intelligence services is simply not credible. Indeed, it is not the first time the Prime Minister has invoked espionage as a convenient excuse for jailing those considered undesirable. All the available evidence points to the Prime Minister himself as the mastermind behind the wiretapping operation, with the chief of state security, Saso Mijalkov—the Prime Minister's cousin—being the executor and superintendent.

Regardless of who is behind the wiretapping, the transcripts that have been released so far provide ample evidence of a ruling party that has deliberately ignored the institutional process and separation of powers. It operates by its own rules and violates all basic standard of democracy and even decency. The coarse and even profane language used by party officials in some of the released tapes would not be out of place in a banana republic.

In particular, the conversations between the Prime Minister, other ministers and party officials relating to the organization of the elections contain evidence of systematic tampering with the electoral register, distorted ballot counting, and ways of forcing the Roma community to go and cast their votes for the ruling party. The derogatory language used notably by the Minister of Interior when referring to the Roma community is nothing short of racism.

In a report entitled *Recommendations of the Senior Experts' Group on systematic Rule of Law issues relating to the communications interception revealed in Spring 2015*,[8] which had been prepared at the request of the European Commission and was made public on 19 June 2015, it was stated that

> The interception scandal has revealed a massive invasion of fundamental freedoms including the right to participate in public affairs and to vote, the right of equal access to public services, the rights to privacy and the protection of data, as well as the right to an independent and impartial judiciary.

The report further highlighted that the senior government and party officials were apparently directly involved in:

> illegal activities including electoral fraud, corruption, abuse of power and authority, conflict of interest, blackmail, extortion (pressure on public employees to vote for a certain party with the threat to be fired), criminal damage, severe procurement procedure infringements aimed at gaining an illicit profit, nepotism and cronyism. (p. 6)

The report also refutes the Prime Minister's claim that foreign intelligence services were responsible for the wiretapping: 'The recordings are also of a quality, scale and number to be generally acknowledged to have been made inside the national intelligence service's facilities' (p. 5).

Unfortunately, the unwitting victims of this latest scandal are the citizens of the country. They are treated as pawns in a ruthless power play controlled by the ruling party, which has put its own narrow party interests ahead of the interests of the country and its citizens.

In the short term, the only credible way out of this crisis would be for the current government to resign, and be replaced by a technical government that would prepare the country for proper elections free from the irregularities and intimidation that have marred previous elections. Despite a number of attempts at mediation both by the European Commission and a delegation from the European Parliament, the Prime Minister has refused to step down. A provisional agreement was reached on 2 June 2015 between the political party leaders for early elections to be held in April 2016. However, this depends on an agreement being reached on the transitional arrangements, including the nature and composition of a transitional government to be set up prior to the elections.

Regardless of whether a final agreement will be reached, it will in any case take many years before the extensive damage perpetrated by this regime is repaired. It will require painstaking efforts by the international community together with moderate voices and civil society organizations to restore public confidence in institutions and political process, and for the restoration of a more tolerant society based on respect for the rule of law.

Notes

1. The Ohrid Framework Agreement is the peace agreement signed 13 August 2001; it brought an end to the armed conflict between the (Albanian) National Liberation Army and the Macedonian Security Forces.
2. The European Commission has been recommending the European Council to open accession negotiations with Macedonia since 2009.
3. Gruevski was re-elected in 2008, 2011 and 2014, each time in a snap election.
4. Index available from: https://index.rsf.org/#!/
5. Official Gazette of the Republic of Macedonia, number 50/2010.
6. It happened to be the Orthodox and Catholic Easters, a rare occasion when they coincide.
7. Call was published in the Official Gazette no.143 of 29 October 2010.
8. Report available at: http://ec.europa.eu/enlargement/news_corner/news/news-files/20150619_recommendations_of_the_senior_experts_group.pdf

References

Kacarska, S. (2015). Losing the rights along the way: The EU–Western Balkans visa liberalisation. *European Politics and Society, 16*(3), 363–378.

Mole, R. C. M. (2016). Nationalism and homophobia in Central and Eastern Europe. In K. Slootmaeckers, H. Touquet, & P. Vermeersch (Eds.), *The EU enlargement and gay politics*. London: Palgrave Macmillan.

Slootmaeckers, K., & Touquet, H. (2016). The co-evolution of EU's eastern enlargement and LGBT politics: An ever gayer union? In K. Slootmaeckers, H. Touquet, & P. Vermeersch (Eds.), *The EU enlargement and gay politics*. London: Palgrave Macmillan.

The Former Yugoslav Republic of Macedonia 2009 progress report, SEC (2009) 1335, final.

The Former Yugoslav Republic of Macedonia 2010 progress report, SEC (2010) 1332, final.

The Former Yugoslav Republic of Macedonia 2014 progress report, COM (2014) 700, final.

VMRO-DPMNE. (2008). *ПРОГРАМА НА ВМРО+ДПМНЕ ЗА ПРЕРОДБА 2008–2012: ПРЕРОДБА ВО 100 ЧЕКОРИ. НАДГРАДЕНА И ПРОШИРЕНА* [*Program of VMRO-DPMNE for Rebirth 2008–2012: Rebirth in 100 Steps. Upgraded and Expanded*]. Retrieved from http://vmro-dpmne.org.mk/wp-content/uploads/2013/08/Programa%202008%20WEB.pdf.

World Bank (2013). *South East Europe regular economic report (No. 4): From double-dip recession to fragile recovery*. Washington, DC: World Bank.

INDEX

234   INDEX

Made in the USA
Middletown, DE
22 April 2022

64655644R00146